STEAM
POWER
Workbooks

## GAIL GIBBONS'

## MONARCH BUTTERFLY

# WORKBOOK

HOLIDAY HOUSE • NEW YORK

## Dear Parents and Teachers,

We are delighted to share the outstanding work of nonfiction author Gail Gibbons with you, and with the children in your care. This workbook is based on Gibbons' popular *Monarch Butterfly*, which teaches children in grades K–2 the fundamentals of the insect life cycle.

Inside this workbook, you will find activities that reinforce not just basic science concepts, but also skills learned in grades K–2. Kids can enjoy learning how butterflies develop from an egg to a caterpillar and then how they molt and transform. They will learn where populations of monarch butterflies live and can fill in the routes monarch butterflies take as they migrate in North America. The book also includes labeled steps for raising your own monarch butterfly in a jar.

All the activities in this workbook have been approved by early primary education experts and reinforce the skills being taught at these grade levels. We hope you agree with us that Gail Gibbons is a master of explaining how the world works to young readers and listeners, and we hope you and the children in your life enjoy this workbook. Please visit our Gail Gibbons website at GailGibbonsbooks.com. We'd love to hear how you are using this book, so let us know at info@holidayhouse.com.

Thank you,

The Editors at Holiday House Books

# Contents

*Gail Gibbons' Monarch Butterfly Workbook* copyright © 2022 by Holiday House Publishing, Inc.
Text and illustrations from *Monarch Butterfly* copyright © 1989 by Gail Gibbons

Spot art from *Flowers* copyright © 2018 by Gail Gibbons
HOLIDAY HOUSE is registered in the U.S. Patent and Trademark Office.

Printed and bound in September 2021
at Toppan Leefung, DongGuan, China.

The artwork was created on watercolor paper
with black ink, watercolors, and colored pencil.

www.holidayhouse.com

First Edition
1 3 5 7 9 10 8 6 4 2

ISBN: 978-0-8234-5096-1 (workbook)

# HOW A MONARCH BUTTERFLY BEGINS

In the summertime, monarch butterflies lay their eggs. They only lay eggs on milkweed plants.

MILKWEED

Butterflies usually lay eggs on the plants that their caterpillars will eat. Color the milkweed plant green.

# WHERE IT BEGINS

The eggs look like dots.
Monarch eggs are small, white, and shiny.
They stick like glue to the milkweed leaves.
The eggs can stay on the leaves through wind and rain.
Trace and write the words "egg" and "leaf."

egg                    leaf

After a few days, the monarch's egg hatches.
Out crawls a small caterpillar, also called a larva.

The caterpillar eats its eggshell.
Then it begins to eat the milkweed leaf.

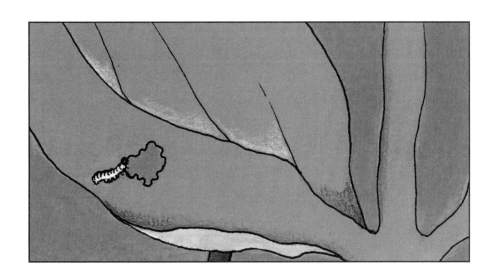

# MOLTING

After hatching, the caterpillar eats and grows.

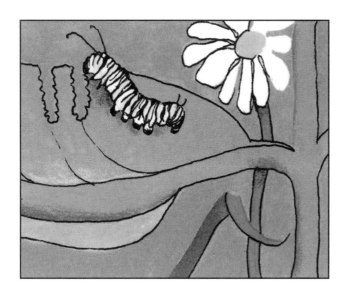

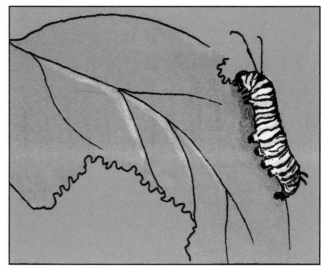

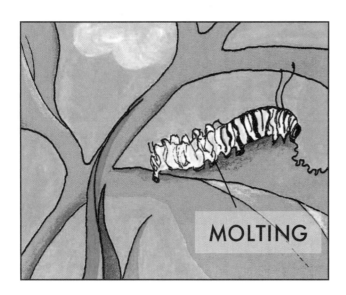

MOLTING

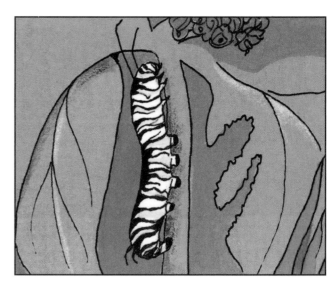

When it gets too big for its old skin, it breaks out of it.
New skin is underneath. This is called molting.

The monarch caterpillar eats milkweed leaves for two weeks. It grows to be two inches long.

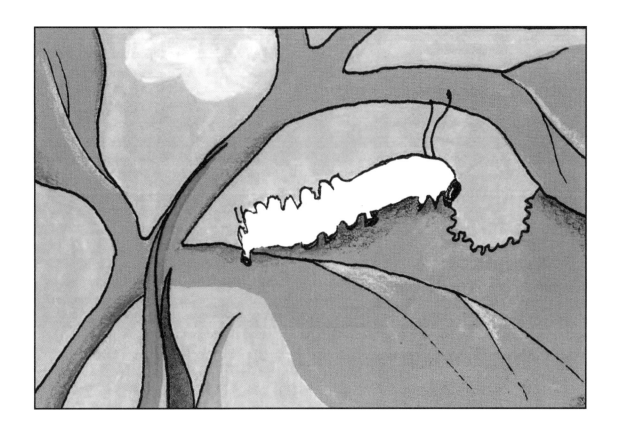

Color in the caterpillar. Circle its molting skin.

Trace and write the words "skin" and "molting."

skin                    molting

# METAMORPHOSIS

When the caterpillar is full-grown, it stops eating.
It hangs upside down.
The caterpillar's skin splits open and falls off.
It is now a chrysalis (KRISS-uh-liss) or pupa (PEW-pa).

**CATERPILLAR HANGING UPSIDE DOWN**

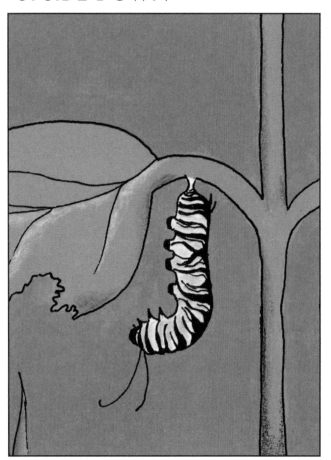

**CHRYSALIS** or **PUPA**

At first, the chrysalis is long and soft.
It shrinks and becomes hard.
It becomes light green with gold dots.
Inside, the butterfly begins to grow.

Color the chrysalis below.

After two weeks, the chrysalis begins to wiggle.
It splits open.

The butterfly begins to pull itself out.
At first, the wings are crumpled and stuck together.
The butterfly pumps a liquid into its wings.

Then it waits for its wings to dry and harden.
After a few hours, the butterfly moves slowly.

Circle the butterfly.

Then it beats its wings and flutters into the sky.
Color this picture that shows the butterflies in flight.

# METAMORPHOSIS

Metamorphosis is a process some animals go through to become adults.

The butterfly has gone through metamorphosis.

The monarch changes from an egg to a caterpillar to a chrysalis or pupa to an adult butterfly.

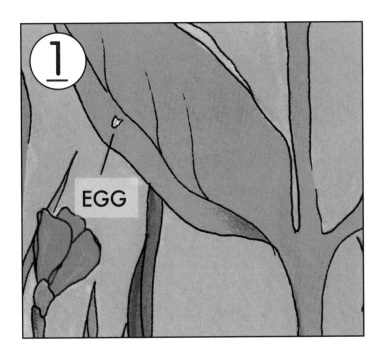

egg

caterpillar

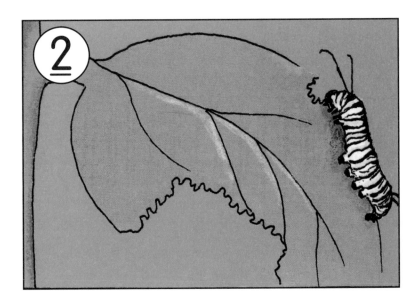

Trace and write the names of the four steps:
egg, caterpillar, chrysalis, and butterfly.
Then practice writing the words.

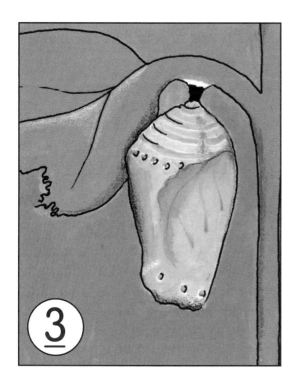

chrysalis

butterfly

# THE MONARCH BUTTERFLY METAMORPHOSIS TIMELINE

It takes about five weeks for a monarch butterfly's egg to become a butterfly.

The egg stays on a leaf for about 3 to 7 days before a caterpillar crawls out.

The caterpillar eats leaves for about 2 weeks.

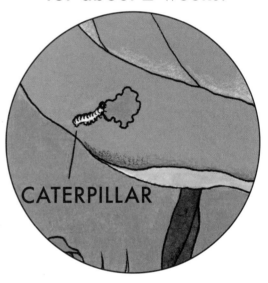

Then the chrysalis forms. It hardens and changes color during the next 2 weeks.

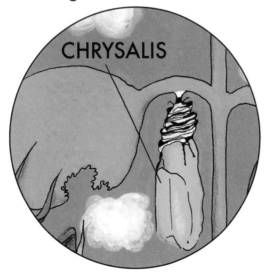

After about 5 weeks, the monarch butterfly emerges!

# Draw the stages on this metamorphosis timeline:

### Draw and write "egg"
### (3 to 7 days)

### Draw and write "caterpillar"
### (weeks 2 and 3)

### Draw and write "chrysalis"
### (weeks 4 and 5)

### Draw and write "butterfly"
### (week 6)

# MIGRATION

Monarch butterflies that hatch in the spring and early summer only a live a few weeks.

Monarchs that hatch later in the summer will take a long trip to a warmer place in the fall.

This trip is called migration.

Monarchs fly from the northern part of the U.S. and Canada to places like Florida, southern California, and Mexico. In the spring, they migrate back. The arrows on the map show the routes monarch butterflies travel. Color these routes in.

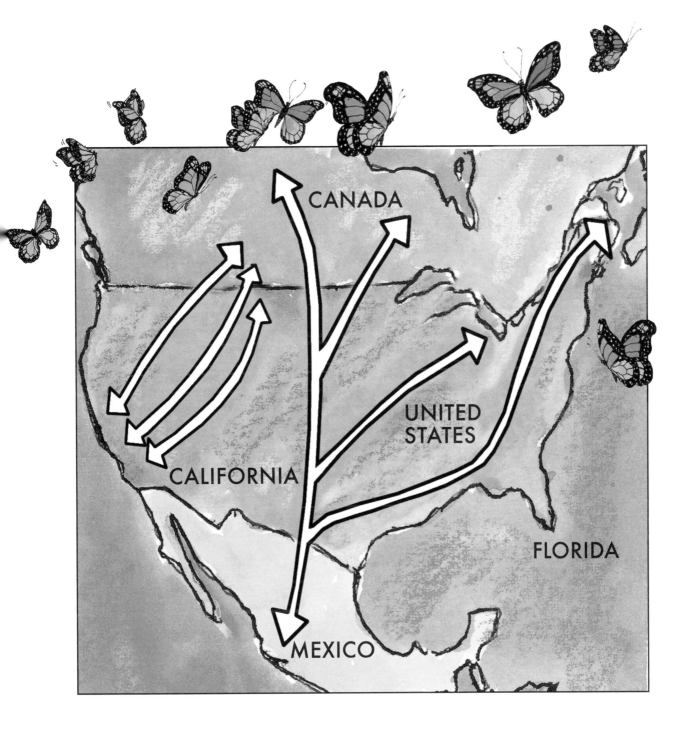

In the south, during the winter months, the monarch butterflies cluster together. There are thousands of them in many trees. The trees are sometimes called butterfly trees.

Trace and write the words "butterfly tree."

butterfly tree

In the spring, the butterflies migrate back. They fly north again, to where fields of milkweed plants grow. At night, they rest in trees.

Some cities have monarch festivals.

Plan your garden. Draw, color, and label the flowers you would like in your window box to attract butterflies.

How many wings does a monarch butterfly have?
Circle the correct number below

1     2     3     4

# HOW DOES A MONARCH BUTTERFLY EAT?

A butterfly has a tube to the mouth called a proboscis.
It uses the proboscis like a straw to drink.
Monarchs suck up a sweet juice called nectar from flowers.
A butterfly can roll up its proboscis or straighten it to drink.
The feelers or antennae are important parts for a butterfly.
Butterflies use their feet and their antennae to smell.
The antennae also help butterflies keep their balance.

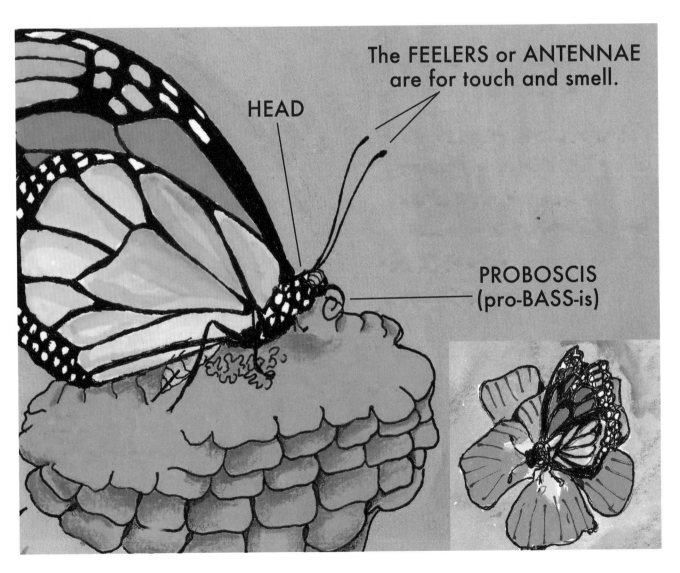

HEAD

The FEELERS or ANTENNAE
are for touch and smell.

PROBOSCIS
(pro-BASS-is)

Can you help the butterfly get to the nectar?

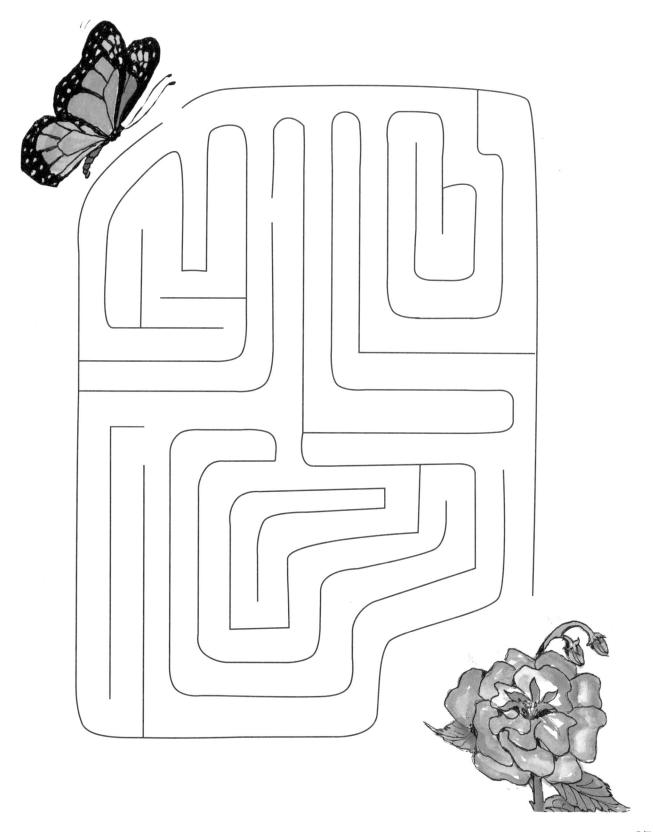

# BODY PARTS OF A MONARCH BUTTERFLY

The thorax is where the legs and wings are attached.

The abdomen contains the butterfly's organs, such as its heart and digestive system.

The head of a butterfly has its eyes, antennae or feelers, and proboscis.

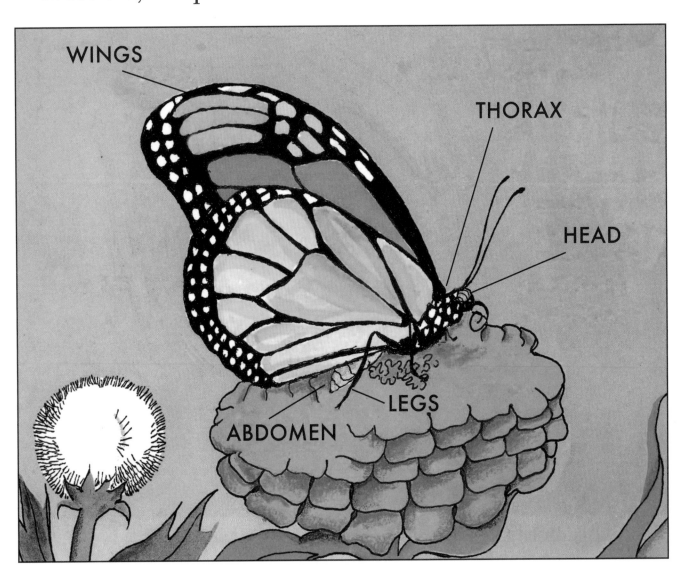

WINGS

THORAX

HEAD

LEGS

ABDOMEN

Using the words in the box below, write the parts of a monarch butterfly on the lines provided.

| | | | |
|---|---|---|---|
| thorax | head | legs | abdomen |
| proboscis | | wings | antennae |

Trace the words "butterfly," "caterpillar," "larva," and "milkweed."

butterfly

caterpillar

larva

milkweed

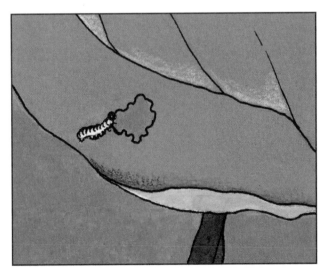

Help the butterfly find the milkweed.

It takes about 30 days for an egg to become an adult butterfly. Put the steps of a monarch butterfly's life cycle in order, from 1 to 4.

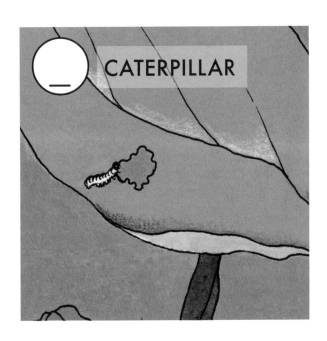

CATERPILLAR

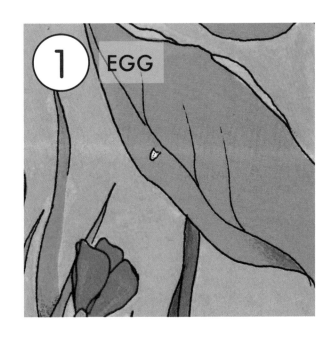

1 EGG

ADULT BUTTERFLY

CHRYSALIS

Milkweed plants are poisonous to many creatures, but not to monarch butterflies, who eat the leaves when they are catepillars. Monarch butterflies are poisonous to many creatures, too. Their enemies know this. A monarch's bright orange color warns others to leave it alone. Some of the monarch butterfly's enemies are frogs, mice, birds, spiders, grasshoppers, and lizards.

Trace and write the names of the monarch's predators.

frogs                    mice

birds

spiders

grasshoppers    lizards

Butterflies are good pollinators.
Their food is the sweet nectar from flowers.
They move from one flower to the next, spreading pollen around. This pollen helps make seeds to grow new plants.

butterfly

flower

seeds

People plant milkweed to attract butterflies to a butterfly garden. Draw some milkweed plants in this garden.

# MONARCH BUTTERFLIES AROUND THE WORLD

NORTH AMERICA

ATLANTIC OCEAN

PACIFIC OCEAN

SOUTH AMERICA

Monarch butterflies live in different parts of the world. Color in the blank places where they live in orange.

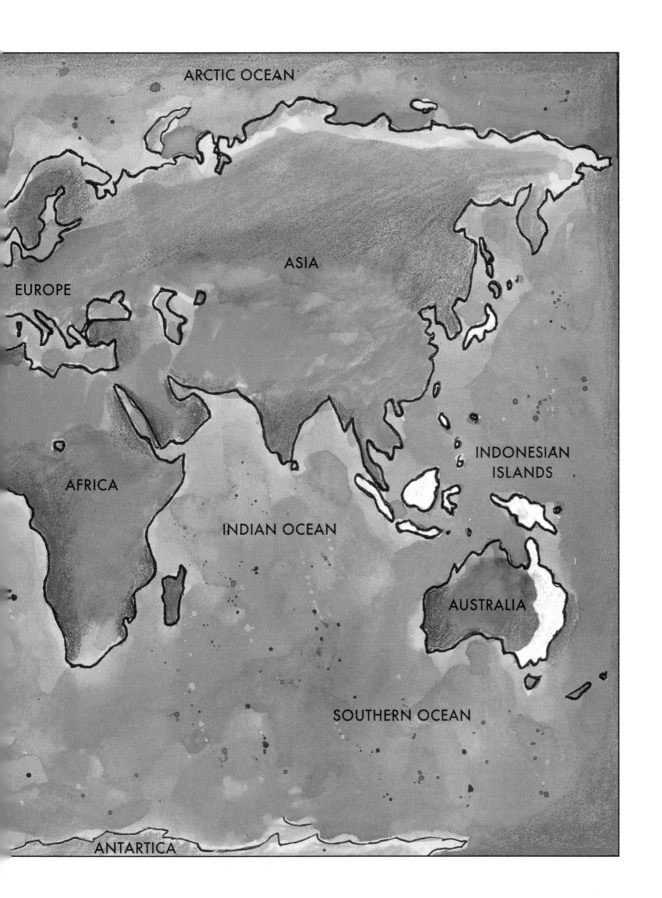

# HOW TO DRAW A MONARCH BUTTERFLY

See the steps below to draw a monarch butterfly.

1

2

3

4

5

6

# Draw a monarch butterfly in steps.

1

2

3

4

5

6

# WHICH ARE MONARCHS?

Circle the monarch butterflies.

# HOW TO RAISE A MONARCH BUTTERFLY

### MAKE A HOME FOR YOUR MONARCH CATERPILLAR

Find a big, clean glass jar with a metal lid. Have an adult help you pound several holes in the lid with a hammer and nail so air can get inside the jar.

### HOW TO FIND YOUR MONARCH CATERPILLAR

Late July and August are the best times to find a monarch caterpillar. Go to a field where milkweed plants grow. Look underneath the milkweed leaves. When you find a monarch caterpillar, pick it up very gently.

### HOW TO CARE FOR YOUR MONARCH CATERPILLAR

Pick four or five leaves off the milkweed plant and put them into the jar for the caterpillar to eat. Then, carefully put the caterpillar in the jar and put the lid on. Keep the jar out of the sun, where it might get too hot. Each day, have someone watch the caterpillar while you clean its home. Replace the old leaves with new ones. Then put the caterpillar back inside the jar.

## YOUR CATERPILLAR WILL CHANGE INTO A CHRYSALIS

When the caterpillar is full-grown, it will hang upside down from the lid of the jar, shed its skin, and form its chrysalis. Don't touch the chrysalis.

## THE CHRYSALIS WILL CHANGE INTO A MONARCH BUTTERFLY

In about two weeks, you will be able to see through the chrysalis. It is time for the monarch butterfly to come out. When it does, it will need a few hours for its wings to grow and dry.

## HOW TO RELEASE YOUR BUTTERFLY OUTSIDE

A monarch butterfly doesn't want to be a pet. Carefully let it climb out of the jar onto your finger. When it is ready to go, it will fly up into the sky. Or you can leave the opened jar outside in a safe place.

# Answer Key

## Page 25

How many wings does a monarch butterfly have?
Circle the correct number below

1    2    3    (4)

25

## Page 27

Can you help the butterfly get to the nectar?

29

# Answer Key

## Page 29

Using the words in the box below, write the parts of a monarch butterfly on the lines provided.

| thorax | head | legs | abdomen |
| proboscis | wings | antennae |

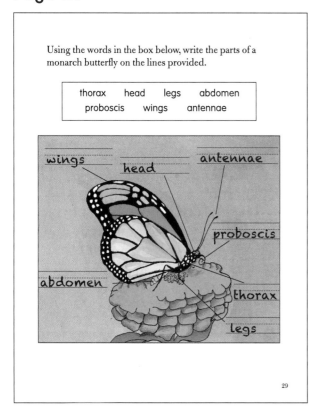

wings
head
antennae
proboscis
abdomen
thorax
legs

29

## Page 31

Help the butterfly find the milkweed.

31

# Answer Key

## Page 32

It takes about 30 days for an egg to become an adult butterfly. Put the steps of a monarch butterfly's life cycle in order, from 1 to 4.

 **2** CATERPILLAR

 **1** EGG

 **4** ADULT BUTTERFLY

 **3** CHRYSALIS

## Page 35

People plant milkweed to attract butterflies to a butterfly garden. Draw some milkweed plants in this garden.

BUTTERFLY GARDEN

## Page 36–37

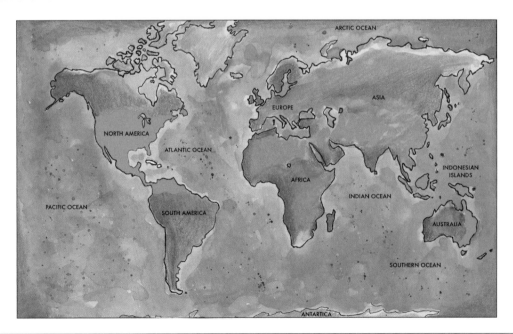

**MONARCH BUTTERFLIES AROUND THE WORLD**

Monarch butterflies live in different parts of the world. Color in the blank places where they live in orange.

# Answer Key

Page 40-41

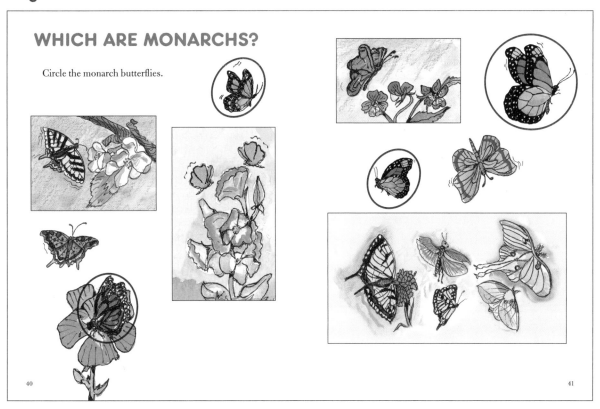

# Young Naturalist Certificate

## Congratulations!

You have learned about the life of monarch butterflies. You have learned all the stages of their life cycle and how they go through metamorphosis. You've learned to identify and write the parts of their body. You've learned what they eat and how far they travel during their lives. You are now a young naturalist, a student in the study of nature.

_____
*Name*

_____
*Date*

# PTCB Exam Study Guide 2022-2023
## Pharmacy Technician Certification Prep Book with Practice Test Questions [Includes Detailed Answer Explanations]

J. M. Lefort

Written and edited by APEX Publishing.

ISBN 13: 9781637750179
ISBN 10: 163775017X

APEX Publishing is not connected with or endorsed by any official testing organization. APEX Publishing creates and publishes unofficial educational products. All test and organization names are trademarks of their respective owners.

The material in this publication is included for utilitarian purposes only and does not constitute an endorsement by APEX Publishing of any particular point of view.

For additional information or for bulk orders, contact info@apexprep.com.

# Table of Contents

# Test Taking Strategies

## 1. Reading the Whole Question

A popular assumption in Western culture is the idea that we don't have enough time for anything. We speed while driving to work, we want to read an assignment for class as quickly as possible, or we want the line in the supermarket to dwindle faster. However, speeding through such events robs us from being able to thoroughly appreciate and understand what's happening around us. While taking a timed test, the feeling one might have while reading a question is to find the correct answer as quickly as possible. Although pace is important, don't let it deter you from reading the whole question. Test writers know how to subtly change a test question toward the end in various ways, such as adding a negative or changing focus. If the question has a passage, carefully read the whole passage as well before moving on to the questions. This will help you process the information in the passage rather than worrying about the questions you've just read and where to find them. A thorough understanding of the passage or question is an important way for test takers to be able to succeed on an exam.

## 2. Examining Every Answer Choice

Let's say we're at the market buying apples. The first apple we see on top of the heap may *look* like the best apple, but if we turn it over we can see bruising on the skin. We must examine several apples before deciding which apple is the best. Finding the correct answer choice is like finding the best apple. Although it's tempting to choose an answer that seems correct at first without reading the others, it's important to read each answer choice thoroughly before making a final decision on the answer. The aim of a test writer might be to get as close as possible to the correct answer, so watch out for subtle words that may indicate an answer is incorrect. Once the correct answer choice is selected, read the question again and the answer in response to make sure all your bases are covered.

## 3. Eliminating Wrong Answer Choices

Sometimes we become paralyzed when we are confronted with too many choices. Which frozen yogurt flavor is the tastiest? Which pair of shoes look the best with this outfit? What type of car will fill my needs as a consumer? If you are unsure of which answer would be the best to choose, it may help to use process of elimination. We use "filtering" all the time on sites such as eBay® or Craigslist® to eliminate the ads that are not right for us. We can do the same thing on an exam. Process of elimination is crossing out the answer choices we know for sure are wrong and leaving the ones that might be correct. It may help to cover up the incorrect answer choice. Covering incorrect choices is a psychological act that alleviates stress due to the brain being exposed to a smaller amount of information. Choosing between two answer choices is much easier than choosing between all of them, and you have a better chance of selecting the correct answer if you have less to focus on.

## 4. Sticking to the World of the Question

When we are attempting to answer questions, our minds will often wander away from the question and what it is asking. We begin to see answer choices that are true in the real world instead of true in the world of the question. It may be helpful to think of each test question as its own little world. This world may be different from ours. This world may know as a truth that the chicken came before the egg or may assert that two plus two equals five. Remember that, no matter what hypothetical nonsense may be in the question, assume it to be true. If the question states that the chicken came before the egg, then choose your answer based on that truth. Sticking to the world of the question means placing all of our biases and assumptions aside and relying on the question to guide us to the correct answer. If we are simply looking for answers that are correct based on our own judgment, then we may choose incorrectly. Remember an answer that is true does not necessarily answer the question.

## 5. Key Words

If you come across a complex test question that you have to read over and over again, try pulling out some key words from the question in order to understand what exactly it is asking. Key words may be words that surround the question, such as *main idea, analogous, parallel, resembles, structured,* or *defines.* The question may be asking for the main idea, or it may be asking you to define something. Deconstructing the sentence may also be helpful in making the question simpler before trying to answer it. This means taking the sentence apart and obtaining meaning in pieces, or separating the question from the foundation of the question. For example, let's look at this question:

> Given the author's description of the content of paleontology in the first paragraph, which of the following is most parallel to what it taught?

The question asks which one of the answers most *parallels* the following information: The *description* of paleontology in the first paragraph. The first step would be to see *how* paleontology is described in the first paragraph. Then, we would find an answer choice that parallels that description. The question seems complex at first, but after we deconstruct it, the answer becomes much more attainable.

## 6. Subtle Negatives

Negative words in question stems will be words such as *not, but, neither,* or *except.* Test writers often use these words in order to trick unsuspecting test takers into selecting the wrong answer—or, at least, to test their reading comprehension of the question. Many exams will feature the negative words in all caps (*which of the following is NOT an example*), but some questions will add the negative word seamlessly into the sentence. The following is an example of a subtle negative used in a question stem:

> According to the passage, which of the following is *not* considered to be an example of paleontology?

If we rush through the exam, we might skip that tiny word, *not,* inside the question, and choose an answer that is opposite of the correct choice. Again, it's important to read the question fully, and double check for any words that may negate the statement in any way.

## 7. Spotting the Hedges

The word "hedging" refers to language that remains vague or avoids absolute terminology. Absolute terminology consists of words like *always, never, all, every, just, only, none,* and *must.* Hedging refers to words like *seem, tend, might, most, some, sometimes, perhaps, possibly, probability,* and *often.* In some cases, we want to choose answer choices that use hedging and avoid answer choices that use absolute terminology. It's important to pay attention to what subject you are on and adjust your response accordingly.

## 8. Restating to Understand

Every now and then we come across questions that we don't understand. The language may be too complex, or the question is structured in a way that is meant to confuse the test taker. When you come across a question like this, it may be worth your time to rewrite or restate the question in your own words in order to understand it better. For example, let's look at the following complicated question:

Which of the following words, if substituted for the word *parochial* in the first paragraph, would LEAST change the meaning of the sentence?

Let's restate the question in order to understand it better. We know that they want the word *parochial* replaced. We also know that this new word would "least" or "not" change the meaning of the sentence. Now let's try the sentence again:

Which word could we replace with *parochial,* and it would not change the meaning?

Restating it this way, we see that the question is asking for a synonym. Now, let's restate the question so we can answer it better:

Which word is a synonym for the word *parochial*?

Before we even look at the answer choices, we have a simpler, restated version of a complicated question.

## 9. Predicting the Answer

After you read the question, try predicting the answer *before* reading the answer choices. By formulating an answer in your mind, you will be less likely to be distracted by any wrong answer choices. Using predictions will also help you feel more confident in the answer choice you select. Once you've chosen your answer, go back and reread the question-and-answer choices to make sure you have the best fit. If you have no idea what the answer may be for a particular question, forego using this strategy.

## 10. Avoiding Patterns

One popular myth in grade school relating to standardized testing is that test writers will often put multiple-choice answers in patterns. A runoff example of this kind of thinking is that the most common answer choice is "C," with "B" following close behind. Or, some will advocate certain made-up word patterns that simply do not exist. Test writers do not arrange their correct answer choices in any kind of pattern; their choices are randomized. There may even be times where the correct answer choice will be the same letter for two or three questions in a row, but we have no way of knowing when or if this might happen. Instead of trying to figure out what choice the test writer probably set as being correct, focus on what the *best answer choice* would be out of the answers you are presented with. Use the tips above, general knowledge, and reading comprehension skills in order to best answer the question, rather than looking for patterns that do not exist.

# FREE Videos/DVD OFFER

Achieving a high score on your exam depends on both understanding the content and applying your knowledge. **Because your success is our primary goal, we offer FREE Study Tips Videos, which provide top-notch test taking strategies to help optimize your testing experience.**

Our simple request is that you email us feedback about our book in exchange for the strategy-packed videos.

To receive your **FREE Study Tips Videos**, scan the QR code or email freevideos@apexprep.com. Please put "FREE Videos" in the subject line and include the following in the email:

   a. The title of the book

   b. Your rating of the book on a scale of 1-5, with 5 being the highest score

   c. Any thoughts or feedback about the book

Thank you!

# Introduction to the PTCE®

## Function of the Test

Passing the Pharmacy Technician Certification Exam® (PTCE®) is required to be certified as a Certified Pharmacy Technician (CPhT) by the Pharmacy Technician Certification Board (PTCB). The certification is nationally accredited and designed for use in the United States and its territories. While State Boards of Pharmacy set the legal scope of practice for CPhTs in each state, many employers require their pharmacy technicians to have CPhT certification. The PTCE® is a multiple-choice test designed by the PTCB to validate knowledge, increase the quality of patient care, and expand employment and advancement opportunities.

Eligibility for the PTCE® can be achieved in two ways. The first eligibility option is taking a PTCB-Recognized Education/Training Program (or being set to complete one within 60 days). This requirement may also be met with a Pharmacy degree pending an additional eligibility review. The second eligibility option is accumulating a minimum of 500 hours of equivalent work experience as a pharmacy technician. Candidates must also live in the United States or its territories and disclose any criminal history or actions taken against them by a government agency or other authority.

## Test Administration

Candidates must apply to take the PTCE® exam by creating an account on the PTCB website. After an account is successfully created, the candidate can login, complete the application for the PTCE® test, and pay the application fee. Once the application is approved, candidates can schedule and take the PTCE® online or in person at one of more than 1,400 Pearson Professional Centers. Exams are offered year-round.

If a candidate wishes to retake the exam, they must wait 60 days before applying for the second and third attempts and 6 months for each subsequent attempt. If the candidate fails the test 4 times, they will be required to submit evidence of an adequate preparation plan to the PTCB for review and approval before applying to take the test again.

## Test Format

The PTCE® is computer-based multiple-choice exam with 80 scored questions and 10 unscored questions for a total of 90 questions. Each question has 4 possible answers with 1 correct or best available answer. The test will take 2 hours to complete: a 5 minute tutorial, 1 hour and 50 minutes exam time, and a 5 minute post-exam survey. There are 4 knowledge areas covered in the PTCE®: medications (40% of the exam), federal requirements (12.5% of the exam), patient safety and quality assurance (26.25% of the exam), and order entry and processing (21.25% of the exam). Test questions will not be grouped by knowledge area but will be mixed randomly throughout the exam. The 10 unscored questions will not be marked and will also be mixed randomly with the scored questions in the exam.

## Scoring

Scores will be available online one to three weeks after completing the exam. The candidate's score will be based only on the 80 scored questions on the PTCE® exam. Using a modified-Angoff method, passing scores are scaled to account for slight variations in difficulty across different versions of the exam. A passing scaled score is 1,400; the possible scores based on the exam outline are between 1,000 and 1,600.

# Study Prep Plan for the PTCE®

**1** **Breathe**
*Reducing stress is key when preparing for your test.*

**2** **Build**
*Create a study plan to help you stay on track.*

**3** **Begin**
*Stick with your study plan. You've got this!*

**1 Week Study Plan**

| Day 1 | Day 2 | Day 3 | Day 4 | Day 5 | Day 6 | Day 7 |
|---|---|---|---|---|---|---|
| Medications | Dosage and Administration Instructions | Federal Requirements | Patient Safety and Quality Assurance | Order Entry and Processing | Practice Test | Take Your Exam! |

**2 Week Study Plan**

| Day 1 | Day 2 | Day 3 | Day 4 | Day 5 | Day 6 | Day 7 |
|---|---|---|---|---|---|---|
| Medications | Therapeutic Equivalence | Dosage and Administration Instructions | Narrow Therapeutic Index (NTI) Medications | Federal Requirements | Federal Requirements for Restricted Drug Programs and Related... | Patient Safety and Quality Assurance |

| Day 8 | Day 9 | Day 10 | Day 11 | Day 12 | Day 13 | Day 14 |
|---|---|---|---|---|---|---|
| Issues that Require Pharmacist Intervention | Hygiene and Cleaning Standards | Order Entry and Processing | Equipment/ Supplies Required for Drug Administration | Practice Test | Answer Explanations | Take Your Exam! |

**30 Day Study Plan**

| Day 1 | Day 2 | Day 3 | Day 4 | Day 5 | Day 6 | Day 7 |
|---|---|---|---|---|---|---|
| Medications | Analgesic Agents | Therapeutic Equivalence | Common and Life-Threatening Drug Interactions and Contraindications | Dosage and Administration Instructions | Medication Side Effects | Drug Stability |

| Day 8 | Day 9 | Day 10 | Day 11 | Day 12 | Day 13 | Day 14 |
|---|---|---|---|---|---|---|
| Narrow Therapeutic Index (NTI) Medications | Proper Storage of Medications | Practice Questions | Federal Requirements | Federal Requirements for Controlled Substances | Federal Requirements for Restricted Drug Programs and Related... | Practice Questions |

| Day 15 | Day 16 | Day 17 | Day 18 | Day 19 | Day 20 | Day 21 |
|---|---|---|---|---|---|---|
| Patient Safety and Quality Assurance | Error Prevention Strategies | Issues that Require Pharmacist Intervention | Event Reporting Procedures | Types of Prescription Errors | Hygiene and Cleaning Standards | Practice Questions |

| Day 22 | Day 23 | Day 24 | Day 25 | Day 26 | Day 27 | Day 28 |
|---|---|---|---|---|---|---|
| Order Entry and Processing | Basic Formulas, Conversions, and Calculations | Sig Codes, Symbols, Abbreviations, and Medical Terminology | Equipment/ Supplies Required for Drug Administration | Lot Numbers, Expiration Dates, and National Drug Code (NDC) Numbers | Practice Questions | Practice Test |

| Day 29 | Day 30 |
|---|---|
| Answer Explanations | Take Your Exam! |

# Medications

## Generic Names, Brand Names, and Classifications of Medications

### Generic and Brand-Name Nomenclature

The United States Adopted Names (USAN) Council is an organization that defines and authorizes the generic or nonproprietary naming of pharmaceutical drugs. The council is composed of multiple representatives including one member from each of the following organizations: the Food and Drug Administration (FDA), the United States Pharmacopeia (USP), the American Pharmacists Association (APhA), and the American Medical Association (AMA). Nomenclature for prescription drugs begins with the pharmaceutical company that develops the drug. The developer will apply for a nonproprietary name that will become the formal generic name of the product once it is approved by the USAN. After the drug in question proves to be effective, the developer may apply for a patented proprietary or brand name.

Once the patent is expired, however, the medication can be manufactured and sold by other companies under different proprietary names. The generic drug bupropion hydrochloride, for example, is marketed and sold under two distinctly different brand names, Wellbutrin and Zyban. Therefore, every medication can have only one generic name but may be produced under multiple brand names upon patent expiration. In the absence of a standardized classification system among prescription medications, nonproprietary medications are named according to stems, prefixes, infixes, and suffixes established and approved by the USAN. The stems are used to group nonproprietary medications that have a similar therapeutic or pharmacological effect. The stem used for antifungal medications is -conazole, for example, fluconazole and ketoconazole.

## Commonly Prescribed Medications

| Brand Name | Generic | Classification | Indication |
|---|---|---|---|
| **Analgesic Agents** | | | |
| Tylenol | Acetaminophen | Non-NSAID Analgesic | Pain (acute) |
| Advil/Motrin | Ibuprofen | NSAID | Pain/Inflammation |
| Celebrex | Celecoxib | NSAID | Pain/Inflammation |
| Feldene | Piroxicam | NSAID | Pain/Inflammation |
| Indocin | Indomethacin | NSAID | Pain/Inflammation |
| Lodine/Lodine XL | Etodalac/Etodalac XL | NSAID | Pain/Inflammation |
| Mobic | Meloxicam | NSAID | Pain/Inflammation |
| Naprosyn/Aleve | Naproxen/Naproxen Sodium | NSAID | Pain/Inflammation |
| Relafen | Nabumetone | NSAID | Pain/Inflammation |
| Toradol | Ketorolac Tromethamine | NSAID | Pain/Inflammation |
| Duragesic | Fentanyl | Opioid | Pain (chronic) |
| Lortab/Vicodin/Lorcet | Hydrocodone/APAP | Opioid | Pain (acute/chronic) |
| MS Contin | Morphine Sulfate ER | Opioid | Pain (chronic) |
| Oxycontin | Oxycodone ER | Opioid | Pain (chronic) |
| Percocet/Roxicet | Oxycodone/APAP | Opioid | Pain (acute) |
| Tussionex | Hydrocodone/Chlorpheniramine Polistirex | Opioid | Pain (acute) |
| Ultram/Ultram ER | Tramadol/Tramadol ER | Opioid | Pain (acute/chronic) |
| Tylenol w/Codeine | APAP/Codeine | Opioid/Non-NSAID Analgesic | Pain (acute) |
| Ultracet | Tramadol/APAP | Opioid/Non-NSAID Analgesic | Pain (acute) |
| Vicoprofen | Hydrocodone/ibuprofen | Opioid/NSAID | Pain (acute) |
| Ecotrin/Bufferin | Aspirin | Salicylate | Pain (acute) |
| **Anti-Infective Agents** | | | |
| Stromectol | Ivermectin | Anthelmintic | Parasitic infection |

| Macrodantin/Macrobid | Nitrofurantoin/Nitrofurantoin ER | Antibiotic-Antiseptic (urinary) | Bacterial infection |
|---|---|---|---|

## Anti-Infective Agents (Cont.)

| | | | |
|---|---|---|---|
| Keflex | Cephalexin | Antibiotic-Cephalosporin (1$^{st}$ generation) | Bacterial infection |
| Ceftin | Cefuroxime Axetil | Antibiotic-Cephalosporin (2$^{nd}$ generation) | Bacterial infection |
| Omnicef | Cefdinir | Antibiotic-Cephalosporin (3$^{rd}$ generation) | Bacterial infection |
| Avelox | Moxifloxacin | Antibiotic-Fluoroquinolone | Bacterial infection |
| Cipro/Cipro XR | Ciprofloxacin | Antibiotic-Fluoroquinolone | Bacterial infection |
| Levaquin | Levofloxacin | Antibiotic-Fluoroquinolone | Bacterial infection |
| Biaxin/Biaxin XL | Clarithromycin | Antibiotic-Macrolide | Bacterial infection |
| Zithromax/Zmax/Azasite | Azithromycin | Antibiotic-Macrolide | Bacterial infection |
| Amoxil | Amoxicillin | Antibiotic-Penicillins | Bacterial infection |
| Augmentin/Augmentin XR | Amoxicillin-Clavulanate | Antibiotic-Penicillins | Bacterial infection |
| Pen-Vee K | Penicillin V Potassium | Antibiotic-Penicillins | Bacterial infection |
| Bactrim/Septra (SS/DS) | Sulfamethoxazole-Trimethoprim | Antibiotic-Sulfonamide | Bacterial infection |
| Vibramycin | Doxycycline | Antibiotic-Tetracycline | Bacterial infection |
| Flagyl/Flagyl ER | Metronidazole/Metronidazole ER | Antibiotic/Antiprotozoal-Nitroimidazole (1$^{st}$ generation) | Bacterial/Parasitic infection |
| Diflucan | Fluconazole | Antifungal | Fungal infection |
| Mycostatin/Nystop | Nystatin | Antifungal | Fungal infection |
| Nizoral | Ketoconazole | Antifungal | Fungal infection |
| Combivir | Zidovudine-Lamivudine | Antiretroviral | Viral infection (HIV) |
| Truvada | Emtricitabine-Tenofovir | Antiretroviral | Viral infection (HIV) |
| Epclusa | Sofosbuvir-Velpatasvir | Antiviral | Viral infection (HCV) |
| Harvoni | Ledipasvir-Sofosbuvir | Antiviral | Viral infection (HCV) |
| Tamiflu | Oseltamivir | Antiviral | Viral infection (influenza) |
| Valtrex | Valacyclovir | Antiviral | Viral infection (HSV) |
| Zovirax | Acyclovir | Antiviral | Viral infection (HSV) |

## Cardiovascular Agents

| | | | |
|---|---|---|---|
| Zetia | Ezetimibe | Absorption Inhibitor | Hyperlipidemia |
| Accupril | Quinapril | ACE Inhibitor | Hypertension |
| Altace | Ramipril | ACE Inhibitor | Hypertension |
| Lotensin | Benazepril | ACE Inhibitor | Hypertension |
| Vasotec | Enalapril | ACE Inhibitor | Hypertension |
| Zestril | Lisinopril | ACE Inhibitor | Hypertension |
| Accuretic | Quinapril/HCTZ | ACE Inhibitor/Diuretic | Hypertension |
| Lotensin HCT | Benazepril/HCTZ | ACE Inhibitor/Diuretic | Hypertension |
| Zestoretic | Lisinopril/HCTZ | ACE Inhibitor/Diuretic | Hypertension |
| Coumadin | Warfarin | Anticoagulant | Blood thinner |
| Eliquis | Apixaban | Anticoagulant | Blood thinner |
| Xarelto | Rivaroxaban | Anticoagulant | Blood thinner |
| Aggrenox | Aspirin/Dipyridamole | Antiplatelet | Blood thinner |
| Plavix | Clopidogrel | Antiplatelet | Blood thinner |
| Avapro | Irbesartan | ARB | Hypertension |
| Benicar | Olmesartan | ARB | Hypertension |
| Cozaar | Losartan | ARB | Hypertension |
| Diovan | Valsartan | ARB | Hypertension |
| Avalide | Irbesartan/HCTZ | ARB/Diuretic | Hypertension |
| Benicar HCT | Olmesartan/HCTZ | ARB/Diuretic | Hypertension |
| Diovan HCT | Valsartan/HCTZ | ARB/Diuretic | Hypertension |
| Hyzaar | Losartan/HCTZ | ARB/Diuretic | Hypertension |
| Bystolic | Nebivolol | Beta Blocker | Hypertension |
| Coreg/Coreg CR | Carvedilol/Carvedilol CR | Beta Blocker | Hypertension |
| Lopressor | Metoprolol Tartrate | Beta Blocker | Hypertension |

| Tenormin | Atenolol | Beta Blocker | Hypertension |
|---|---|---|---|

## Cardiovascular Agents (Cont.)

| Toprol XL | Metoprolol Succinate | Beta Blocker | Hypertension |
|---|---|---|---|
| Norvasc | Amlodipine | CCB (Dihydropyridines) | Hypertension |
| Procardia/Procardia XL | Nifedipine/Nifedipine ER | CCB (Dihydropyridines) | Hypertension |
| Calan/Calan SR | Verapamil/Verapamil ER | CCB (Non-dihydropyridines) | Hypertension |
| Cardizem/Cardizem CD | Diltiazem | CCB (Non-dihydropyridines) | Hypertension |
| Klor-Con | Potassium | Electrolyte | Hypokalemia |
| Tricor | Fenofibrate | Fibrate | Hyperlipidemia |
| Lanoxin | Digoxin | Glycoside | CHF/Antiarrhythmic |
| Lasix | Furosemide | Loop Diuretic | Edema |
| Crestor | Rosuvastatin | Statin | Hyperlipidemia |
| Lipitor | Atorvastatin | Statin | Hyperlipidemia |
| Pravachol | Pravastatin | Statin | Hyperlipidemia |
| Zocor | Simvastatin | Statin | Hyperlipidemia |

## Respiratory Agents

| Allegra | Fexofenadine | Antihistamine | Allergy |
|---|---|---|---|
| Claritin | Loratadine | Antihistamine | Allergy |
| Zyrtec | Cetirizine | Antihistamine | Allergy |
| Combivent | Albuterol/Ipratropium | Bronchodilator | Asthma/COPD |
| Spiriva | Tiotropium | Bronchodilator | COPD |
| Ventolin | Albuterol | Bronchodilator | Asthma/COPD |
| Advair Diskus | Fluticasone Propionate/Salmeterol | Bronchodilator/Steroid | Asthma/COPD |
| Symbicort | Budesonide/Formoterol | Bronchodilator/Steroid | Asthma/COPD |
| Singulair | Montelukast | Leukotriene Inhibitor | Asthma |
| Flonase | Fluticasone | Steroid | Asthma/Allergy |
| Nasonex | Mometasone | Steroid | Asthma/Allergy |
| Pulmicort | Budesonide | Steroid | Asthma/COPD |
| Rhinocort | Budesonide | Steroid | Asthma/COPD |

## Genitourinary Agents

| Avodart | Dutasteride | 5-alpha-reductase Inhibitor | BPH |
|---|---|---|---|
| Proscar | Finasteride | 5-alpha-reductase Inhibitor | BPH |
| Detrol/ Detrol LA | Tolterodine/Tolterodine LA | Antispasmodic (urinary) | Overactive bladder |
| Ditropan/Ditropan XL | Oxybutynin/Oxybutynin XL | Antispasmodic (urinary) | Overactive bladder |
| Myrbetriq | Mirabegron | Antispasmodic (urinary) | Overactive bladder |
| Flomax | Tamsulosin | Selective Alpha Blocker | BPH |
| Uroxatral | Alfuzosin | Selective Alpha Blocker | BPH |
| Cialis | Tadalafil | Vasodilator | Erectile dysfunction |
| Viagra | Sildenafil | Vasodilator | Erectile dysfunction |

## Gastrointestinal Agents

| Lomotil | Diphenoxylate/Atropine | Antidiarrheal | Diarrhea |
|---|---|---|---|
| Compro | Prochlorperazine | Antiemetic | Nausea/Vomiting |
| Zofran | Ondansetron | Antiemetic | Nausea/Vomiting |
| Reglan | Metoclopramide | Antiemetic (Prokinetic) | GERD/Nausea/Vomiting |
| Pepcid | Famotidine | Antihistamine | GERD |
| Phenergan | Promethazine | Antihistamine | Nausea/Vomiting |
| Aciphex | Rabeprazole | Proton Pump Inhibitor | GERD |
| Nexium | Esomeprazole | Proton Pump Inhibitor | GERD |
| Prevacid | Lansoprazole | Proton Pump Inhibitor | GERD |
| Prilosec | Omeprazole | Proton Pump Inhibitor | GERD |
| Protonix | Pantoprazole | Proton Pump Inhibitor | GERD |

## Endocrine Agents (Hormones & Modifiers)

| Androgel | Testosterone transdermal | Androgen Hormone | Hypogonadism |
|---|---|---|---|
| Depo-Testosterone | Testosterone injectable | Androgen Hormone | Hypogonadism |
| Glucophage/Glucophage XR | Metformin/Metformin ER | Antidiabetic | Diabetes Mellitus, Type II |

| Janumet | Sitagliptin/Metformin | Antidiabetic | Diabetes Mellitus, Type II |
|---|---|---|---|

## Endocrine Agents (Hormones & Modifiers) (Cont.)

| Januvia | Sitagliptin | Antidiabetic | Diabetes Mellitus, Type II |
|---|---|---|---|
| Onglyza | Saxagliptin | Antidiabetic | Diabetes Mellitus, Type II |
| Amaryl | Glimepiride | Antidiabetic (Sulfonylurea) | Diabetes Mellitus, Type II |
| Glucotrol/Glucotrol XL | Glipizide/Glipizide XL | Antidiabetic (Sulfonylurea) | Diabetes Mellitus, Type II |
| Actos | Pioglitazone | Antidiabetic (Thiazolidinediones) | Diabetes Mellitus, Type II |
| Actonel | Risedronate | Bisphosphonate | Osteoporosis |
| Boniva | Ibandronate | Bisphosphonate | Osteoporosis |
| Fosamax | Alendronate | Bisphosphonate | Osteoporosis |
| Deltasone | Prednisone | Corticosteroid (systemic) | Anti-inflammatory |
| Medrol | Methylprednisolone | Corticosteroid (systemic) | Anti-inflammatory/Allergy |
| Estrace | Estradiol | Estrogen Hormone | Osteoporosis/Menopause |
| Premarin | Conjugated Estrogens | Estrogen Hormone | Osteoporosis (Postmenopausal) |
| Humulin R | Insulin Regular | Insulin (fast-acting) | Diabetes Mellitus, Type I/II |
| Levemir | Insulin Detemir | Insulin (intermediate-acting, long-acting) | Diabetes Mellitus, Type I/II |
| Humulin N | Insulin NPH | Insulin (intermediate-acting) | Diabetes Mellitus, Type I/II |
| Lantus | Insulin Glargine | Insulin (long-acting) | Diabetes Mellitus, Type I/II |
| Toujeo | Insulin Glargine | Insulin (long-acting) | Diabetes Mellitus, Type I/II |
| Tresiba | Insulin Degludec | Insulin (long-acting) | Diabetes Mellitus, Type I/II |
| Apidra | Insulin Glulisine | Insulin (rapid-acting) | Diabetes Mellitus, Type I/II |
| Humalog | Insulin Lispro | Insulin (rapid-acting) | Diabetes Mellitus, Type I/II |
| Novolog | Insulin Aspart | Insulin (rapid-acting) | Diabetes Mellitus, Type I/II |
| Ocella/Yasmin/Yaz | Ethinyl Estradiol/Drosperinone | Oral Contraceptive | Birth control |
| Ortho Tri-Cyclen Lo | Norgestimate/Ethinyl Estradiol | Oral Contraceptive | Birth control |
| Depo-Provera | Medroxyprogesterone | Progestin Contraceptive | Birth control |
| Evista | Raloxifene | Selective Estrogen Receptor Modulator | Osteoporosis (Postmenopausal) |
| Armor Thyroid | Desiccated Thyroid | Thyroid Hormone (porcine) | Hypothyroidism |
| Synthroid/Levoxyl | Levothyroxine | Thyroid Hormone (synthetic t4) | Hypothyroidism |

## Musculoskeletal Agents

| Colcrys | Colchicine | Antigout | Gout |
|---|---|---|---|
| Uloric | Febuxostat | Antigout (Xanthine Oxidase Inhibitor) | Gout |
| Zyloprim | Allopurinol | Antigout (Xanthine Oxidase Inhibitor) | Gout |
| Flexeril | Cyclobenzaprine | Muscle Relaxant | Muscle spasms |
| Robaxin | Methocarbamol | Muscle Relaxant | Muscle spasms |
| Skelaxin | Metaxalone | Muscle Relaxant | Musculoskeletal pain (acute) |
| Soma | Carisoprodol | Muscle Relaxant | Musculoskeletal pain (acute) |

## Psychotropic Agents

| Cogentin | Benztropine | Acetylcholine/Histamine Receptor Antagonist | Parkinson's disease |
|---|---|---|---|
| Ativan | Lorazepam | Antianxiety (Benzodiazepine) | Anxiety/Insomnia |
| Klonopin | Clonazepam | Antianxiety (Benzodiazepine) | Anxiety |
| Restoril | Temazepam | Antianxiety (Benzodiazepine) | Insomnia |
| Valium | Diazepam | Antianxiety (Benzodiazepine) | Anxiety |
| Xanax | Alprazolam | Antianxiety (Benzodiazepine) | Anxiety |
| Depakote | Divalproex Sodium | Anticonvulsant | Seizure disorders |
| Dilantin | Phenytoin | Anticonvulsant | Seizure disorders |
| Keppra | Levetiracetam | Anticonvulsant | Seizure disorders |
| Lamictal | Lamotrigine | Anticonvulsant | Seizure disorders |
| Tegretol | Carbamazepine | Anticonvulsant | Seizure disorders |
| Trileptal | Oxcarbazepine | Anticonvulsant | Seizure disorders |

## Psychotropic Agents (cont.)

| Wellbutrin | Bupropion Hydrochloride | Antidepressant (NDRI) | Depression/Smoking cessation |
|---|---|---|---|
| Cymbalta | Duloxetine | Antidepressant (SNRI) | Depression/Fibromyalgia |
| Effexor | Venlafaxine | Antidepressant (SNRI) | Anxiety/Depression |
| Celexa | Citalopram | Antidepressant (SSRI) | Anxiety/Depression |
| Lexapro | Escitalopram | Antidepressant (SSRI) | Anxiety/Depression |
| Paxil | Paroxetine | Antidepressant (SSRI) | Anxiety/Depression |
| Prozac | Fluoxetine | Antidepressant (SSRI) | Anxiety/Depression |
| Zoloft | Sertraline | Antidepressant (SSRI) | Anxiety/Depression |
| Haldol | Haloperidol | Antipsychotic (1st generation) | Psychosis |
| Abilify | Aripiprazole | Antipsychotic (2nd generation) | Schizophrenia/Bipolar disorder |
| Geodon | Ziprasidone | Antipsychotic (2nd generation) | Schizophrenia/Bipolar disorder |
| Latuda | Lurasidone | Antipsychotic (2nd generation) | Schizophrenia/Bipolar disorder |
| Risperdal | Risperidone | Antipsychotic (2nd generation) | Schizophrenia/Bipolar disorder |
| Seroquel | Quetiapine | Antipsychotic (2nd generation) | Schizophrenia/Bipolar disorder |
| Zyprexa | Olanzapine | Antipsychotic (2nd generation) | Schizophrenia/Bipolar disorder |
| Aricept | Donepezil | Cholinesterase Inhibitor | Alzheimer's disease |
| Mirapex | Pramipexole | Dopamine Agonist | Parkinson's disease |
| Requip | Ropinirole | Dopamine Agonist | Parkinson's disease |
| Sinemet | Carbidopa/Levodopa | Dopamine Agonist | Parkinson's disease |
| Namenda | Memantine | NMDA Receptor Antagonist | Alzheimer's disease |
| Ambien | Zolpidem | Sedative (Hypnotic) | Insomnia |
| Lunesta | Eszopiclone | Sedative (Hypnotic) | Insomnia |
| Adderall | Dextroamphetamine/Amphetamine | Stimulant (NDRI) | ADD/ADHD |
| Concerta | Methylphenidate | Stimulant (NDRI) | ADHD |
| Focalin | Dexmethylphenidate | Stimulant (NDRI) | ADHD |
| Quillivant XR | Methylphenidate XR | Stimulant (NDRI) | ADHD |
| Ritalin | Methylphenidate | Stimulant (NDRI) | ADHD |
| Vyvanse | Lisdexamfetamine | Stimulant (NDRI) | ADHD |

## Ophthalmic Agents

| Alphagan P | Brimonidine | Alpha Agonist | Glaucoma/Ocular HTN |
|---|---|---|---|
| Combigan | Brimonidine/Timolol | Alpha Agonist/Beta Blocker | Glaucoma/Ocular HTN |
| Tobradex | Tobramycin/Dexamethasone Ophthalmic | Aminoglycoside/Corticosteroid | Bacterial infection/Inflammation |
| Vigamox | Moxifloxacin Ophthalmic | Antibiotic-Fluoroquinolone | Bacterial conjunctivitis |
| Zymar | Gatifloxacin Ophthalmic | Antibiotic-Fluoroquinolone | Bacterial conjunctivitis |
| Azasite | Azithromycin Ophthalmic | Antibiotic-Macrolide | Bacterial conjunctivitis |
| Cosopt | Dorzolamide/Timolol | Beta Blocker/Carbonic Anhydrase Inhibitor | Glaucoma/Ocular HTN |
| Restasis | Cyclosporine | Calcineurin Inhibitor | Dry eye |
| Pred Forte | Prednisolone Acetate | Corticosteroid | Ocular inflammation |
| Lumigan | Bimatoprost | Prostaglandin Analog | Glaucoma/Ocular HTN |
| Travatan | Travaprost | Prostaglandin Analog | Glaucoma/Ocular HTN |
| Xalatan | Latanoprost | Prostaglandin Analog | Glaucoma/Ocular HTN |

## Otic Agents

| Cortisporin | Neomycin/Polymyxin B/ Hydrocortisone Otic | Aminoglycoside/Corticosteroid | Otitis externa |
|---|---|---|---|
| DermOtic | Fluocinolone Otic | Corticosteroid | Otitis eczema |
| Ciprodex | Ciprofloxacin/Dexamethasone Otic | Fluoroquinolone/Corticosteroid | Bacterial otitis |

| | | | |
|---|---|---|---|
| Cipro HC | Ciprofloxacin/Hydrocortisone Otic | Fluroquinolone/Corticosteroid | Bacterial otitis |

## Classifications of Medications

Drugs are commonly classified according to the area of the body they act on as well as the mechanism of action, or how they work in the body. However, there is no standardized method of classifying medications, so classifications may vary depending on the referenced source.

### Common Medication Classification Schemes

**Analgesics**
- Non-aspirin, non-NSAID
- NSAIDs
- Opiates
- Salicylates

**Anti-Infectives**
- Anthelmintics
- Antibiotics
- Antifungals
- Antimycobacterials
- Antiprotozoals (parasitic)
- Antivirals

**Antineoplastics**

**Cardiovascular Agents**
- ACE inhibitors
- Antianginals
- Antiarrhythmics
- Anticoagulants/thrombolytics
- Antihyperlipidemics
- Antihypertensives
- Beta blockers
- Calcium channel blockers
- Diuretics
- Vasodilators
- Vasopressors

**Endocrine Agents (Hormones & Modifiers)**
- Adrenal agents
- Androgens
- Contraceptives
- Estrogens
- Insulins
- Oral antidiabetics
- Progestins
- Thyroid & parathyroid agents

**Gastrointestinal Agents**
- Antacid/antiulcer agents
- Antidiarrheals
- Antiemetics
- Enzymes
- Laxatives/stool softeners

**Genitourinary Agents**
- Phosphodiesterase inhibitors
- Urinary tract agents

**Hematological Agents**
- Hematopoietic agents
- Hemostatic agents

**Immunobiologic Agents**
- Immune globulins
- Vaccines

**Musculoskeletal Agents**
- Antigout agents
- Muscle relaxants
- Osteoporotics

**Neurological Agents**
- ADD and ADHD agents
- Anti-Alzheimer's agents
- Anti-epileptics
- Anti-migraine agents
- Antiparkinson agents

**Ophthalmic & Otic Agents**
- Antiglaucoma agents
- Other opthalmics
- Otics

**Psychotropic Agents**
- Antianxiety agents
- Antidepressants
- Antipsychotics
- Drug dependency
- Sedatives/hypnotics

**Respiratory Agents**
- Antihistamines
- Antitussives
- Bronchodilators
- Decongestants
- Expectorants/mucolytics

(Source: "The Pharmacy Technician" 4th Edition, APhA Basic Pharmacy & Pharmacology Series)

## Analgesic Agents

Analgesic agents are a class of medications that can be used to treat acute pain, chronic pain, inflammatory conditions, or a combination of the three. This class of medications consists of three types of peripherally acting analgesics—non-steroidal anti-inflammatory drugs (NSAIDs), salicylates, and non-aspirin/non-NSAID medications—and opiates, which act on the central nervous system (CNS).

NSAIDs are a class of analgesics used to treat pain and inflammation. This class of medications includes meloxicam (Mobic), celecoxib (Celebrex), ibuprofen (Advil or Motrin), and naproxen (Aleve).

Salicylates are analgesic agents used to treat acute pain; they are generally considered to be NSAIDs as well. Salicylates include the over the counter (OTC) medication aspirin, which is sold under such brand names as Ecotrin, Bayer, and St. Joseph's.

Non-aspirin/non-NSAID analgesic drugs include the OTC pain reliever acetaminophen, more commonly referred to by the brand name Tylenol. Acetaminophen is considered a non-NSAID analgesic because it has pain-relieving properties but does not treat inflammation.

Opiates are powerful analgesic agents that include morphine and codeine as well as opiate-derived agents such as fentanyl. Most of these pain medications are labeled Schedule II narcotics by the Drug Enforcement Agency (DEA) due to their significant potential for abuse. Opiate combination medications such as the hydrocodone/acetaminophen combinations Norco and Vicodin also fall under the Schedule II status.

## Cardiovascular Agents

Cardiovascular agents cover a broad range of medical conditions that affect the circulatory system. They include antihypertensives, vasopressors, anticoagulants, antihyperlipidemics, antianginals, and antiarrhythmics.

Antihypertensives are medications that are used to treat high blood pressure and can be further classified by how they act in the body. Beta blockers, for example, are a class of antihypertensives that lower blood pressure by reducing the rate and force by which the heart beats and contracts. Atenolol (Tenormin) is an example of a beta blocker.

Calcium channel blockers (CCBs) are another class of antihypertensives that inhibit ion movement into the heart muscle, which reduces the force of contraction, allowing blood vessels to dilate. The antihypertensive medications that decrease blood pressure by dilating blood vessels, allowing blood to flow more freely, are referred to as vasodilators.

Diuretics are a class of antihypertensive medication that decreases blood volume, which, in turn, decreases blood pressure. Diuretics act by inhibiting sodium and chloride salt reabsorption. Water is pulled into the kidneys along with the sodium and chloride salt and eliminated from the body through urine, resulting in decreased blood volume.

Finally, angiotensin-converting enzyme (ACE) inhibitors are antihypertensives that act to relax blood vessel walls by preventing the conversion of the enzyme angiotensin I to angiotensin II, an enzyme that narrows blood vessel walls.

Vasopressors, in contrast, contract or narrow blood vessels to raise blood pressure. Examples include epinephrine (used in EpiPens to treat severe allergic reactions) and phenylephrine.

Anticoagulants are medications that are used to prevent the formation of clots in the blood, thereby reducing the risk of heart attack and stroke. Anticoagulants are often referred to as blood thinners; however, they do not actually thin the blood but rather slow down the clotting processes in the body. Examples of anticoagulants include warfarin and heparin. Thrombolytics, on the other hand, act by dissolving existing blood clots in the body. Thrombolytics are not considered blood thinners but are typically classified with anticoagulants because they also reduce the risk of stroke and heart attack.

Antihyperlipidemics are medications used to treat high cholesterol, and they include a group of medications often referred to as statins. Atorvastatin (Lipitor) is one example of a statin.

Antianginals are used to treat ischemic chest pains referred to as angina. There are several types of antianginals including nitrates, calcium channel blockers, beta blockers, and ranolazine.

Antiarrhythmics are a class of medications prescribed for conditions that include irregular heart rhythms such as tachycardia, bradycardia, and atrial fibrillation. There are four main subclassifications of antiarrhythmic drugs: sodium channel blockers (Class I), beta blockers (Class II), potassium channel blockers (Class III), and calcium channel blockers (Class IV).

## Anti-Infective Agents

Anti-infective agents are medications that are used to treat bacterial, fungal, parasitic, viral, and protozoal infections in the body. It is important that the anti-infective agent prescribed is specific to the type of infection present.

Antibiotics are medications used for the treatment of bacterial infections; they act by suppressing the growth of microorganisms in the body. Antibiotics can further be classified by how they work. Bacteriostatic antibiotics such as tetracyclines, amphenicols, sulfonamides, and macrolides inhibit the growth and reproduction ability of bacteria. Bactericidal antibiotics such as cephalosporins, fluoroquinolones, glycopeptides, and penicillins work by killing the bacteria, usually by attacking the cell wall or the contents of the cell itself.

Antifungals are prescribed for fungal infections involving yeast and molds. Most often they are prescribed for candidiasis or common yeast infections, oral thrush, and ringworm infections. Examples of antifungal medications include fluconazole (Diflucan), nystatin (Mycostatin, Nystop), and ketoconazole (Nizoral).

Anthelmintics are prescribed for parasitic infections such as strongyloidiasis or roundworm infestations and includes ivermectin (Stromectol). They are often prescribed prophylactically for patients traveling abroad to prevent parasitic infections.

Antiviral medications are used to treat a broad range of ailments including shingles, hepatitis, and human immunodeficiency virus (HIV). The primary objective of an antiviral medication is to inhibit the replication of the virus in the body. Examples of antiviral medications used to treat viral infections include valacyclovir (Valtrex), ledipasvir/sofosbuvir (Harvoni), and lopinavir/ritonavir (Kaletra).

Antiprotozoals are a class of medications used to treat parasitic infections such as scabies. Metronidazole (Flagyl) is an antibiotic medication commonly prescribed for both bacterial and protozoal infections.

## Respiratory Agents

Respiratory agents are used to treat conditions or infections that disrupt a patient's normal airway or breathing process. Respiratory agents include antihistamines, antitussives, bronchodilators, decongestants, expectorants, and mucolytics. These classes of medications are used to treat ailments such as allergies; bacterial or viral infections such as croup, bronchitis, and pneumonia; and chronic conditions such as asthma, chronic obstructive pulmonary disorder (COPD), and emphysema.

Antihistamines are respiratory agents used to treat chronic or seasonal allergies associated with irritants such as pet dander, pollen, or dust. A few examples of commonly prescribed antihistamines include loratadine (Claritin), cetirizine (Zyrtec), and hydroxyzine (Atarax). Antihistamines such as diphenhydramine, more commonly referred to by its brand name Benadryl, may be prescribed to treat reactions to insect bites, food allergies, or allergic reactions to other medications.

Antitussives are a class of respiratory agent used to suppress coughs. Antitussives are used for both a wet or productive cough in which phlegm is present and a dry or non-productive cough without phlegm. Examples of antitussives include the prescription medications benzonatate (Tessalon Perles) and dextromethorphan, which is sold under various OTC brand names such as Delsym and Robitussin.

Bronchodilators are a class of respiratory medications that alleviate bronchospasms by opening the airways in the lungs, relieving the narrowing of the bronchi, and allowing improved movement of oxygen in the lungs. Albuterol (ProAir HFA) and levalbuterol (Xopenex) are bronchodilators that are inhaled, while theophylline (Theo-dur) is an orally administered bronchodilator. The bronchodilator and decongestant ephedrine is a regulated ingredient under the Combat Methamphetamine Epidemic Act (CMEA), which mandates purchase limitations and requires that the product be kept behind the pharmacy counter. For example, Bronkaid is an OTC medication indicated for the treatment of asthma symptoms that contains the expectorant guaifenesin and the bronchodilator ephedrine.

Decongestants are a class of respiratory agent used to reduce congestion and drainage of the nasal passages. Decongestant medications include pseudoephedrine (Sudafed) and phenylephrine (Sudafed PE). Pseudoephedrine is an access restricted medication and is regulated by CMEA because it is the precursor ingredient used to produce methamphetamine.

Expectorants and mucolytics are respiratory medications used to help relieve chest congestion. Expectorants increase the water content of mucus, thinning it out and making it easier for the body to cough up. Guaifenesin (Mucinex) is an expectorant. Mucolytic medications such as acetylcysteine (Mucomyst) decrease the viscosity or thickness of bronchial mucus in the lungs, allowing it to be more easily cleared from the body.

## Endocrine Agents

Endocrine agents are medications that act on or modify the hormone secreting glands in the body including the adrenal glands, the gonads, the pancreas, the pituitary gland, the thymus gland, the thyroid, and the parathyroid glands.

Adrenal agents include a class of medications called corticosteroids. Natural secretion of corticosteroids such as hydrocortisone and methylprednisolone by the adrenal gland helps regulate metabolic functions, stress responses, and immune system responses like inflammation. Adrenal agents may be prescribed for many different ailments including adrenal insufficiency, contact dermatitis, and rheumatoid arthritis. Examples of corticosteroids include hydrocortisone (Cortef), prednisone (Sterapred), and methylprednisolone (Medrol).

Androgen agents affect both male and female gonads. They include the male sex hormone testosterone, which is used to treat the effects of male hypogonadism or low testosterone. Examples of this class of medication include the transdermal testosterone hormone replacement Androgel as well as the injectable formulation testosterone cypionate (Depo-Testosterone). Androgen replacement medications can also be used to treat some breast cancers in women.

Contraceptives are a class of medications used to prevent pregnancy, regulate menstrual cycles in women, and treat severe acne by increasing the levels of the female sex hormones estrogen and progesterone in the body. They come in various dosage forms including implants, oral tablets, injectables, and transdermal patches. Oral contraceptives like the generic norgestimate/ethinyl estradiol may be marketed under several brand names including Sprintec, Ortho Tri-Cyclen, and Previfem.

Estrogen agents are used in contraceptives and may be used by women to relieve menopausal symptoms such as hot flashes, night sweats, and vaginal dryness. Estrogen medications may also be used to prevent bone loss or osteoporosis in postmenopausal women. An example of an estrogen medication is estradiol (Estrace).

Progestin agents may be used to prevent ovulation and are often found in contraceptives with estrogens. They can also treat menopausal symptoms in women and include the medications progesterone (Prometrium) and medroxyprogesterone (Provera).

Insulins are a class of medication used to control blood glucose in the body when the pancreas does not produce sufficient natural insulin (commonly known as diabetes). They are further classified by their duration of action. Lispro (Humalog), for instance, is a rapid-acting insulin, while glargine (Lantus) is a long-acting insulin.

Oral antidiabetics are non-insulin diabetes medications that are used to control blood glucose levels. Examples of oral antidiabetic medications include metformin (Glucophage) and saxagliptin (Onglyza).

The pituitary gland, often referred to as the master gland, is a major hormone producer and regulator. It produces hormones that signal other parts of the body to produce additional hormones. Collectively, these hormones carry out major functions of the brain and body such as managing blood pressure, regulating skeletal and muscular growth, producing breastmilk after childbirth, and regulating internal hydration levels. Therefore, medications and agents that act on the pituitary gland must be carefully monitored. These medications typically aim to address issues that affect the function of the pituitary gland. Most commonly, dysfunction occurs as a result of tumors on or near the pituitary gland that interfere with hormone function. Dopamine agonists are a class of medication that bind to dopamine receptors in the brain when pituitary tumors are present. These can help reduce tumor size and normalize the production of prolactin, a hormone that is responsible for many reproductive and postpartum processes.

The most commonly prescribed dopamine agonists include bromocriptine (Cycloset and Parlodel) and cabergoline (Dostinex). Somatostatin analogs are another class of medication used to shrink pituitary tumors. These work by mimicking the hormone somatostatin, which can help in cases where the pituitary gland is producing excess cortisol, metabolic, and growth hormones. The most commonly prescribed somatostatin analogs include octreotide (Sandostatin), lanreotide (Somatuline), and pasireotide (Signifor LAR). In addition, patients may be prescribed classes of drugs that do not act directly on the pituitary gland or associated tumors, but instead act on the hormone pathway that has been disrupted. These classes of drugs include steroidogenesis inhibitors and cortisol receptor blockers. Steroidogenesis inhibitors reduce high cortisol production and include osilodrostat (Isturisa), mitotane (Lysodren), and aminoglutethimide (Cytadren). Cortisol receptor blockers work by blocking the pathway of cortisol to tissues in the body. Mifepristone (Korlym) is a cortisol receptor blocker.

The thymus gland is an important part of the immune system in childhood. Pediatric patients with dysfunctional thymus glands are immunocompromised, as they have limited adaptive immunity. The primary function of the thymus is to produce and mature T-cells, which are responsible for mounting specific immune responses against foreign agents in the body. These processes occur with the production of the hormone thymosin. These processes are highly active until puberty, after which thymus function slows down considerably; by age 75, it completely ceases.

Medications that act on the thymus gland primarily focus on regulating thymosin or other related immune system pathways; however, patients who develop thymus cancers may also be prescribed medications that act on the thymus. Thymalfasin or thymosin alpha 1 (Zadaxin) is classified as a peptide drug and is the most commonly used medication to enhance thymosin production in patients who are immunocompromised. In thymus-related cancers, the primary class of drugs that are administered to act on the cancerous cells on or near the thymus are chemotherapeutics. Medications include doxorubicin (Adriamycin), cisplatin (Platinol), and cyclophosphamide (Cytoxan). These are generally paired with a class of drugs known as corticosteroids, which help maintain steroid levels during the treatment process. The mostly commonly used drug for this purpose is prednisone (Deltasone).

Thyroid and parathyroid agents include medications used to treat thyroid disorders. Levothyroxine (Synthroid, Levothroid, and Levoxyl), for example, is used to treat an underactive thyroid or hypothyroidism. Methimazole (Tapazole) is used for the treatment of an overactive thyroid, also called hyperthyroidism.

## Gastrointestinal Agents

Gastrointestinal agents are a class of medications used to treat disorders of the digestive system including the stomach, esophagus, and intestinal tract. Gastrointestinal agents include antacids, acid reducers or antiulcer agents, antidiarrheals, antiemetics, digestive enzymes, laxatives, and stool softeners.

Antacids and antiulcer agents are medications used for the treatment of several gastrointestinal conditions including dyspepsia, also known as heartburn or indigestion; duodenal and gastric ulcers; and gastroesophageal reflux disease (GERD). Calcium carbonate (TUMS) and aluminum hydroxide (Maalox) are short-acting antacids used to treat indigestion and are available as OTC medications. Examples of antiulcer medications include the proton pump inhibitors (PPIs) esomeprazole (Nexium) and pantoprazole (Protonix).

Antidiarrheal agents are medications used for the treatment or prevention of diarrhea. Examples of antidiarrheal agents include the Schedule V controlled substance diphenoxylate/atropine (Lomotil), while loperamide (Imodium) and bismuth subsalicylate (Kaopectate) are common OTC antidiarrheals. This classification sometimes includes probiotics such as Florastor as well.

Antiemetic agents are a class of medications used to treat nausea, vomiting, and motion sickness. Examples of antiemetic medications include promethazine (Phenergan), ondansetron (Zofran), and meclizine (Bonine).

Enzymes are a class of gastrointestinal agents used to treat patients that have exocrine pancreatic insufficiency, a condition in which the production of pancreatic enzymes is not adequate to aid in the digestion of food and nutrient absorption. Pancrelipase is an enzyme agent used to treat exocrine pancreatic insufficiency and is the active pharmaceutical ingredient in Creon, Zenpep, and Pancreaze.

Laxatives are gastrointestinal agents used to treat constipation, and stool softeners are a particular type of laxative. There are several different types of laxatives that work in different ways and are useful for treating different levels of constipation. Laxatives can work by increasing the water content and bulk of the stool (fiber), increasing the amount of water in the intestine (osmotic laxatives), stimulating the intestinal muscles to contract (stimulant laxatives), or, less commonly, lubricating the intestinal walls and surface of the stools (lubricant laxatives). Suppositories and enemas may also be considered laxatives. Stool softeners (emollient laxatives) work by softening the surface of the stool, allowing for greater water absorption and softer stools. Examples of prescription laxative medications include lactulose (Kristalose) and mesalamine (Asacol). Bisacodyl is an OTC laxative that is marketed under the brand names Dulcolax and Fleet Enema, while docusate sodium (Colace) is an OTC stool softener.

## Genitourinary Agents

Genitourinary agents are a class of medications that are used to treat conditions that affect the urinary tract and genitals. This class of medications covers conditions such as kidney stones, erectile dysfunction, incontinence, and benign prostatic hyperplasia (BPH).

Phosphodiesterase inhibitors are a class of genitourinary agents that may be used for the treatment of erectile dysfunction and BPH. This class of medications includes sildenafil (Viagra), tadalafil (Cialis), and vardenafil (Levitra).

Urinary tract agents are a broad class of medications that includes medications to treat BPH, dysuria (painful urination), and overactive bladder (OAB). Phenazopyridine (Pyridium) is a urinary tract medication used to treat dysuria caused by urinary tract, bladder, and kidney infections. Tamsulosin (Flomax), dutasteride (Avodart), and alfuzosin (Uroxatral) are urinary tract agents used to treat BPH in men. Examples of urinary tract drugs used to treat overactive bladder include oxybutynin (Ditropan), tolterodine (Detrol), and mirabegron (Myrbetriq).

## Neurological Agents

Neurological medications are those that affect the nervous system and are typically prescribed for neurological disorders including attention deficit disorder (ADD), dementia, seizure disorders such as epilepsy, fibromyalgia, multiple sclerosis (MS), Parkinson's disease, and migraines.

ADD agents and attention deficit hyperactivity disorder (ADHD) agents are neurological medications that are used to treat inattentiveness, hyperactivity, impulsivity, and other behavioral disorders. These neurological agents are further classified as stimulants due to their effects on the central nervous system. Examples of ADD and ADHD agents include methylphenidate (Concerta) and atomoxetine (Strattera).

Anti-Alzheimer's agents are medications that are used to improve cognitive function in patients with dementia and Alzheimer's disease. Memantine (Namenda) and donepezil (Aricept) are anti-Alzheimer's medications.

Anticonvulsants (also known as antiseizure drugs or antiepileptic drugs) are medications used to treat neurological disorders such as epilepsy and other non-epileptic seizure disorders. Examples include carbamazepine (Tegretol XR, Equetro, Tegretol) and topiramate (Topamax), among many others.

While there is currently no cure for fibromyalgia, symptoms such as pain and insomnia can be treated with various types of antidepressants including serotonin and norepinephrine reuptake inhibitors (SNRIs) such as duloxetine (Cymbalta) and milnacipran (Savella), selective serotonin reuptake inhibitors (SSRIs) such as fluoxetine (Prozac) and paroxetine (Paxil), and tricyclics such as amitriptyline (Elavil). Anticonvulsants such as pregabalin (Lyrica) and gabapentin (Neurontin) may also be prescribed.

Multiple sclerosis (MS) is another disease that currently does not have a cure; however, medications can help manage the disease and delay its progression. Steroids such as methylprednisolone (Solu-Medrol) and prednisone (Detlasone) help with recovery from MS attacks. Drugs that modify the progression of the disease include injectable medications such as beta interferons (Avonex, Betaseron) and glatiramer acetate (Copaxone, Glatopa); oral medications such as fingolimod (Gilenya), teriflunomide (Aubagio), and dimethyl fumarate (Tecfidera); and infused medications such as alemtuzumab (Lemtrada) and natalizumab (Tysabri).

Antiparkinson agents include carbidopa/levodopa (Sinemet) and ropinirole (Requip). Disease progression in patients with Parkinson's is unfortunately unresponsive to drug therapy. Therefore, current medications are intended to improve quality of life in patients with Parkinson's disease.

Anti-migraine agents are neurological medications used to treat severe migraine headaches. A few examples include Aimovig, Emgality, and sumatriptan (Imitrex).

## Psychotropic Agents

Psychotropic agents are medications prescribed for the treatment of psychological disorders including anxiety, depression, bipolar disorder, schizophrenia, and drug and alcohol dependency.

Antianxiety agents are a class of medications that are used to treat anxiety-related restlessness, tension, and panic attacks. Benzodiazepines are short-acting psychotropic medications that are often used for the treatment of anxiety and are one of the most frequently prescribed antianxiety agents. Examples of antianxiety agents include the benzodiazepines alprazolam (Xanax) and lorazepam (Ativan).

Antidepressants are medications that may be used to treat varying degrees of depression, mood disorders, anxiety disorders, and seasonal affective disorder (SAD). Commonly prescribed antidepressants include escitalopram (Lexapro) and venlafaxine (Effexor).

Antipsychotics are psychotropic medications used to treat bipolar disorder and schizophrenia. Quetiapine (Seroquel) and aripiprazole (Abilify) are commonly prescribed for the treatment of these psychological disorders.

Drug dependency such as alcoholism can be treated with psychotropic agents such as disulfiram (Antabuse). Opioid dependency and alcoholism are both conditions that can be treated with the psychotropic agent naltrexone (Vivitrol).

## Musculoskeletal Agents

Musculoskeletal agents are used to treat gout, rheumatoid arthritis, osteoporosis, muscle spasms, tendonitis, and numerous other disorders that affect the joints, bones, and muscles in the body.

Antigout agents are prescribed for the treatment of gout, a buildup of uric acid in the joints that causes painful inflammation. Commonly prescribed medications for gout include allopurinol (Zyloprim) and colchicine (Colcrys).

Disease-modifying antirheumatic drugs (DMARDs) treat the chronic inflammation associated with rheumatoid arthritis, an inflammatory and autoimmune disease. Examples include hydroxychloroquine (Plaquenil) and methotrexate (Rheumatrix, Trexall). Steroids such as prednisone (Rayos) and betamethasone (Celestone) can also be prescribed to treat inflammation. Various types of biologic response modifiers or biologics, a subset of DMARDs, such as etanercept (Enbrel), infliximab (Remicade), and adalimumab (Humira) can help stop the progression of the disease.

Osteoporotic agents are medications that are used to treat osteoporosis as well as osteoarthritic conditions that affect the body's bone density, range of motion loss, and bone deformities. Alendronate (Fosamax) and ibandronate (Boniva) are osteoporotic medications.

Muscle relaxants are musculoskeletal agents often prescribed for the treatment of acute and chronic muscle spasm conditions. Cyclobenzaprine (Flexeril) and carisoprodol (Soma) are examples of muscle relaxers prescribed for the treatment of muscle spasticity.

Tendonitis, or the inflammation of a tendon, can often be treated with analgesics and NSAIDs to manage pain and reduce inflammation. In more severe cases corticosteroids such as methylprednisolone or cortisone may be prescribed.

## Therapeutic Equivalence

Rising prescription drug costs have heightened the need for patients to seek out more affordable options. Unfortunately, brand-name medications can be very expensive, partly because of the expense of developing a new pharmaceutical drug. The development process of bringing a drug to market is lengthy and can cost millions of dollars. When a brand-name medication's patent expires, however, competitors can begin manufacturing its generic equivalent. Generic medications must meet the same standards for safety, efficacy, purity, potency, etc., as their brand-name counterparts, but they do not incur the same startup costs as the brand-name medication since the initial research, safety, efficacy, and clinical trials have already been performed. Generic medications are therefore more cost effective to produce and provide significant cost savings for the patient.

Generic medications are essentially a copy of their brand-name counterparts and must meet various criteria to be considered equivalent; in particular, they must be both bioequivalent and pharmaceutically equivalent to the brand medication.

### Bioequivalence and Bioavailability

The bioequivalence of a generic medication is a measurement of its bioavailability when compared to the name brand medication. The bioavailability of a drug can be defined as the rate and extent to which the active pharmaceutical ingredient of a drug reaches systemic circulation and the intended site of action under similar therapeutic conditions. Slight variations in the manufacturing process can affect the bioavailability of a medication. For example, various manufacturers might use different inactive ingredients in a drug formulation, also called excipients. Excipients include fillers, binding agents, preservatives, and dyes; these can all affect the absorption and distribution of the active ingredient in the body. Additionally, the physical particle size of an active ingredient can vary across manufacturers, which can cause differences in a medication's bioavailability. The bioavailability of a medication also varies by dosage form. Bioavailability must be the same for two medications to be considered bioequivalent. If the difference in bioavailability between two medications is significant, then they cannot be considered bioequivalent.

### Pharmaceutical Equivalents

Pharmaceutically equivalent medications are those that not only contain exactly the same active pharmaceutical ingredient, including the same salt form, but also exactly the same quantity of the active pharmaceutical ingredient. The medications must be of the same dosage formulations and have same routes of administration as well. Pharmaceutically equivalent medications are not, however, required to include the same inactive ingredients and therefore may vary in their shape, color, and scoring configurations. Variations in the inactive ingredients such as flavors, fillers, and preservatives can affect the medication's beyond-use date or expiration date, however. The generic hypertension medication lisinopril is pharmaceutically equivalent to its brand-name counterpart, Zestril.

### Therapeutic Equivalents

Therapeutically equivalent medications must not only meet the criteria of pharmaceutically equivalent and bioequivalent medications, but they must also generate an identical therapeutic effect in the body. In addition, therapeutically equivalent medications must have the same dosage, routes of administration, safety profile, and clinical efficacy. Lastly, therapeutically equivalent medications must be manufactured per the FDA's Current Good Manufacturing Practices (CGMP) and be properly labeled.

## Pharmaceutical Alternatives

Pharmaceutical alternative medications contain the same active ingredient, but they may be of different strengths, different dosage formulations, and different salt or ester complexes. The beta blockers metoprolol tartrate (Lopressor) and metoprolol succinate (Toprol XL) are different salt forms of the same active pharmaceutical ingredient (metroprolol). Metoprolol tartrate is available in 50 mg and 100 mg immediate release tablets, while metoprolol succinate is available in 25 mg, 50 mg, 100 mg, and 200 mg extended-release tablets. Therefore, metoprolol tartrate and metoprolol succinate are examples of pharmaceutical alternative medications.

## Generic Substitution and FDA Orange Book

The FDA's *Approved Drug Products with Therapeutic Equivalence Evaluations*, a publication often referred to as the Orange Book, compiles safety, efficacy, and equivalency data for FDA-approved medications. It is a useful online resource about the therapeutic equivalence of FDA-approved drugs.

Generic substitution is the dispensing of a therapeutically equivalent medication in place of its branded counterpart. A prescription written for the antihyperlipidemic medication Crestor, dispensed as the generic rosuvastatin, is an example of a generic substitution. In general, automatic generic substitution is a common practice in pharmacy. The practice is aimed at keeping prescription drug costs low for patients and insurance companies. However, in some cases patients and insurance companies may prefer to fill the branded product over the generic. Prescribers can also choose to require a pharmacy to dispense the brand medication when medically necessary.

Prescribers, pharmacies, and insurance companies use product selection codes when writing and processing prescription orders. Dispense as written (DAW) codes are used when generic substitution is not preferred or the brand-name medication is medically necessary. For example, when prescribing narrow therapeutic index (NTI) medications, prescribers will write the prescription using the code DAW-1, in which generic substitution is not allowed by the prescribing physician. DAW-1 can also be used when a specific generic manufacturer is preferred. The chart below lists the various DAW codes that may be used.

| Dispense as Written (DAW) Product Selection Codes | |
|---|---|
| 0 | No product selection indicated |
| 1 | Substitution not allowed by prescriber |
| 2 | Substitution not allowed; patient requested brand drug be dispensed |
| 3 | Substitution allowed; pharmacist selected drug dispensed |
| 4 | Substitution allowed; generic drug not in stock |
| 5 | Substitution allowed: brand drug dispensed as generic |
| 6 | Override |
| 7 | Substitution not allowed; brand drug mandated by law |
| 8 | Substitution not allowed; brand drug not available in marketplace |
| 9 | Other |

(Source: https://ushik.ahrq.gov/ViewItemDetails?itemKey=200387000&system=sdo)

Insurance companies require pharmacies to use DAW product selection codes properly during the adjudication process (processing prescription drug claims) to ensure that the proper reimbursement is made. It is important to always document the code on the hard copy when a substitution is made in the event the insurance company audits the pharmacy. While product selection and generic substitution are common practices across much of the country, the rules and regulations regarding which drugs can be substituted can vary by state. It is therefore important to understand the generic substitution regulations in one's own state.

## Common and Life-Threatening Drug Interactions and Contraindications

A drug interaction is any interaction that occurs between a medication and another substance that disrupts or enhances the medication's pharmacological effects on the body or that causes unintended side effects in the body. Types of drug interactions include drug-drug interactions, drug-disease interactions, drug-dietary supplement interactions, drug-laboratory interactions, and drug-nutrient interactions.

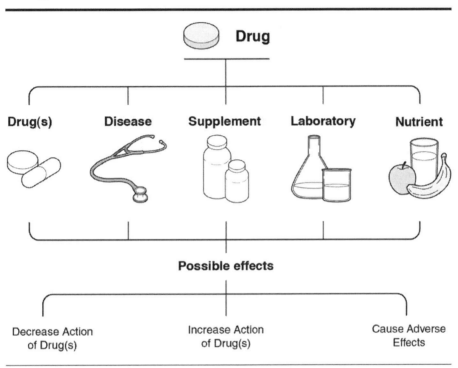

Source: National Institute of Health (NIH). https://aidsinfo.nih.gov/h/fact-sheets/21/95/what-is-a-drug-interaction-

## Drug-Drug Interactions

Drug-drug interactions occur when one of two or more drugs administered concomitantly affects the pharmacokinetics or therapeutic effect of another. The more medications a patient takes, the greater the likelihood of a drug-drug interaction. The coadministration of medications can result in antagonistic effects, additive effects, synergistic effects, or potentiation effects. An antagonistic effect is one in which one drug impedes the effect of another. An additive effect is one in which the combined use of two or more medications with similar therapeutic actions is equivalent to the sum of effects of the drugs if taken independently. A synergistic effect is one in which the combined use of two or more medications with similar therapeutic action is greater than the sum of effects of the drugs if taken independently. Potentiation is an effect in which a drug or substance administered alone has no therapeutic activity but increases the therapeutic action of another drug when combined. Depending on the medications involved, these interactions can be beneficial or harmful.

Some commonly seen antagonistic drug interactions can be avoided or lessened with medication adjustments. Azithromycin and Vivotif are a good example of a drug-drug interaction in which an antibiotic can render a live vaccine ineffective. Patients that travel to areas where typhoid is prevalent are typically prescribed the oral live vaccine Vivotif. They may also be given a prescription for antibiotics for prophylactic use such as azithromycin. The azithromycin can inactivate the vaccine, leaving the patient unprotected and at risk for contracting typhoid. This type of interaction is one that can be avoided simply by adjusting the time of medication administration. Another example of a common antagonistic drug-drug interaction is that between antibiotics and contraceptives. Patients that are taking contraceptives and are prescribed an antibiotic are advised to use a backup method of contraception since the antibiotic can decrease the hormonal effectiveness of the contraceptive.

While some antagonistic drug-drug interactions can be limited or avoided by changing the time of administration of each drug, other more serious drug interactions can be life-threatening and should be monitored or avoided altogether. An example of a life-threatening antagonistic drug-drug interaction is the interaction that occurs between theophylline and the antibiotic ciprofloxacin. Ciprofloxacin inhibits the metabolic breakdown of theophylline by the liver, causing a toxic buildup of the drug in the body, which can lead to serious complications including death.

Antagonistic interactions can also yield positive therapeutic outcomes. Naloxone (Narcan), for example, is an opioid antagonist that produces an antidotal effect, reversing the effects of opioids. This type of drug interaction has proven greatly beneficial for first responders and hospitals when treating patients experiencing a suspected opioid overdose. Another example of an interaction that delivers an antidotal effect is the dietary supplement vitamin K. Vitamin K is essential for developing blood clotting factors in the body, and it can be administered to reverse the effects of the blood thinner warfarin.

The second type of drug-drug interactions is additive interactions. These can be positive, for example, taking both acetaminophen and an NSAID such as naproxen (Aleve) for pain relief. The combined effect of the two different types of analgesics is the same as if they were taken separately, but because they treat pain in different ways, patients often experience greater relief with the combination of medications than by taking each separately. However, additive interactions can also be harmful. If two types of NSAIDs are taken together, such as naproxen and a salicylate (aspirin), the risk of stomach bleeding that each has individually combines, making the side effect much more likely to occur.

Synergistic drug-drug interactions can also be beneficial or life-threatening. Multiple medications are often combined to treat complex diseases such as cancer, and physicians may also prescribe multiple antimicrobials at one time to increase the effectiveness of treatments for some infections. On the other hand, serious, life-threatening synergistic interactions can also occur. One example is combining warfarin with NSAIDs such as aspirin. Both medications individually increase the risk of excessive bleeding and, when combined, the risk becomes exponentially greater than if a patient took each medication separately.

The final type of drug-drug interaction is potentiation. One positive example of a potentiated medication is Augmentin, a combination of the antibiotic amoxicillin and the enzyme inhibitor clavulanic acid. Amoxicillin administered alone can undergo enzymatic degradation in the presence of resistant microorganisms. Clavulanic acid, however, inhibits the enzyme degradation of amoxicillin, which not only increases the duration of the antibiotic's effect but also broadens the spectrum of microorganisms it can be used to treat.

## Drug-Disease Interactions

Some medical conditions or disease states can result in interactions with medications; these are referred to as drug-disease interactions. Diseases that present potential drug-disease interactions are typically those in which the patient exhibits some form of compromised organ function, which can hinder the body's ability to break down or metabolize a medication effectively and prevent the body from receiving the full therapeutic value of the drug. For example, patients with cirrhosis of the liver have compromised hepatic systems, which may affect the liver's ability to metabolize medications effectively. This can lead to a toxic buildup of a drug or its metabolites (byproducts of metabolism) in the body.

Toxicity can also occur in patients with kidney disease since the kidney is an organ that filters and clears the body of metabolites. Vancomycin, a narrow therapeutic index antibiotic, should be monitored in patients with renal impairment or chronic kidney disease (CKD) to avoid nephrotoxicity, since the drug clears the body through the kidneys.

Drug-disease interactions can also occur in patients with digestive conditions such as inflammatory bowel disease (IBD). These diseases can cause a thickening of the intestinal wall, resulting in decreased absorption of some medications.

Patients with cardiovascular diseases such as hypertension should avoid pseudoephedrine, the active ingredient found in multiple OTC cold and allergy medications, because it causes constriction of the blood vessels (vasoconstriction). While constriction of the blood vessels relieves nasal and sinus congestion, it also elevates blood pressure, which can be unsafe for patients with hypertension.

## Drug-Dietary Supplement Interactions

Drug–dietary supplement interactions are those that occur between a prescription medication and a dietary supplement. Dietary supplements are typically OTC products including vitamin supplements, mineral supplements, enzyme supplements, amino acid supplements, and herbal supplements. Dietary supplements are regulated by the FDA but are classified as foods, not medications; therefore, they do not undergo the same clinical trials as legend medications (medications approved by the FDA). While the FDA requires dietary supplements to be labeled as such, there are no federal regulations that require manufacturers of dietary supplements to prove the safety and effectiveness of their products through clinical trials or other tests. As a result, many things about dietary supplements are unknown. However, there are some dietary supplements with known significant interactions. St. John's Wort, for example, is an herbal supplement often taken to improve mood or treat mild depression. There is strong evidence to suggest St. John's Wort can decrease the effectiveness of many medications, including the immunosuppressant medication cyclosporine, which is used to prevent organ rejection in transplant patients.

## Drug-Laboratory Interactions

In drug-laboratory interactions, a medication interferes with laboratory tests, causing skewed or incorrect test results. Drug-laboratory interactions can result in a missed diagnosis and unnecessary testing, which can be costly. Prescription medications that are likely to interfere with laboratory test results include antibiotic medications, hormone medications, psychotropic medications, and antihypertensive medications. For instance, hypercalcemia (elevated calcium levels in the blood) and frequent urination are both common side effects of the antihypertensive medication hydrochlorothiazide. These side effects are also common symptoms of parathyroid disease. Some antibiotic medications can produce a drug-laboratory interaction, for example, first-generation cephalosporins such as cephalexin. This class of antibiotic can interfere with laboratory tests that are used to detect glucose or ketones in the urine as well as serum creatinine diagnostics, incorrectly indicating the presence of other medical conditions.

## Drug-Nutrient Interactions

Drug-nutrient interactions can occur when a medication interacts with the nutrients obtained from food and drink. For example, grapefruit juice can decrease the absorption of thyroid medications such as levothyroxine. It is therefore best to avoid grapefruit juice or wait to drink it at least one full hour after taking the medication. The interaction between grapefruit juice and other medications such as oxycodone or simvastatin is much more severe. A natural chemical found in grapefruit juice prevents an enzyme from metabolizing or deactivating oxycodone and simvastatin in the GI tract, allowing greater absorption of the medication in the gut. Greater absorption of the medication therefore results in an unwanted increase in the medication's effects on the body. Alcohol is another substance that can produce an unwanted drug-nutrient interaction when taken with medications, including the antifungal metronidazole. Taking metronidazole and consuming alcohol can cause excessive, sometimes violent, vomiting. This occurs because the drug blocks an enzyme that breaks down alcohol in the body. The vomiting is a result of the body not being able to fully digest the alcohol.

## Contraindications

A medication or therapeutic treatment is said to be contraindicated if it may cause harm to the patient. Misoprostol, for example, is a medication often prescribed for gastrointestinal conditions such as chronic constipation or as an ulcer preventative; however, it is contraindicated in pregnant individuals because it can cause ripening of the cervix, resulting in the loss of a pregnancy.

## Dosage and Administration Instructions

To best perform their role, pharmacy technicians should be familiar with other characteristics of prescription medications in addition to brand and generic names. It is important to also understand the strengths, doses, dosage forms, administration routes, and durations of therapy for commonly prescribed medications. In addition, the pharmacy technician must be aware of any special handling requirements and administration instructions for specific medications.

## Strength and Dose

The strength of a medication is the amount of active pharmaceutical ingredient present in a specific dosage formulation or unit of medication. The dose of a medication is the amount of medication delivered during a specific administration. Therefore, the strength and the dose of a drug are not necessarily the same. The strength of a drug is conveyed in terms of the medication's dosage form. The strength of a tablet or capsule is thus expressed as the number of grams or milligrams of active ingredient per tablet or capsule, for example, 250 mg tablets, while the dose would be one tablet.

Insulin is a medication that follows a standardized measurement; insulin strengths are expressed in terms of their concentration. Since insulin is delivered in units per milliliter, insulin strengths are expressed as the number of units per milliliter of fluid. The most common insulin is U-100 insulin, in which one milliliter of fluid contains one hundred units of insulin. For example, an insulin order may be written to administer as follows:

| |
|---|
| U-100 Insulin |
| Inject 15 units SQ QID |

The strength on this order is 100 units/ml, and the dose is 15 units. (In the example above, SQ means that the medication should be injected under the skin (subcutaneously) and QID means four times per day. So, the patient should receive 15 units of insulin at 100 units/ml subcutaneously four times per day.) While U-100 insulin is the most common strength, U-200, U-300, and U-500 insulins may also be available.

## Dosage Formulations and Routes of Administration

Pharmacy medications are available in many different dosage formulations, or the physical form of the medication. Dosage formulations are developed in tandem with an intended delivery method or route of administration including oral (solid and liquid), non-oral liquid, rectal, vaginal, topical, and inhaled.

Oral dosage formulations include solids and liquids and may be delivered via immediate release or modified release. Solid oral dosage formulations include tablets, capsules, and orally disintegrating tablets (ODTs). Tablets are solid formulations that are composed of the active pharmaceutical ingredient and excipients (inactive ingredients) that have been compressed into a hard tablet. Capsules are dosage formulations that involve packing the active ingredient and any excipients into a cellulose or gelatin-based capsule. Orally disintegrating tablets are solid formulations composed of the active pharmaceutical ingredient and excipients that dissolve when placed on the patient's tongue. Liquid oral dosage formulations include suspensions, solutions, elixirs, syrups, and reconstitutable powders.

Oral dosage formulations, both solid and liquid, may be immediate release or may have a modified release mechanism. An immediate release medication is one in which the active ingredient is released in a relatively short period of time; a medication with a modified release mechanism enables a slower release of the active ingredient. Medications with a modified release mechanism are commonly referred to with one of the following designations: long-acting (LA), sustained action (SA), extended-release (ER or XR), controlled release (CR), or sustained release (SR).

Non-oral liquid dosage formulations include otic and ophthalmic solutions and suspensions. The route of administration for otic drops is the ear; ophthalmic drops are placed in the eye. However, it is not uncommon for physicians to prescribe ophthalmic drops for use in the ear if the medication is deemed medically appropriate. It is important to note that ophthalmic drops are sterile whereas otic drops are not; therefore, while ophthalmic drops can be used in the ear, otic drops should never be used in the eye.

Other non-oral liquid dosage formulations include nasal sprays and injectables. While the dosage formulations are similar in that they are solutions or suspensions, the medications have different routes of administration. Nasal sprays are solutions or suspensions that are instilled in the nasal cavity and are usually administered in a metered dose actuator or sprayer that delivers the specified dose. Injectables are dosage formulations that may be administered by several routes including subcutaneously (SQ), intramuscularly (IM), and intravenously (IV).

Rectal routes of administration include dosage formulations such as suppositories, creams, foams, ointments, and enemas. Suppositories are semisolid dosage forms in which the active drug is added to an excipient that dissolves when inserted rectally. Rectal creams, foams, and ointments are topical dosage formulations that are applied rectally to treat conditions like hemorrhoids. Enemas are liquid formulations, emulsions, solutions, etc., that are administered rectally, typically to relieve constipation.

Vaginal routes of administration include dosage formulations such as vaginal suppositories, tablet inserts, and intrauterine devices (IUDs). Other medications administered vaginally include topical creams, ointments, and foams. These formulations are used to deliver anti-infectives, contraceptives, and hormone therapies.

Topical dosage formulations are applied to the skin or a mucous membrane. Topical dosage formulations include the same previously mentioned creams, foams, and ointments, but they also include topical solutions, gels, and transdermal patches. The acne medication clindamycin/benzoyl peroxide (BenzaClin) and the NSAID gel diclofenac (Voltaren Gel) are topical dosage gels. An example of a topical transdermal delivery system or patch include the Schedule II narcotic fentanyl (Duragesic), which is applied to the skin to treat chronic pain.

Inhaled dosage formulations include aerosols that are delivered via a nebulizer or metered dose inhalers (MDI). In some cases, inhalant formulations need to be administered using an adapter or spacer to ensure the aerosol is inhaled into the lungs rather than swallowed.

Advancements in pharmaceutical dosage formulations have provided numerous therapeutic advantages, including reduced side effects and better medication adherence. Patients struggling to maintain a complex medication regimen, for instance, might benefit from extended-release dosage formulations that reduce dosing from twice daily to once daily or even once monthly. Alternatives such as oral suspensions, chewable tablets, and orally disintegrating tablets can be prescribed for patients who cannot swallow tablets or capsules. Medications such as Hyzaar, which combines the medication Losartan with the diuretic hydrochlorothiazide in one tablet, can also reduce the number of medications a patient is required to take daily. Reducing the number of daily doses or medications required is more cost effective for patients as well.

## Duration of Drug Therapy

Duration of therapy refers to the length of time a medication should be continued. Maintenance medications do not normally have a therapy duration since patients remain on them for life. Most courses of antibiotics, however, are administered over a few days to weeks depending on the type of infection being treated. For example, oseltamivir (Tamiflu) is typically prescribed as shown in the following illustration. In this example, the duration of therapy is five days.

---

Tamiflu 75 mg Cap

Take 1 Cap PO BID x 5 days for influenza

---

In the illustration above, Cap indicates that the dosage formulation is a capsule (rather than a powder that must be reconstituted into an oral suspension), PO indicates that the medication should be taken by mouth, and BID means twice a day. So, the patient should take one 75 mg capsule of Tamiflu by mouth twice a day for five days to combat influenza. If the Tamiflu prescription were written for prophylactic use instead of treatment of confirmed influenza, the medication would be taken once per day and the duration would be ten days.

## Administration Instructions and Special Handling

Administration instructions for a medication should be written clearly to avoid any medication errors. The administration instructions should include the dose of medication to be given per administration, the route of administration, the frequency, the duration of therapy, the indication (the condition the medication is treating), and any auxiliary directions such as "take with food," "shake well," etc.

When handling prescription medications, it is important to understand which medications are considered hazardous and take the necessary precautions when handling them. The National Institute for Occupational Safety and Health (NIOSH) is a federal research agency that operates under the United States Center for Disease Control (CDC). Its mission is to create a safer workplace environment through research. Established by the Occupational Safety and Health Act (OSHA) of 1970, NIOSH researches and develops numerous recommendations, including the NIOSH list of hazardous medications.

In general, medications on the NIOSH list are those that display some degree of carcinogenicity, genotoxicity, teratogenicity, reproductive toxicity, or organ toxicity. Carcinogenicity is the ability of a chemical substance or drug to cause cancer or induce tumors. Genotoxicity refers to the ability of a chemical substance or drug to be damaging to genetic material such as DNA. Teratogenicity is the ability of a chemical substance or drug to cause fetal deformities or other developmental malformations in a fetus. Reproductive toxicity is the ability of a chemical substance or drug to alter aspects of male and female reproductive systems including fertility, sex alteration, and the ability to maintain a pregnancy. Organ toxicity is the ability of a chemical substance or drug to cause organ damage or failure at even low doses. The NIOSH list also includes new drugs whose toxicity profile and structure are comparable to drugs already included in the list.

The NIOSH list is divided into three main groups of medications. The first group is antineoplastic drugs. This group includes mostly cytotoxic medications (medications that are toxic to cells), but also includes many medications that have hazardous reproductive effects in both men and women. Cytotoxic agents are used to treat cancer as well as other medical conditions like rheumatoid arthritis and psoriasis. The medications letrozole (Femara) and methotrexate are, among other things, used to treat patients with breast cancer. Methotrexate is also commonly used for the treatment of rheumatoid arthritis.

The second group includes non-antineoplastic drugs that exhibit one or more of the NIOSH characteristics. Most non-antineoplastic drugs in this group exhibit some degree of reproductive toxicity and teratogenic or other developmental effects, and they may also be carcinogenic. The hormone medication estradiol and other estradiol-containing drugs are examples of non-antineoplastic drugs that can increase the risk of several types of cancers. The anticonvulsant medications divalproex (Depakote) and carbamazepine (Tegretol) are examples of non-antineoplastic hazardous drugs that can cause teratogenic and congenital birth defects if pregnant individuals are exposed to them.

The third group of medications on the NIOSH list includes non-antineoplastic drugs that cause predominantly reproductive effects in both men and women. Finasteride (Proscar or Propecia) is a non-antineoplastic medication used to treat benign prostate hyperplasia (BPH) as well as male pattern baldness. Simply handling broken or crushed Finasteride tablets can be hazardous to pregnant individuals because it can cause birth defects in the male fetus. Another example of a non-antineoplastic hazardous medication is the antidepressant paroxetine (Paxil). If administered to a pregnant individual, it can cause congenital abnormalities in the fetus.

Due to the harmful nature of antineoplastic and non-antineoplastic hazardous medications, it is necessary to use the proper personal protective equipment (PPE) when working with them. For many of these hazardous medications, proper PPE includes gloves but may also include gowns, goggles, face shields, and masks. The PPE required while working with hazardous drugs can depend on the dosage formulation being handled and the degree to which the drug must be manipulated.

For example, capsules and tablets often have powder or residues on them. The residues of a medication can also settle in the bottom of stock bottles. These residues can be a danger when the medication is dispensed. Poorly transported medications can result in damage to drugs, including broken or crushed tablets and burst capsules. These powders and residues can be absorbed through the skin, or particles can be inhaled. Wearing gloves is therefore essential when counting hazardous medications. In addition to wearing gloves, it is best to wear a mask when cutting or crushing tablets for use in compounded medications to avoid inhaling any drug particles that may be released into the air.

The more hazardous a medication is deemed to be, such as with cytotoxic chemotherapy drugs, or the more a medication must be manipulated, such as with compounded hazardous drugs, the greater the PPE requirement for the individual.

## Medication Side Effects

Side effects, adverse effects, and allergies are all physical effects of a drug on the body that occur secondary to the medication's intended therapeutic effect. Side effects of varying severity are usually known and may even be beneficial, whereas adverse effects and allergies are typically unpredictable and always detrimental or even dangerous. It is therefore important to understand the differences between common side effects, severe side effects, adverse effects, and allergies.

## Side Effects

Drug manufacturers are required to disclose all known side effects experienced by trial participants during clinical testing, whether common or severe. Nearly all medications produce side effects to some degree, including prescription medications, OTC medications, and dietary supplements. Human variabilities such as age, gender, race, and genetic makeup can influence the degree to which a patient responds to medication and which side effects they experience. The side effects of some medications may be mild and manageable for some patients but severe for others. Some side effects may be more common or occur more frequently in certain patients than in others.

The most common type of side effects experienced is gastrointestinal distress including constipation, diarrhea, and nausea. Other commonly experienced side effects of medications include headaches, dry mouth, and dizziness. These common side effects may be mild, last only a short period of time, or completely subside with continued use. Medication counseling should be offered to patients regarding the side effects of a medication so that they understand which side effects should concern them and which are normal reactions to their medications. Without such counseling, harmless side effects may seem alarming to an uninformed patient. For example, the harmless side effect of discolored urine typically occurs with the analgesic phenazopyridine, an analgesic indicated for dysuria (painful urination).

Sometimes, a medication's common side effects may be more severe or last for the entire duration of therapy. Common side effects of the antibiotic medication ciprofloxacin (Cipro) include diarrhea, vomiting, and insomnia. Antibiotics in general are medications that can disrupt the delicate balance of the gastrointestinal system, and these side effects occur often with this class of medication.

Medications can also produce serious side effects in some patients. Severe side effects are typically known potential negative effects that were observed during clinical trials and may include hemorrhage, suicidal thoughts, seizures, or abnormal arrythmias. The narrow therapeutic index anticoagulant warfarin (Coumadin), for example, is indicated for medical conditions such as deep vein thrombosis (DVT), pulmonary embolism (PE), and stroke prevention. Minor bleeding is a common side effect experienced by patients taking warfarin; however, excessive uncontrolled bleeding or hemorrhage can sometimes occur and lead to death.

Although many side effects are undesirable, they may occasionally benefit some patients. For example, the medication mirtazapine (Remeron), which is indicated for the treatment of depression, also produces increased appetite and weight gain. Although considered an off-label use of the medication, these side effects can be beneficial for patients suffering from eating disorders such as anorexia.

## Adverse Effects

An adverse effect of a medication is one that is typically unpredictable as well as being unintended, undesired, and often harmful to the patient. Adverse reactions may be patient specific intolerances or reactions that occur even when a medication is taken as prescribed. Examples of adverse reactions to medications include arrythmias, seizures, and organ damage; allergic reactions are also examples of an adverse reaction. A patient should report any adverse effects to their physician or to MedWatch. MedWatch and the FDA's Adverse Event Reporting System, or FAERS, compile reported data regarding adverse events to identify possible after-market safety concerns regarding a medication.

## Allergies

An allergy is defined as a reaction or overreaction by the immune system in response to something it interprets as a foreign substance. The time required for the body to develop an allergic reaction to a medication can vary depending on the severity of the allergy as well as other factors such as the route of administration; the allergic reaction can occur immediately after administration or it could take hours. Allergies to medications can be mild, presenting simply as a rash, or they can be extremely severe, resulting in an anaphylactic reaction. Anaphylactic reactions are systemic immune system responses and typically occur within minutes of medication administration.

Signs of anaphylaxis may include mild symptoms such as runny nose, hives, and rash, but they can escalate to more severe symptoms quickly. Severe anaphylaxis can cause swelling of the throat, difficulty breathing, rapid heartbeat, and fatal cardiac arrest. If a patient has an allergic reaction to a medication—for example, the fluoroquinolone antibiotic levofloxacin (Levaquin)—it is likely they will also be allergic to similar drugs in the same class. It is therefore a pharmacy best practice to verify and document known allergies to medications to prevent dispensing a similar medication that could also trigger an allergic reaction.

## Indications of Medications and Dietary Supplements

### Indications of Medications

A medication's indication refers to the condition or disease state the medication is intended to treat or has been approved to treat by the FDA. The indication can be for the treatment of a specific medical condition in general or it may be more targeted such as a specific population with the medical condition. Zolpidem (Ambien) is a medication indicated for the treatment of short-term insomnia. Another example, polyethylene glycol (MiraLAX), is an OTC medication that is indicated for the treatment of constipation. Some medications may only be safe and effective for a specific age group, ethnicity, etc., and may be approved with a limitation of use disclaimer. For instance, children are often excluded in clinical trials until a medication has been fully tested in adult subjects. The labeling will therefore contain a limitation of use statement which states that the safety and effectiveness have yet to be determined in pediatric patients. This statement does not mean the medication is unsafe or ineffective for use in pediatric patients; it simply means the drug was not tested in the pediatric population and its safety and effectiveness are therefore undetermined.

While the FDA ultimately determines whether a medication has been proven to be safe and effective, it is not responsible for the actual testing. The Kefauver-Harris Amendment of 1962 states that drug manufacturers are responsible for all testing and research to determine the safety and efficacy of their products. Drug manufacturers determine the potential benefits of a medication through rigorous research protocols. They then use the known information they have about a drug's effects on the body to determine potential uses during the research and developmental stages of the medication. Once enough data has been gathered from animal studies, the manufacturer can begin clinical trials using human subjects. If the drug is then determined to be a safe and effective treatment for a specific condition, the drug manufacturer can submit the findings to the FDA to gain approval for its intended use. The FDA's Center for Drug Evaluation and Research (CDER) is the organization responsible for evaluating the drug manufacturer's clinical data to ensure that the drug's potential benefits for its intended demographic outweigh the risks associated with its use.

Ideally, the broader the indication, the broader the marketing value of a medication. The FDA's approval of a drug indication allows the manufacturer to include the information in its drug literature including the drug label, the package insert, and any marketing materials. A drug manufacturer cannot market a medication for an indication that has not been approved by the FDA; this is often referred to as "off-label use."

The off-label use of a medication is the use of a prescription drug for an indication or indications other than those approved by the FDA. A common misconception regarding the off-label use of medications is that a medication is not approved by the FDA because it is unsafe or ineffective. The reality is that the manufacturer simply did not test and/or submit clinical data to the FDA for approval regarding other medical conditions. Since research and development of drugs can be costly, a drug manufacturer may limit the parameters of its testing, such as excluding certain routes of administration, dosage forms, or specific human populations. Again, these restrictions do not mean the product is unsafe or ineffective; they just mean there is no clinical data to support the use of the medication in any other manner than what has been FDA approved.

It is common for physicians to prescribe medications for off-label use. An example of a medication often prescribed for an off-label indication is trazodone (Desyrel). Trazodone is a medication that has been approved by the FDA to treat depression; however, it is often prescribed to treat sleep disturbances in geriatric patients, which is an unapproved off-label indication. Other examples of off-label use include clonidine (Catapres), which has FDA approval for the treatment of hypertension but is also used for the off-label indications of ADHD, migraine headaches, and restless leg syndrome (RLS).

Aside from safety and efficacy, an important and sometimes overlooked consequence of off-label prescribing is the cost of using an unapproved drug. Prescribers may not be aware that health insurance companies often will not cover the cost of a medication for an off-label or unapproved indication.

## Indications of Dietary Supplements

Dietary supplements are OTC products that include ingredients such as vitamins, minerals, botanicals, amino acids, and enzymes. Dietary supplements fall under guidelines set forth by the Dietary Supplement Health and Education Act of 1994 (DSHEA), an amendment to the Federal Food, Drug, and Cosmetic Act. DSHEA is responsible for ensuring that manufacturers of dietary supplements follow guidelines from an official drug compendium such as the United States Pharmacopeia (USP). Dietary supplements, however, are not required to undergo the same standards of clinical testing as prescription medications.

The FDA's role in the regulation of dietary supplements begins after the supplement is brought to market and is more focused on consumer protection from adulterated or misbranded dietary supplements. The FDA does not approve dietary supplements for the treatment of specific medical conditions, nor does the FDA allow the manufacturer to market dietary supplements for such purposes.

Manufacturers of dietary supplements are not required to prove their products are safe and effective through clinical trials or other testing, but they must properly label the products as dietary supplements. In addition, any claims printed on the product label must have a disclaimer specifically stating the claims are not approved by the FDA. The manufacturer can make general health claims as well as nutrient content and function claims regarding dietary supplements.

Vitamin C, which is a dietary nutrient, is known to support or boost the immune system. The immune system benefit of vitamin C is an example of a health claim as well as a functional claim that can be made by the manufacturer.

| Common Indications of Dietary Supplements | |
|---|---|
| **Calcium** | Reduce bone loss |
| **Iron** | Anemia |
| **Vitamin C** | Immune system health |
| **Fish oil** | Cardiovascular health |
| **Vitamin D** | Reduce bone loss |
| **Turmeric** | Anti-inflammatory properties |
| **Glucosamine** | Osteoarthritis |
| **Coenzyme Q10** | Antioxidant properties |
| **Vitamin B12** | Blood cell/nerve health |
| **Zinc** | Immune system health |
| **Echinacea** | Immune system health |
| **Folate (vitamin B9)** | Reduces risk of birth defects |
| **St. John's Wort** | Mood enhancement |
| **Fiber** | Digestive health |
| **Magnesium** | Healthy nerve/muscle function |
| **Vitamin B6** | Red blood cell formation |
| **L-Arginine** | Cardiovascular health |
| **Vitamin E** | Immune system health |
| **Lactobacillus** | Probiotic |

## Drug Stability

It is important for prescription medications to not only preserve their potency or therapeutic efficacy over the course of their shelf life but also to remain safe to administer. Environmental storage factors such as pH, temperature, light exposure, and humidity can lead to degradation of a medication's active ingredient. Some of the consequences of a medication's loss of stability include the loss of potency of the active ingredient, formation of toxic compounds due to degradation of ingredients, changes in bioavailability of the active ingredient due to degradation, microbial contamination, and inconsistent medication delivery due to loss of uniformity. Drug stability testing is therefore conducted to ensure that the storage conditions for a medication maintain the drug's integrity from the time the medication is packaged until it expires.

Stability data for pharmaceuticals and pharmaceutical ingredients are established during the drug development process using rigorous stability testing protocols. These stability protocols help determine the limitations of an active pharmaceutical ingredient under various conditions and evaluate long-term stresses and accelerated methods. Stability testing procedures must be developed and conducted in ways that mimic the conditions in which the medication will be handled and stored and provide important information such as the drug's stability under different levels of temperature, moisture, and light. The results of stability research determine storage specifications for a medication, such as which kind of closed container system should be used.

## Oral Suspensions

Suspensions are liquid formulations that are composed of an insoluble active ingredient suspended in an aqueous base. The insoluble medication is referred to as the internal phase of the suspension; the aqueous base is called the external phase. The attributes of a stable suspension include relatively small particle size, equal or uniform distribution of suspended particles that settle slowly, and sediment or particles that are easily redistributed with gentle shaking. Oral suspensions that have lost stability may exhibit caking of the internal phase or changes in viscosity, taste, odor, and color.

## Reconstitutable Medications

Reconstituted oral suspensions are packaged as dry powders and reconstituted with purified water when they are dispensed. Prior to dispensing, the dry powder form might have a stable shelf life of several years. However, once the medication is reconstituted with water, its stability is decreased and its beyond-use date is significantly shortened. The chance for microbial growth increases as well. Oral antibiotic suspensions such as azithromycin (Zithromax) and amoxicillin/clavulanic acid (Augmentin) are common medications that require reconstitution but have different storage and stability requirements once mixed with water. Azithromycin oral suspension is stable for only ten days once mixed with water but does not require refrigeration after mixing. Augmentin oral suspension is only stable for seven days after reconstitution and should be refrigerated after mixing.

## Insulin Medications

Insulin solutions used for the treatment of diabetes are an example of drugs that must be transported and stored under refrigerated conditions until they are administered. Insulin is composed of proteins that can break down if not stored properly, resulting in an ineffective or non-therapeutic medication. Insulin vials that are not stored under proper conditions can also become contaminated with microbial growth; therefore, it is important to understand how to store such medications.

All insulins must be refrigerated prior to use; however, most vials of insulin can be left at room temperature and will remain stable for some time after opening. Aspart (Novolog) and lispro (Humalog) are rapid-acting insulins that can retain stability for twenty-eight days at room temperature once they have been opened. Detemir (Levemir) is a long-acting insulin that can maintain stability for up to forty-two days at room temperature after opening.

The stability of insulin pens after opening can range anywhere from ten days to fifty-six days at room temperature, with most remaining stable for twenty-eight days. Humulin N insulin pens have an expiration date of fourteen days at room temperature after opening; others like glargine (Toujeo) and degludec (Tresiba) are stable for up to forty-two days and fifty-six days, respectively. Differences in insulin stability and storage vary greatly; therefore, it is best to consult the package insert or a pharmacist with questions.

## Injectable Medications

Injectable medications are packaged in a variety of ways, including prefilled syringes and vials. Prefilled syringes are ideal for easy medication administration and typically retain stability since they do not require reconstitution with a diluent. Factors that might contribute to loss of stability in prefilled syringes include extreme temperatures and light. Damage to the prefilled syringe itself, for example a compromised seal or plunger, can result in contamination of the medication. Many prefilled plastic syringes have seals made of rubber, which can sometimes react with or leach into the active ingredient if not stored properly.

Medications that are packaged in vials may either be single dose vials (SDVs) or multi-dose vials (MDVs). Some injectable medications are packaged in a vial as an aqueous suspension or solution and do not require reconstitution. A safely stored injectable medication that is packaged as a suspension in a single dose vial is likely to maintain its stability or therapeutic capability better than either a multi-dose vial or a reconstituted formulation. Single dose vials are also less likely to result in microbial contamination since the seal is punctured once for a single administration. With multi-dose vials, the chance of microbial contamination increases with every dose that is drawn from the vial, which can introduce bacteria to the patient and ultimately hinder the therapeutic value of the drug. The steroid medication methylprednisolone acetate (Depo-Medrol) is an injectable medication that is available in an SDV or an MDV. Regardless of the dosage formulation, it is important to visually inspect injectable medications and note any precipitate formation, leaking seals, cracks in the vial, etc., prior to administering.

Injectable antibiotic medications are often packaged as dry powders in glass vials; these require reconstitution with a diluent prior to administration. It is important to use the correct diluent to reconstitute injectable antibiotics since they can chemically react with the active ingredient, resulting in many unwanted effects such as precipitate formation, crystallization, and loss of therapeutic potency. A few examples of diluents used to reconstitute injectable medications include sodium chloride (normal saline) for injection, sterile water for injection, bacteriostatic water for injection, and lidocaine. Common antibiotics that are reconstituted for injection include ceftriaxone (Rocephin) and vancomycin. Ceftriaxone is compatible with several diluents, including sodium chloride and sterile water. Ceftriaxone, however, should never be reconstituted with diluents that contain calcium, such as Ringer's solution (saline solution with sodium chloride, calcium chloride, and potassium chloride), as this can result in dangerous particulate formation.

Once reconstituted, the stability of the medication is significantly reduced and becomes dependent upon several factors including the final reconstituted concentration of drug, the storage temperature, and the type of container it is stored in.

## Vaccinations

Vaccine administration plays an increasing role in community pharmacy. Vaccinations are a critical line of defense against preventable diseases such as measles, influenza, and meningitis, to name a few. An important part of an effective vaccine administration program is ensuring that vaccines retain their potency and have not been compromised. If a vaccine is to deliver its intended benefit of disease immunity and remain stable, it must be properly stored at all times. To ensure the stability during the life cycle of a vaccine, cold chain protocol must be followed by all involved handlers of a vaccine, including manufacturers, distributors, and administrators.

## Cold Chain Flowchart

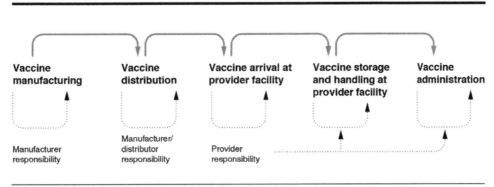

Source: https://www.cdc.gov/vaccines/hcp/admin/storage/toolkit/storage-handling-toolkit.pdf

Markers of an effective vaccine cold chain system include adequately trained staff that can handle vaccines using established standard operating procedures (SOPs), an inventory management program that is both accurate and efficient, and suitable refrigeration or freezer units with proper temperature monitoring equipment. A refrigeration unit used for the storage of vaccines such as the flu vaccine or HPV vaccine should be kept at a consistent temperature of between 2°C and 8°C (36°F to 46°F). Most vaccines that are required to remain frozen should be kept at a consistent temperature between -50°C and -15°C (-58°F to 5°F).

Varivax, the vaccine for chickenpox or varicella, and Zostavax, the shingles vaccine, must be transported and stored frozen. Unfortunately, this may require special freezers to properly maintain stability as most household freezers are not capable of reaching -50°C (-58°F). Varivax and Zostavax are also vaccines that require reconstitution with a sterile diluent prior to administration. The improper handling of the required diluent can also lead to decreased stability and effectiveness of the vaccines. It is important to note that while the vaccines Zostavax and Varivax should be kept frozen, the diluents used to reconstitute them should not be frozen.

Vaccines should never be stored or transported at temperatures above or below those recommended by the vaccine manufacturer. Temperature excursions or fluctuations outside the specified parameters can lead to decreased stability of the vaccine. Additional consequences of improper vaccine storage include microbial contamination, formation of toxic impurities due to chemical reactions, and ultimately a patient that is not fully protected due to an ineffective vaccine. One of the difficulties with determining whether a vaccine has been compromised and lost stability is that often there are no visible signatures. Contaminated vials might contain precipitates or appear cloudy; however, this is not necessarily an accurate indicator as to whether the vaccine has been compromised since this can be the normal appearance for some vaccines.

## Narrow Therapeutic Index (NTI) Medications

The therapeutic index (TI) of a medication is an expression of the drug's margin of safety. A medication's therapeutic index is determined by quantitatively comparing the blood concentration of a drug at a therapeutic dose to the blood concentration of a drug at a toxic dose. This ratio can be expressed using the following equation:

$$TI = \frac{Toxic\ dose}{Effective\ dose} = \frac{TD_{50}}{ED_{50}}$$

In this equation, $TD_{50}$ represents the toxic dose for 50% of observed subjects, and $ED_{50}$ represents the effective dose for 50% of observed subjects. Narrow therapeutic index (NTI) medications are those in which the difference between the medication's therapeutic dose and its lethal dose is exceptionally small.

A narrow window between a medication's efficacy and toxicity can make dosing difficult. Medications with narrow therapeutic indexes are used to treat a variety of medical conditions including seizure disorders, systemic infections, and cardiovascular diseases. Patients taking narrow therapeutic index medications require a higher degree of monitoring to ensure therapeutic levels are achieved and to prevent serious complications from their use.

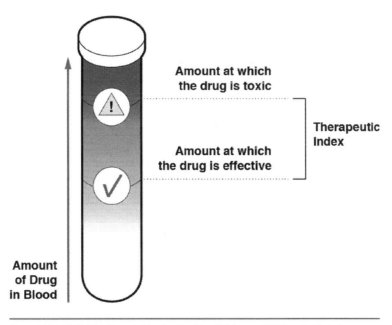

Source: https://aidsinfo.nih.gov/understanding-hiv-aids/glossary/865/therapeutic-index

Medications with a narrow therapeutic index are available in multiple strengths, but the difference between the strengths are extremely small. For instance, oral thyroid medications such as levothyroxine (Synthroid, Tirosint) are dosed in micrograms. These medications are available in as many as thirteen different strengths, depending on the brand, and can range from 13 mcg to 300 mcg. With these medications, a slight difference in dose can have a significant effect on therapeutic concentrations. Maintenance medications, however, can have a broad therapeutic margin of safety, or high therapeutic index value, and therefore do not require significant monitoring of values. For example, the cholesterol medication atorvastatin (Lipitor), a statin drug, can typically be monitored with a simple, annual cholesterol screening. Atorvastatin is available in a broad range of strengths, from 10 mg tablets up to 80 mg tablets, a difference of 70 mg between the lowest and highest doses. The variety of strengths is acceptable because atorvastatin is relatively safe due to its broad therapeutic range and minimal therapeutic monitoring requirements.

Warfarin (Coumadin), an anticoagulant medication, is a narrow therapeutic index medication that is indicated for the treatment of DVT, pulmonary embolism (PE), thromboembolism, and stroke prophylaxis. Often referred to as a blood thinner, warfarin essentially slows down the clotting process by inhibiting the production of clotting factors such as the protein prothrombin or factor II. The danger associated with warfarin dosing that is too low is that it can result in too much clotting, leading to the formation of blood clots that can cause an embolism or stroke. Too high a dose, however, can result in too little clotting of the blood and the potential for uncontrolled bleeding or hemorrhage. Warfarin tablets are available in strengths that range from 1 mg tablets to 10 mg tablets. Warfarin dosing is further complicated by its various interactions with other medications, dietary supplements, and some foods, which can make it extremely challenging to achieve the correct therapeutic dose.

Patients taking warfarin require frequent monitoring of their blood clotting, which is done by performing a PT/INR test to ensure levels are therapeutic. The prothrombin test (PT) and the partial thromboplastin time (PTT) are tests that are often performed together and are used to verify how long it takes for the blood to clot. The international normalized ratio (INR) is a method of calculating the results of a PT test; the INR ranges from zero to five. Variations in PT reagents used by different laboratories can lead to variations in the results. The INR was established to standardize testing results and account for these variations.

The standard therapeutic target INR value for a patient taking warfarin is between two and three. An INR value below two can increase the risk of clot formation while an INR above three can result in excessive bleeding. Other variables that might affect the INR value for patients taking warfarin include other medications, dietary supplements, and foods. Warfarin has numerous interactions, including an increase in bleeding, with NSAIDs such as the OTC medications aspirin and ibuprofen as well as with prescription NSAIDs such as meloxicam (Mobic). The dietary supplement garlic should also be avoided by patients taking warfarin since garlic can also lead to an increase in bleeding. It is also best to avoid foods that are high in vitamin K such as leafy greens since they can affect therapeutic levels of warfarin in the body.

Drug manufacturers have put in place a few safety measures to help prevent medication dispensing errors of some narrow therapeutic index medications since such errors can cause serious injury. For instance, all manufacturers of the brand-name drug Coumadin and the generic drug warfarin use a color-coding system such as the one below to designate the strength of the tablets. This feature is in addition to having the strength imprinted on the tablet.

| Coumadin/Warfarin Tablet Color Scheme | |
|---|---|
| Tablet Strength | Tablet Color |
| 1 mg | Pink |
| 2 mg | Lavender |
| 2.5 mg | Green |
| 3 mg | Tan |
| 4 mg | Blue |
| 5 mg | Peach (Light orange) |
| 6 mg | Teal (Blue-green) |
| 7.5 mg | Yellow |
| 10 mg | White |

Similarly, manufacturers of thyroid medications such as levothyroxine, Synthroid, and Levoxyl color code their tablets to make the strengths recognizable by all manufacturers, including generic manufacturers.

## Physical and Chemical Incompatibilities

Non-sterile compounding is the preparation of a medication by mixing or altering multiple ingredients into a uniform dosage formulation. Often a medication is compounded when a commercially available product does not meet a patient's needs. Commonly compounded preparations include oral solutions, suspensions, and topical medications. There are various concerns regarding compatibility as well as other limitations that must be considered when preparing non-sterile medications. Improper preparation of these medications can potentially affect the stability, efficacy, and safety of the compound. There are two types of incompatibility that can arise when compounding non-sterile medications: physical incompatibilities and chemical incompatibilities.

## Physical Incompatibilities

Physical incompatibilities may prevent product uniformity, which can affect a preparation's stability and also result in changes in odor, taste, and overall palatability. Insolubility, incorrect electrical charges, and immiscibility are common physical incompatibilities that can be overcome with proper technique and the use of appropriate solvents, wetting agents, surfactants, etc.

Insolubility affects liquid compounded preparations called solutions, one-phase systems in which the solute (the active pharmaceutical ingredient) is completely dissolved in the solvent (an aqueous medium such as purified water), creating a homogenous mixture. Often this means incorporating bulk powders, pulverized tablets, or the contents of a capsule into a liquid medium. Solubility is essentially the number of milliliters of a solvent needed to dissolve one gram of the solute (a solute that is unable to dissolve in a solvent is said to be insoluble). When the dissolution of a solute in a solvent reaches the maximum amount under a given set of conditions, the solution is said to be saturated, while exceeding this maximum amount yields a supersaturated solution.

Saturated and supersaturated solutions are not thermodynamically stable and can cause the active ingredient to precipitate out of solution, resulting in a loss of therapeutic integrity. It is possible that the amount of powder required for a preparation might be physically impossible to incorporate into the specific volume of liquid required to achieve the desired concentration. It is therefore important to understand the solubility properties of ingredients and any excipients included in the compounded preparation since some may not be compatible.

Unmatched electrical charges affect suspensions, or non-sterile compounded preparations in which the active pharmaceutical ingredient is suspended in a liquid medium. A suspension is referred to as a two-phase system since the active ingredient (internal phase) is not dissolved into the aqueous medium (external phase) but rather suspended in it. Suspensions are therefore ideal formulations for insoluble active ingredients.

For suspensions, it is important that the active ingredient remain uniformly dispersed in the suspension vehicle to ensure the patient receives the correct therapeutic dose. Uniform dispersion of the particles in a suspension is the result of the attraction and repulsion of electrical charges. The electrical charges of the active pharmaceutical ingredient, suspension vehicle, and excipients must be compatible with each other or else the active ingredient can clump together or settle. Reducing the particle size of the active ingredient and/or use of a wetting agent can help to ensure an equal dispersion of the active ingredient into the suspension vehicle.

The two methods of reducing particle size, whether tablets or powders, are trituration and levigation. Trituration is a dry method in which tablets or bulk powders are ground into smaller particles using a mortar and pestle. The wet method, referred to as levigation, is essentially the same as trituration except a small amount of a wetting or levigating agent is added to the active ingredient while it is being ground into a fine powder. This process not only reduces particle size but also helps the active ingredient incorporate more completely into the suspension vehicle. The addition of viscosity enhancers and flocculating agents can help create a more uniformly distributed product. Viscosity enhancers thicken the suspension, which slows the rate of sedimentation. Neutral electrolytes or flocculating agents are used to prevent caking of the particles, ensuring a more stable suspension.

Immiscibility, or the inability of two substances to form a homogenous mixture, affects topical gels, lotions, and creams—non-sterile emulsion preparations that can be difficult to prepare when using two or more components (or phases). An emulsifying agent, also called a surfactant, can be used when combining non-polar or hydrophobic liquids with polar or hydrophilic liquids. An emulsifying agent is amphiphilic, meaning one end is attracted to water or is polar and the other repels water or is non-polar. This amphiphilic property of an emulsifying agent decreases interfacial tension allowing a barrier to form between the dispersed phase (the internal or dispersed component) and the continuous phase (the external component or disbursement medium) of the preparation. An emulsifying agent can therefore aid in the stabilization of the topical preparation.

It is important to use both the correct type and the correct amount of an emulsifying agent. Failure to do so may disrupt the interfacial tension, causing the separation of the two phases. Disruption of the barrier created between the two phases can cause a cracked emulsion in which the oil and water layers separate into two distinct layers. Coalescence can also occur with the breakdown of an emulsion's interfacial tension, causing small droplets of the internal phase to combine, resulting in larger droplets. Coalescence results in an irreversible loss of uniformity, which affects the efficacy of the emulsion preparation.

## Chemical Incompatibilities

Chemical incompatibilities in non-sterile compounded preparations occur when the combination of ingredients or the compounding process results in a chemical reaction. Chemical incompatibility can affect the preparation's therapeutic effectiveness, potency, or integrity and may also lead to precipitation of the drug, changes in pH, or formation of toxic non-therapeutic compounds. For example, some medications are only stable within a specific pH range. Outside the specified pH range, the drug can begin to degrade. Therefore, if two active pharmaceutical ingredients are stable at different pH values, they cannot be combined into one preparation due to their chemical incompatibility.

Omeprazole (Prilosec) is a proton pump inhibitor (PPI) that can be compounded as a non-sterile oral suspension and is used to reduce stomach acid in pets and pediatric patients. The bulk powders used to prepare the omeprazole oral suspension can begin to degrade under low pH (acidic) conditions, so it must be compounded with the proper alkaline base, such as sodium bicarbonate, to prevent chemical incompatibility, which might affect the pH of the suspension. To remain stable and effective, the suspension should maintain an ideal pH between 8 and 8.5. A pH value in this range is necessary to prevent degradation of the active ingredient as well as enhance absorption of the medication.

Chemical incompatibilities caused by improper dilution or reconstitution of injectable medications can also result in precipitate formation and crystallization. Chemical incompatibility can result from using the incorrect diluent to reconstitute a medication or using the incorrect quantity of a diluent. Administering a medication that has crystallized or precipitated can lead to tissue irritation at the IV site and therapeutic failure. In addition, the patient may be exposed to toxic solutions and particulates that can enter the bloodstream through the IV line, causing a potentially fatal embolism. It is therefore important to note any changes in color, cloudiness, or particulate formation after reconstituting injectable medications, since these can often be observable characteristics of a chemical incompatibility. When administering reconstituted injectable drugs intravenously, it is important to flush the IV lines prior to administration to prevent inadvertently mixing medications or diluents. It is also important to verify compatibility if two medications must be administered concurrently.

Sodium bicarbonate is used to treat metabolic acidosis and is an example of an intravenous solution that can not only cause other medications to precipitate but can also render medications such as epinephrine completely inactive.

## Proper Storage of Medications

Proper storage of pharmaceutical drugs is necessary first to ensure that the safety, efficacy, stability, and overall integrity of a medication is maintained. Factors that can affect the integrity of a medication include extreme temperatures, light, moisture, and improper ventilation. Second, proper storage of pharmaceutical drugs ensures that only authorized personnel can access restricted medications.

## Temperature Ranges

Prescription medications should be transported and stored at a consistent controlled temperature according to the manufacturer's product specifications. Every medication has a recommended room temperature range established by the drug manufacturer during stability testing. These guidelines provide information for potential temperature excursions. Improper storage of pharmaceutical medications can cause the degradation of the active pharmaceutical ingredient or the breakdown of excipients and fillers; these chemical reactions can have detrimental effects on the delivery of the medication, rendering the medications therapeutically ineffective. Chemical reactions can also create unknown impurities in the medication that may be toxic to patients. Therefore, it is always important to verify the storage requirements of medications and adhere to them.

For most solid dosage formulations such as tablets and capsules, the controlled room temperature is between 20°C-25°C (68°F-77°F). This temperature range also applies to shelf stable oral suspensions and solutions. Medications that are stable at these temperature ranges are generally permitted excursions within five degrees Celsius or nine degrees Fahrenheit of this range (15°C-30°C or 59°F-86°F). Temperature excursions can vary, however, especially across dosage formulations; therefore, it is best to verify the temperature requirements found on the package labeling.

Most refrigerated medications should be transported and stored at a consistent temperature of 2°C-8°C (36°F-46°F). It is important to follow cold chain protocols for medications that require refrigeration prior to use, including insulins and some vaccines. Medications such as insulin generally have an expiration date established by the manufacturer that could be up to one or two years from the manufactured date. However, once the medications are no longer refrigerated, the expiration date is significantly reduced, often to under a month, whether opened or not.

## Moisture and Ventilation

Many medications can be severely degraded if they are exposed to excessive moisture or to too little moisture. Too much humidity may result in desterilization, destabilization, degradation, and the formation of toxic compounds in medications. The side effects may be visible in powders or solid dosages such as pills or caplets; however, these effects are not always visibly apparent. As an example, blood glucose strips may give incorrect readings if they are exposed to humidity. Low humidity conditions, on the other hand, can dry out medications, causing them to crumble or stick together, and can also change the effects of the solvents used in compounds. Medications should be maintained at relative humidity levels of 50-60 percent to remain therapeutically effective. Keeping medication in its originally packaging; storing medication in a cool, dry location; and making sure that the storage location for medication is well ventilated can all help prevent medication degradation.

## Proper Storage of Light-Sensitive Medications

Exposure to light can not only decrease the potency of a light-sensitive medication's active pharmaceutical ingredient (API) and its overall therapeutic effect, but the medication can also undergo chemical reactions that result in potentially toxic metabolites. Therefore, an active pharmaceutical ingredient that is susceptible to light, whether natural lighting or artificial lighting, should be stored in a special container that blocks light, such as an amber vial. An example of a light-sensitive medication is the macrolide antibiotic erythromycin; due to their light sensitivity, erythromycin tablets are often packaged in dark plastic containers.

## Proper Storage of Restricted Access Medications

Safety and security are important factors when considering proper storage methods for medications that have restricted access, such as controlled substances and federally restricted products. The DEA guidance on the proper storage requirements for Schedule II controlled substances, which include narcotic medications fentanyl (Duragesic) and hydromorphone (Exalgo), consists of a sturdy, locked cabinet. Schedule III-V controlled substances may be placed in the pharmacy with noncontrolled inventory in a way that will discourage theft or diversion of the controlled substance. While the interpretation of this storage and security policy is typically left up to the practitioner to develop and implement, it is expected that the DEA's minimum standards are to be adhered to using common sense criteria. For instance, pharmacies or hospitals located in high crime areas or those with a history of theft and diversion of medications should carefully consider additional security measures beyond the DEA minimum.

It also is important to consider the volume of Schedule II narcotic medications the pharmacy handles or has on hand at a given time. Pharmacies that are in close proximity to a hospital are more likely to dispense higher quantities of narcotics; therefore, other security considerations might include having a functioning alarm, an auto-locking safe, and a limit on the number of employees with access to the safe. Schedule III through Schedule V controlled substances are typically dispersed in the pharmacy among the noncontrolled medications, which is a perfectly acceptable means of storage according to the DEA.

Other types of restricted access medications are regulated by the Combat Methamphetamine Epidemic Act (CMEA) of 2005, a federal law that places sale restrictions on any OTC medication stored in a pharmacy that contains the active ingredients pseudoephedrine, ephedrine, and phenylpropanolamine. Access to OTC cold and allergy products containing these ingredients is restricted by federal law because the active ingredients are the primary chemicals used in the illegal production of the highly addictive street drug methamphetamine. The CMEA therefore requires these products to be secured in the pharmacy behind the counter or in a locked cabinet. In addition, sales of products containing pseudoephedrine, ephedrine, and phenylpropanolamine are restricted to 3.6 grams per day and require a form of identification in order to purchase.

# Practice Quiz

1. A pharmacy technician is reviewing a patient's medical record and notes a history of taking benzodiazepines. The pharmacy technician is likely to observe medications with which drug suffix?
   a. -pam
   b. -pine
   c. -emide
   d. -cillin

2. A pharmacy technician notes "Coreg" written on a prescription. The pharmacy stocks the generic form of the medication. Which medication will be dispensed to the patient?
   a. Propranolol
   b. Carvedilol
   c. Losartan
   d. Valsartan

3. A patient reports developing a dry cough since the last time they filled their prescription. The pharmacy technician refers the patient to the pharmacist but knows a dry cough is a common side effect of which antihypertensive drug class?
   a. Alpha Adrenergic Blockers
   b. Beta-Blockers
   c. Angiotensin Converting Enzyme Inhibitors
   d. Loop Diuretics

4. A pharmacy technician is dispensing sumatriptan for a patient. Which condition does this medication treat?
   a. Migraines
   b. Seizures
   c. Anxiety
   d. Depression

5. A patient approaches the pharmacy counter and asks for an over-the-counter recommendation to treat diarrhea. Which medication is the pharmacist likely to recommend?
   a. Bisacodyl
   b. Sennoside
   c. Docusate sodium
   d. Loperamide

# Answer Explanations

**1. A**: Choice *A* is correct because the drug suffix "-pam" is assigned to benzodiazepines, such as diazepam, used in the treatment of anxiety and sleep disorders. Choice *B* is incorrect because the drug suffix "-pine" is assigned to calcium channel blockers for the treatment of hypertension. Choice *C* is incorrect because the drug suffix "-emide" is assigned to loop diuretics used in the treatment of fluid overload and hypertension. Choice *D* is incorrect because "-cillin" is a drug suffix for antibiotics used to treat various infections.

**2. B**: Choice *B* is correct because carvedilol is the generic name for Coreg. It is important for the pharmacy technician to recognize both the generic and brand names of medications. Choice *A* is incorrect because propranolol is the generic name for Inderal, a different type of beta-blocker. Choice *C* is incorrect because losartan is the generic name for Cozaar, an angiotensin II receptor blocker (ARB). Choice *D* is incorrect because valsartan is the generic form of Diovan, which is also an ARB.

**3. C**: Choice *C* is correct because angiotensin converting enzyme inhibitors can cause a dry cough. The development of this side effect is a common cause of medication discontinuation. Choice *A* is incorrect because alpha adrenergic blockers are not known to produce a cough. Common side effects include headache and dizziness. Choice *B* is incorrect because beta-blockers do not produce a dry cough. Common side effects include bradycardia, hypotension, and fatigue. Choice *D* is incorrect because loop diuretics remove excess fluid and can cause dehydration and dry mouth. A cough is not associated with loop diuretics.

**4. A**: Choice *A* is correct because sumatriptan (Imitrex) is an intracranial vasoconstrictor used to treat acute migraines and cluster headaches. Choice *B* is incorrect because seizures are treated with anticonvulsant medications such as phenytoin and carbamazepine. Choice *C* is incorrect because anxiety is treated with benzodiazepines such as alprazolam. Choice *D* is incorrect because depression is treated with various antidepressants such as selective serotonin reuptake inhibitors and tricyclic antidepressants.

**5. D**: Choice *D* is correct because loperamide (Imodium A-D) is an antidiarrheal medication that decreases peristalsis and helps to decrease the loss of fluid and electrolytes via the stool. Choices *A* and *B* are incorrect because bisacodyl (Dulcolax) and sennoside (Ex-Lax) are laxatives. Laxatives have the opposite effect in the gastrointestinal system; they relieve constipation. Choice *C* is incorrect because docusate sodium (Colace) is a stool softener, which prevents constipation.

# Federal Requirements

## Federal Requirements for Handling Substances and Waste

The Environmental Protection Agency (EPA) discourages the disposal of hazardous and nonhazardous pharmaceutical waste using any method that allows the waste to enter the sewage system. When pharmaceutical waste is improperly disposed of, it can pollute drinking water sources and leach into the soil, posing a significant health risk to people and the environment. It is therefore important to not only understand the federal and state regulations regarding proper disposal of waste products, but also to be able to determine which pharmaceutical materials are considered waste. In addition, it is necessary to understand and distinguish between hazardous and nonhazardous waste since the regulations regarding their handling and disposal methods differ.

Federal requirements regarding the proper management of nonhazardous, hazardous, and pharmaceutical waste are outlined by an amendment to the Solid Waste Disposal Act, referred to as the Resource Conservation and Recovery Act (RCRA). The RCRA was passed by the United States Congress in 1976 to further protect public health and the environment from the improper handling and disposal of waste substances, including pharmaceutical wastes. The RCRA regulations are enforced by the EPA, the Occupational Safety and Health Administration (OSHA), the Drug Enforcement Agency (DEA), and the Department of Transportation (DOT), as well as numerous local and state authorities.

RCRA guidelines and recommendations regarding the handling and disposal of waste are outlined in Title 40 of the United States Code of Federal Regulations. The first step in properly handling waste is to determine whether the waste material meets the RCRA's definition of a solid waste. The label "solid waste" does not require the material to be a physical solid under RCRA's definition; solid waste materials can include solids, semisolids, and liquids. The next step in determining how to process waste is to identify whether the waste is 1) hazardous, 2) nonhazardous, or 3) excluded from the RCRA's guidelines for the disposal of solid waste. One example of an exception is household pharmaceutical waste.

According to the RCRA, it is acceptable to dispose of household pharmaceutical waste in the trash with other household waste, even when the waste meets the RCRA's definition of solid waste and may include hazardous or nonhazardous materials. The EPA, however, has recently begun to discourage these disposal methods since they can lead to environmental pollution. Instead, the EPA encourages the public to use pharmaceutical take-back programs offered locally to dispose of household OTC and prescription medications. If the medications must be disposed of in the regular household trash, the recommended method is mixing the medications in with undesirable contents such as cat litter or used coffee grounds and disposing of them with other household waste. Patients who have unwanted or expired controlled substances in the home are also advised to take the medications to a local take-back event for disposal.

Hazardous waste transporters move waste using various transportation routes including public roads, highways, and waterways. The Department of Transportation (DOT) is responsible for ensuring that transporters of hazardous materials comply with all guidelines and protocols for the movement of hazardous waste products among these routes. When transporting hazardous waste between locations, transporters must comply with all DOT requirements regarding transport containers, labeling, manifests, and protocols in case of a hazardous waste spill.

## Hazardous Waste

Federal requirements for the management of hazardous wastes were updated in 2019. Any healthcare facility that makes, stores, or manages hazardous waste pharmaceuticals is required to uphold these regulations established by the United States Environmental Protection Agency (EPA) in conjunction with other federal regulatory bodies such as the Department of Transportation, Drug Enforcement Administration, state-level Environmental Protection Agencies, and state-level Pharmacy Boards. Hazardous wastes are divided into two categories: listed wastes and characteristic wastes. Listed wastes are those that can pose a significant risk to human health or the environment, while characteristic wastes are those that exhibit a particular trait such as toxicity, reactivity, etc.

The EPA divides listed wastes into four categories: F-list, K-list, P-list, and U-list. F-list wastes are those that can be generated through various sources and are said to be non-source-specific. They are not wastes typically generated by pharmacies; however, acetone is an F-list hazardous waste that is sometimes used in pharmaceutical compounding. K-list wastes are source-specific, such as those generated through industrial processes. Of these four categories, P-list and U-list wastes are the primary categories of hazardous wastes that contain pharmaceutical products.

Hazardous pharmaceutical wastes are those that meet one of four qualities defining a hazardous waste. The EPA defines these as ignitability (able to cause a fire), corrosivity (can break down other substances or materials), reactivity (the ability for substance to chemically react with another substance), and toxicity (having a poisonous quality).

Healthcare facilities often store many hazardous pharmaceuticals since, in their intended form, they act as a therapeutic. Should they come into contact with unintended targets, however, they can place humans at high risk. As a result, hazardous pharmaceutical materials and waste should be stored and transported in containers that cannot be easily spilled or broken, even in the context of accidental mishandling. In general, these materials should be stored separately from non-hazardous materials. Accurate and reliable labeling systems are critical for safety. Storage areas should be well-ventilated with frequent hourly air changes, and under negative pressure.

Workers who handle hazardous pharmaceuticals and their waste byproducts should wear personal protective equipment (PPE) that is designed for the substances they are handling. In general, PPE such as gloves, goggles, facial masks, cuffed gowns, and boot covers are required to handle most hazardous substances, while specific substances may have additional PPE requirements. Chemotherapy drugs, for example, require gloves for handling that can specifically withstand the compounds found in these drugs. Substances that are at high risk of splashing may require double gloving. Facilities should have separate, sealable biohazard waste bins to dispose of used PPE after handling hazardous materials and wastes. Healthcare facilities are no longer allowed to dispose of hazardous pharmaceutical waste by flushing it into wastewater sewer streams.

Instead, these facilities must participate in drug buyback or reverse distribution programs in which waste materials are returned to manufacturing distributors, often for a credit to the healthcare facility. These distributors may repurpose active materials while treating expired materials to render then non-hazardous. Other hazardous waste products, such as PPE and medical equipment, may be incinerated or sterilized through autoclaving, irradiation, or other disinfection treatments and then returned to healthcare facility for use. Many public and private organizations provide biohazard waste removal services that stringently follow EPA guidelines to ensure that a facility's pharmaceutical wastes are transported and disposed of safely and lawfully.

The RCRA places limitations on the quantity of these hazardous waste products that can be stored on site at a given facility and limits the duration of storage. Hazardous waste generators are classified according to how much hazardous waste they produce. There are three classifications of waste generators: small quantity generators (SQG), large quantity generators (LQG), and conditionally exempt small quantity generators (CE-SQG). Facilities classified as SQGs are those that generate more than 100 kilograms but less than 1,000 kilograms of non-acute hazardous waste, more than 1 kilogram of acute hazardous waste, and less than 100 kilograms of acute hazardous waste spill residues per month.

LQGs, meanwhile, include facilities that generate more than 1,000 kilograms of non-acute hazardous waste, more than 1 kilogram of acute hazardous waste, and more than 100 kilograms of acute hazardous waste spill residues per month. Under EPA guidelines, CE-SQGs are facilities that generate under 100 kilograms of non-acute hazardous waste, no more than 1 kilogram of acute hazardous waste, and no more than 100 kilograms of hazardous waste spill residues per month. In addition, hazardous waste from CE-SQGs is not subject to storage time limitations and therefore may be stored on site for an indefinite duration if the quantity of waste being stored does not exceed EPA guidelines. Federal regulations require organizations that generate waste, such as hospitals and pharmacies, to be registered with an EPA identification number except for CE-SQG.

The EPA identification number can be obtained from local environmental agencies and allows waste generators to track manifested waste from the time it is generated to the time it is destroyed. In general, most hospitals and pharmacies are categorized as SQGs. A hospital or pharmacy may, however, qualify as an LQG if it is located on the same campus as other hazardous waste generators, such as on a military base or a university campus.

## Hazardous Pharmaceutical Waste

P-list hazardous wastes are considered acutely hazardous and have the potential to cause serious harm, including death. Prescription nicotine products and phentermine are examples of medications that are considered P-list hazardous wastes and must be properly disposed of. Warfarin waste is a listed waste; however, the classification is dependent on the concentration of drug present. Warfarin is considered a P-list hazardous waste if the concentration exceeds 0.3% but is a U-list hazardous waste if the concentrations is less than 0.3%. U-listed hazardous waste is considered non-acute hazardous waste and includes the chemotherapy agents chlorambucil and cyclophosphamide as well as seven other chemotherapeutic agents.

There are currently more than one hundred other chemotherapy agents that are not recognized as hazardous waste under federal RCRA regulations; however, it is recommended that they be treated as such since they can have cytotoxic effects. Other examples of U-listed wastes include the highly acidic glacial acetic acid and the highly basic sodium hydroxide, both of which are corrosive substances used in some compounded formulations. Containers that once held P-listed and U-listed hazardous medications, such as warfarin stock bottles, should also be treated as hazardous waste due to medication residues that may be present in the bottles.

It is important to ensure that hazardous pharmacy waste is stored separately from nonhazardous waste. If nonhazardous waste were to become contaminated with hazardous waste through improper handling, it would need to be disposed of under RCRA hazardous waste guidelines. This mishandling might not have a significant impact on an LQG, but it could have consequences for a CE-SQG since it could change their waste generator status. Hazardous pharmacy waste must also be stored in approved storage containers and should be properly labeled as hazardous waste. Hazardous pharmacy waste is generally stored in a container lined with a thick plastic bag that is free of leaks, and it should be placed away from nonhazardous pharmaceutical waste. Regarding storage of hazardous waste, most pharmacies are not considered large waste generators; therefore, the waste generally stays on site until transport to an approved waste handler such as Stericycle.

SQGs are permitted to store hazardous waste on site for a period up to 180 days prior to disposal by an EPA-approved hazardous waste processor. If an SQG's hazardous waste processor is located 200 miles or more from the facility, then EPA federal regulations allow the hazardous waste to remain on site for up to 270 days. Federal EPA regulations permit LQGs to store their hazardous waste on site for a maximum of 90 days; after that, however, such a facility would need to be designated as a storage facility and a permit would be required.

## Nonhazardous Waste

Nonhazardous wastes are generally solid wastes that do not meet the criteria of a hazardous substance under the RCRA's definition; however, many medications appear on the NIOSH list of hazardous medications without being designated as RCRA hazardous waste. NIOSH hazardous wastes include hormone medications such as progesterone and estrogens and are generally labeled as biohazardous wastes. The RCRA also regulates these nonhazardous pharmaceutical substances and wastes that are generated by pharmacies, hospitals, and clinics. Pharmaceutical waste that is not considered hazardous includes pharmaceutical medications that are obsolete or deemed unsaleable. Obsolete or unsaleable pharmaceutical medications may be damaged or expired but may also include overstocked medications. Pharmaceutical waste might also include any medical device or container that held pharmaceuticals such as empty medication bottles, vials, intravenous tubing, syringes, etc. Pharmaceutical wastes are required to be properly collected, documented, stored, and destroyed. Reverse distribution is the preferred method for handling pharmaceutical waste; a reverse distributor must handle the waste according to policies established by local environmental authorities as well as any EPA guidelines.

## Federal Requirements for Schedules and Prescriptions

The United States Congress enacted the Comprehensive Drug Abuse Prevention and Control Act in 1970 to curb drug abuse in the United States. Title II of this legislation, the Controlled Substances Act (CSA), created regulations regarding the dispensing and distribution of controlled substances, which includes classification schedules of controlled substances as determined by the United States Attorney General. This piece of legislation created the Justice Department's Drug Enforcement Agency (DEA), which enforces these laws and regulations as well as the scheduling system under which controlled substances are grouped. The Controlled Substances Act organizes controlled drugs into five different groups, referred to as "schedules." The scheduling of controlled substances is based on several factors including the drug's potential for abuse, the drug's ability to cause a dependency, and whether the drug has a legitimate medical purpose.

## DEA Controlled Substance Schedules

Title 21 Code of Federal Regulations provides guidance on all aspects of controlled substances including distribution, scheduling, labeling, etc. The five DEA drug schedules for narcotic and non-narcotic drugs are Schedule I, Schedule II/IIN, Schedule III/IIIN, Schedule IV, and Schedule V. The smaller the drug schedule number, the greater the drug's capacity to cause dependency and the greater its potential for abuse.

DEA Schedule I drugs are controlled substances that lack a legitimate medical purpose in the United States and therefore cannot be prescribed by a physician. Schedule I controlled substances are referred to as street drugs; their possession and use are illegal. These drugs are known to be highly addictive, causing significant dependency issues. Schedule I controlled substances include hallucinogens such as lysergic acid diethylamide (LSD) and 3,4-methylenedioxymethamphetamine (Ecstasy). Other examples of Schedule I drugs include opium derivatives such as heroin and marijuana (cannabis). It is important to note that medical marijuana, while illegal on the federal level, has been approved to some degree in various states for medical purposes.

Unlike Schedule I controlled substances, DEA Schedule II/IIN controlled substances have a legitimate medical purpose; therefore, they can be legally prescribed in the United States. Schedule II/IIN controlled substances are used to treat both acute and chronic pain conditions as well as attention deficit disorder (ADD) and attention deficit hyperactivity disorder (ADHD). However, Schedule II/IIN controlled substances also have a significant potential for abuse as well as the ability to cause significant dependency. Schedule II drugs include opiate and opiate derived narcotics. Examples of Schedule II narcotic controlled substances include oxycodone (Roxicodone), hydromorphone (Dilaudid), codeine, methadone (Dolophine), and fentanyl (Duragesic). Schedule IIN is the designation given to non-narcotic controlled drugs, which includes the stimulants lisdexamphetamine (Vyvanse), methylphenidate (Ritalin), and dextroamphetamine/amphetamine (Adderall).

DEA Schedule III/IIIN controlled substances also have the potential for abuse and dependency; however, the risk is lower than those associated with Schedule I, II, and IIN drugs. Abuse of Schedule III/IIIN drugs can lead to mild to moderate dependency. Examples of Schedule III controlled substances include the narcotics buprenorphine (Suboxone, Belbuca) as well as the combination drugs acetaminophen/codeine (Tylenol #3, Tylenol #4) and butalbital/acetaminophen/caffeine/codeine (Fioricet with codeine). Tylenol #3, Tylenol #4, and Fioricet are examples of Schedule III controlled substances that contain codeine, a Schedule II drug. However, per DEA regulations, medications that contain codeine are only classified as Schedule II when the preparation contains greater than ninety milligrams of the drug. Tylenol #3 and Tylenol #4 contain thirty and sixty milligrams of codeine, respectively. Fioricet with codeine contains thirty milligrams of codeine. Schedule IIIN consists of controlled substances that are non-narcotics, such as anabolic steroids containing testosterone. Dronabinol (Marinol) and testosterone gel (Androgel) are both examples of Schedule IIIN controlled substances.

DEA Schedule IV controlled substances include drugs that have a legitimate medical purpose and a lower potential for abuse and dependency than Schedule I, II, IIN, III, and IIIN drugs. This DEA schedule includes a class of medications referred to as benzodiazepines, which are often used in the treatment of anxiety-related disorders. Alprazolam (Xanax), lorazepam (Ativan), and clonazepam (Klonopin) are examples of Schedule IV controlled substances. Other Schedule IV drugs include the anticonvulsant phenobarbital, the muscle relaxer carisoprodol (Soma), and the analgesic tramadol (Ultram).

DEA Schedule V controlled substances include drugs that have the lowest abuse and dependency potential of all the DEA schedules. Schedule V includes pregabalin (Lyrica), lacosamide (Vimpat), and promethazine/codeine. Schedule V medications that contain codeine cannot exceed two-hundred milligrams per dosage unit of one hundred milliliters.

## Federal Requirements for Controlled Substance Prescriptions

Federal and state regulations regarding prescriptions for controlled medications are significantly more restrictive than those for noncontrolled medications. It is important to note that federal regulations may differ from state regulations. When federal laws are different from state pharmacy laws, the more restrictive regulation supersedes the less restrictive one. It is therefore important to refer to the specific state board of pharmacy to ensure proper compliance.

Federal regulations require prescribers or pharmacies that wish to prescribe or dispense controlled medications from Schedules II-V to register with the DEA by filling out DEA Form 224. The DEA is responsible for authorizing registrants and assigning approved registrants a DEA number composed of two letters, six digits, and a check digit, which will always be the last digit in the DEA number. The first letter corresponds to the type of registrant and the second letter corresponds to the first letter of the registrant's last name. The six digits and the check digit are computer generated. To validate a prescriber's DEA number, add the sum of the first, third, and fifth numbers in the DEA number to twice the sum of the second, fourth, and sixth numbers in the DEA number. If the DEA number is a valid one, the result will be a number whose last digit is the same as the last digit in the DEA number (the check digit).

For example, the DEA number for MB123466<u>4</u> can be validated as follows:

$$(1 + 3 + 6) = 10$$

$$2(2 + 4 + 6) = 24$$

$$10 + 24 = 34$$

The result is a valid DEA number since the last number, four, is the same as the check digit.

## Schedule II and IIN Prescriptions

Schedule II and IIN medications can be prescribed only by a practitioner for a legitimate medical purpose, and the practitioner must be registered with the DEA. Federal regulations for Schedule II prescriptions require that the prescription either be written or be transmitted to the pharmacy electronically. Electronic prescribing systems allow practitioners to use DEA-approved prescribing systems to securely transmit prescriptions directly to the pharmacy for dispensing. All controlled substance prescriptions, regardless of the medication's DEA schedule, must include several key elements to be considered valid: the patient's full name and full address, the prescriber's full name and full address, the prescriber's DEA number, the date the prescription was issued, the name of the drug, the strength of the drug, the dosage form of the drug, the quantity authorized, the directions for use, and the number of refills. Lastly, a valid prescription for a controlled substance must include the prescriber's signature. If for any reason the prescription for a controlled substance cannot be accepted electronically, the pharmacy must have a manual signature from the prescriber to dispense the prescription.

In general, federal regulation prohibits Schedule II prescriptions from being refilled. In some settings, however, a Schedule II prescription can be partially filled, for example, for long-term care patients and terminally ill patients. For patients residing in long-term care facilities (LTCFs) or those who are terminally ill, the pharmacy may partially fill a Schedule II medication for up to sixty days from the date it was initially authorized by the physician. In this scenario, the determination "LTCF patient" or "terminally ill" must be documented on the prescription. If the remaining quantity is not used before the sixty days are up, then the remaining quantity is lost, and the patient will need to obtain a new prescription from the prescriber.

For patients who do not meet the criteria of being terminally ill or in a LTCF, a pharmacist can choose to partially fill a Schedule II medication on a written prescription if they do not have the full quantity on hand. However, they must document the date the medication was dispensed and the quantity dispensed on the prescription. The pharmacy must dispense the remaining medication no later than thirty days from the prescription's date of issue. If the pharmacy cannot fulfill the prescription for the authorized quantity within thirty days of the issue date, the remaining medication will be lost. In addition, if a patient requests to fill a Scheduled II prescription for less than the authorized quantity, it will result in the forfeiture of any medication that remains on the prescription.

Verbal authorizations for Schedule II medications are permitted only in an emergency and are restricted to a seventy-two-hour supply of medication. This verbal authorization must be communicated directly between the prescriber authorizing the emergency prescription and the pharmacist. The pharmacist taking the oral emergency authorization is responsible for writing up the verbal prescription. The written authorization must be documented with all the required elements of a Schedule II prescription as well as the designation "Authorization for Emergency Dispensing."

The prescribing physician of the oral emergency authorization is then responsible for ensuring a written or electronic prescription is sent to the pharmacy within seven days of authorizing the emergency order. The pharmacist will then attach the written prescription to the verbal authorization or, if sent electronically, annotate the electronic order with all pertinent information from the initial verbal prescription. If an electronic or written prescription is not received by the pharmacist within the seven-day timeframe, the pharmacist is required to report the prescribing physician to the DEA and local board of pharmacy for failure to follow up with a written or electronic prescription. If a pharmacist fails to report the physician, they can be prohibited from accepting verbal emergency authorizations in the future.

There are currently no federal regulations that restrict the quantity on Schedule II prescriptions, nor is there an expiration statute for the prescriptions. Federal regulations simply require pharmacists to use professional judgement regarding Schedule II prescriptions. Many state laws do, however, have regulations in place that restrict the quantity on a Schedule II prescription as well as how long a prescription is valid. Pharmacists should therefore consider whether the quantity is appropriate for the intended therapy duration and whether the prescription is being filled in a timely manner. For example, a prescription for a Schedule II medication that was issued six months prior may require consultation with the prescriber to verify that dispensing the medication is still appropriate.

While refills are not permitted on Schedule II prescriptions, multiple Schedule II prescriptions can be authorized by a prescriber per DEA regulations. They must be written as separate prescriptions or electronically prescribed separately and must not exceed a ninety-day supply. Each prescription must have the same date of issue and cannot be postdated. Each prescription must state the earliest date that they are permitted to be filled by the pharmacy. Lastly, Schedule II prescriptions, in general, are not allowed to be transferred between pharmacies. However, there is currently debate about allowing transfers of Schedule II prescriptions among state-level pharmacy boards due to the DEA's vague stance on the issue.

## Schedule III-V Prescriptions

Federal regulations for Schedule III, IIIN, IV, and V prescriptions are more lenient than those for Schedule II controlled substances. While they must include the same DEA-required elements on the prescription as the Schedule II prescriptions, they can be dispensed from written, facsimile, e-prescribed, and verbal orders that have been reduced to written form. Schedule III, IIIN, and IV prescriptions are also permitted to be refilled five times or up to six months from the date of issue. Schedule V prescriptions, however, may be refilled as authorized by the prescribing physician and are considered valid for one year after the issue date.

Transfers of Schedule III, IIIN, IV, and V prescriptions that have been previously filled by one DEA-registered pharmacy are permitted to be transferred one time to another DEA-registered pharmacy. However, if two pharmacies share a real-time database, the prescription can be transferred multiple times between the pharmacies that share a computer system until all authorized refills have been exhausted or the prescription expires. The transfer must be a direct communication between a licensed transferring pharmacist and a licensed receiving pharmacist.

The transferring pharmacist is required to void the original prescription and must record the date of transfer; the full name of the transferring pharmacist; the receiving pharmacist's full name; and the receiving pharmacy's name, address, and DEA number. The receiving pharmacist must mark the prescription as a transfer and record the date of transfer; the full name of the transferring pharmacist; the transferring pharmacy's name, address, DEA number, and the prescription number; the receiving pharmacist's full name; the name, address, DEA number, and prescription number of the pharmacy at which the prescription was originally filled; the prescription's original issue date and original dispensing date; the original number of refills and the number of refills remaining; and the date and location of previous refills. If a transfer is received orally, the receiving pharmacist is required to reduce to writing all pertinent information.

## Federal Requirements for Controlled Substances

The handling of controlled substances is highly regulated by the federal government to prevent substance abuse and diversion. The DEA oversees every aspect of controlled substances including distribution, dispensing, and disposal. The federal regulations on controlled substance medications, as outlined in the Controlled Substances Act (CSA), essentially creates a chain of custody between drug manufacturers, drug distributors, and drug dispensers. Each of these entities in the chain of custody must be registered with the DEA in order to manufacture, distribute, or dispense controlled substances.

Schedule I and Schedule II controlled substances can be ordered from a distributor by an individual that holds a DEA registration. Registrants must obtain a DEA Form 222 from the DEA and fill it out to order or transfer Schedule I and II controlled substances. In general, DEA Form 222s are issued based on the pharmacy's volume and are issued with the registrant's pertinent information as well as a serial number. The Form 222 is a triplicate order form that must be completed by pen, computer, or typewriter. When completing a DEA Form 222, the registrant must include the supplier the medications are being ordered from, the number of packages, the package size, and the name and strength of the medication.

At the bottom of the form, the purchaser must fill in the last line that was completed (the line number of the last drug being ordered), then sign and date. The purchaser must make a copy for their records and send the original to the supplier to be filled. Once the order is completed, the first copy is retained by the supplier, the second copy is forwarded to the DEA, and the third copy is retained by the purchaser. DEA registrants can also execute a power of attorney to allow another individual to complete a DEA Form 222 on their behalf. The power of attorney must be kept with ordering records and made available, if necessary, for inspection.

The turnaround time for orders filled in this manner can often be up to three days; therefore, under the authority of the Controlled Substance Act (CSA), the DEA launched an electronic ordering system that permits purchasers to place orders online. The Controlled Substance Ordering System (CSOS) is an electronic record that has numerous benefits for purchasers. The CSOS decreases errors when ordering, enables more frequent orders, permits more line items per order, and is a faster process than the standard paper form. The DEA registrant must obtain a CSOS digital certificate and private key from the DEA Certification Authority in order to place electronic orders for controlled substances. This digital identity enables the encrypted online ordering of Schedule I and II medications.

### Receipt and Storage of Controlled Substances
Upon receipt of Schedule I and II controlled substances, the pharmacy or purchaser must verify and document the package quantities that were received from the supplier on their copy of the DEA Form 222 as well as the dates the drugs were received. Once verified, the medications that were received must be

added to the inventory logbooks and the pharmacy's copy of the DEA Form 222 must be filed with order records. All DEA Form 222s, including executed forms, rejected forms, or damaged forms, must be retained for two years.

The Drug Enforcement Agency provides guidelines and recommendations regarding the storage of controlled substances. Due to their abuse potential, the DEA requires Schedule II controlled substances to be physically secured in a safe or a sturdy, locked cabinet. Several factors may influence the type of storage required, including the volume of medications being stored at a given time, location of the pharmacy, and previous theft or diversion history. Schedule III-V controlled substances may be shelved with noncontrolled substances as long as the placement discourages theft or diversion of the controlled substances.

## Labeling and Dispensing of Controlled Substances

Title 21 of the Code of Federal Regulations requires drug manufacturers to adequately label controlled substances with the DEA schedule they belong to by including the symbol that corresponds to the drug's DEA schedule on the commercial stock bottle. The schedule of the drug must be prominently displayed to make the medication easily identifiable as a controlled medication. The packaging is also required to be sealed to prevent tampering.

When controlled substances are dispensed, federal regulations require the patient's medication label to include the name and address of the pharmacy filling the medication, the patient's name, the prescriber's name, the date of initial fill, the prescription number, directions for use, and any cautionary information. Accurate dispensing of a controlled substance prescription requires validating the prescription, verifying the medication is being prescribed for a legitimate medical purpose, verifying that the prescriber is operating within their scope of practice, ensuring the hard copy has all of the DEA-required elements, accurate data entry of the prescription, and any other steps required by law or by the individual pharmacy. When dispensing controlled substances, it is common practice to perform a double count of the medication, regardless of its DEA schedule, to help prevent over or under dispensing. For Schedule II controlled substances, a physical inventory logbook is used to manually record each prescription. The logbook may include dispensing information such as the prescription number, quantity of medication dispensed, the date it was dispensed, the initials or signature of the pharmacist that dispensed the drug, and a running on-hand balance of the drug dispensed.

## Take-Back Programs

Take-back programs have become a popular and effective method of allowing patients to dispose of unwanted, expired, and unused medications. These programs may include take-back collections, collection kiosks, and mail-in collections, and they are often conducted by local law enforcement, local pharmacies, or local hospitals that are registered with the DEA. Each of these collection programs allow patients to dispose of their unwanted medications, both controlled and noncontrolled. These collection programs are vital to ensuring that unwanted medications, especially controlled substances such as narcotics, are out of households and disposed of properly.

Take-back events are held by local law enforcement and require all aspects of the collection event to be overseen by a member of the law enforcement agency that is conducting the take-back event. This officer is responsible for ensuring all the medication that is collected remains in their custody for the duration of the event until transferred to a disposal facility.

Collection kiosks or drop boxes can be found in local law enforcement offices, pharmacies, hospitals, and other DEA registrants in the community. The collection receptacles must be secured, and they must have an inner liner that meets strict DEA regulations. Per DEA regulations, the liner must be tamper-evident, waterproof, tear-resistant, and sealable upon removal from the collection receptacle. The liner must state its capacity on the outside and must also include a traceable serial number that can be used to track its contents. Once the liner has reached its capacity, two employees of the responsible agency must prepare the contents for destruction by removing the liner and immediately sealing it. The medications are then transferred to a waste processor for destruction.

Mail-back programs allow the patient to discard unwanted medications by sending them to a DEA-registered waste processor or collector via postage paid envelopes. Medication mail-back programs are offered by many waste processors, pharmacies, and local law enforcement agencies. Federal DEA regulations require the medication return envelopes be postage paid as well as preaddressed with the DEA-registered waste collector's address. If the mail-back program is sponsored by a local law enforcement agency, then the postage paid envelope should be preaddressed with the responsible agency's physical address. The mail-back envelope should be similar to the liners used at take-back events in that they must be tear-resistant, waterproof, tamper-evident, sealable, and traceable. The mail-back envelopes should also be non-descript and void of information regarding the contents.

These collection programs do not require that patients or collectors separate noncontrolled medications from controlled medications. Consequently, it is reasonable to assume that each liner or envelope may potentially contain controlled substances. As a result, when the liners or envelopes are acquired by a DEA-registered waste processor, the processor is required to treat the collections as controlled substances and process them according to DEA regulations for rendering controlled substances non-retrievable. The DEA does not specify which method of destruction should be used when destroying controlled substances; it does, however, define "rendering non-retrievable" as destroying the medication to the point where it is completely unusable as a controlled substance or controlled substance analog. Incineration of the controlled medications is the preferred disposal method used by controlled substance waste processors.

## Reverse Distribution

Reverse distribution is the process by which pharmacies dispose of overstocked, expired, or damaged medications. Reverse distributors are required to follow Resource Conservation and Recovery Act (RCRA) guidelines and to be registered with the DEA if they are processors of controlled substances. Reverse distributors not only facilitate the destruction of non-dispensable (or non-saleable) medications but also redistribute saleable medications throughout the supply chain. Pharmacies can sometimes receive credit for returned medications when the medications are processed by a reverse distributor, as long as the medications meet certain criteria to be deemed saleable (e.g., they are a certain number of months away from their expiration date, the bottle is unopened, etc.). Management of saleable medications by a reverse distributor ensures the integrity of redistributed medications and decreases waste. Damaged, recalled, and expired medications are considered non-dispensable pharmaceutical waste.

Controlled substances must be transferred to the reverse distributor for evaluation and destruction if necessary. A DEA Form 222 must be completed in order to transfer Schedule II medications from the pharmacy to the reverse distributor. If the Schedule II medications being transferred are saleable, the reverse distributor can facilitate their return to the manufacturer for credit. The pharmacy must also document the transfer of Schedule III–V medications, noting the date of transfer, the drug, the dosage formulation, the strength, and the quantity. If a manufacturer cannot give credit on surrendered Schedule II–V controlled substances, the controlled substances will be deemed non-distributable and the reverse distributor will be required to dispose of the medications per federal regulations.

Upon destruction of controlled substances, the reverse distributor is required to fill out a DEA Form 41 as verification that the controlled medications have been disposed of. The DEA Form 41 must include the registrant's information as well as a complete inventory of medications that were surrendered for disposal. The reverse distributor must document the National Drug Code (NDC) or DEA Controlled Substance Code for the product, the number of packages or units to be destroyed, the drug formulation, etc. Section B of DEA Form 41 is for medications that were acquired from take-back programs, receptacle collections, and mail-in programs. If the collected medication was acquired from a collection receptacle, the size of the inner liner as well as the serial number or unique tracking number found on the liner must be documented on the DEA Form 41 in Section B.

If the collected medication was acquired from a mail-back envelope that does not include a unique tracking number, the reverse distributor needs to document the address of the law enforcement agency that received the collections as well as the package size. The sealed envelopes and inner liners are prohibited from being unsealed and inventoried and must be destroyed as-is. Once all relevant information has been documented on the DEA Form 41, the reverse distributor must record the location of destruction and the method of destruction, and the form must be signed by the two employees that are required to witness the destruction. The DEA Form 41 does not need to be filed with the FDA (unless requested to do so), but it must be kept on file for at least two years.

Some pharmacies may have the capacity to destroy controlled medications in-house. To do so, they must be registered with the DEA, completely fill out a DEA Form 41, and have two employees witness the destruction. As with reverse distributors, the DEA Form 41 does not need to be filed with the FDA (unless requested to do so), but it must be kept on file for at least two years.

## Loss/Theft/Diversion

Federal DEA regulations require a registrant to notify their region's field division office regarding the loss, theft, or diversion of controlled substances. The notification should be in writing and should be reported within one business day of discovery. Reported losses may be the result of in-transit losses, natural disaster losses, internal diversion, or robbery and theft. Registrants that have suffered a significant loss of controlled substances or disposal receptacles containing controlled substances must complete a DEA Form 106. DEA Form 107 is the form used to report the loss, theft, and diversion of DEA listed chemicals that are used to make controlled substances. These forms must be completed and submitted to the DEA when a significant loss or theft has occurred.

## Federal Requirements for Restricted Drug Programs and Related Medication Processing

Restricted distribution drug programs are those in which access to specific medications or chemical ingredients with serious safety concerns is limited to a small number of distributors. An example of a restricted distribution drug program is Risk Evaluation and Mitigation Strategy program (REMS). Isotretinoin, clozapine, and Sublocade are just a few of the medications that are required to implement a REMS program by the FDA. The Combat Methamphetamine Epidemic Act (CMEA) is another example of a restricted access program, although it is significantly less restrictive than a REMS program. CMEA restricts access to OTC medications that could be used to manufacture methamphetamine and amphetamine, but it restricts patient access to the medications rather than restricting which pharmacies can distribute them.

### Risk Evaluation and Mitigation Strategy (REMS) Programs

Side effects and adverse reactions can occur when taking any medication; however, some medications can pose serious health risks. Medications with potentially serious safety concerns but legitimate medical benefits are evaluated by the FDA to assess the need for a Risk Evaluation and Mitigation Strategy (REMS) program. The FDA reviews several characteristics of the medication, including severe complications of the medication, the severity of the medical condition being treated, and any potential or documented adverse effects in the target patient population, to adequately determine whether a REMS program is required. If, after evaluating a medication, the FDA determines there is a need for a REMS program, the FDA will notify the manufacturer of the medication. The manufacturer is then responsible for the development and implementation of the REMS program. Although the FDA is not involved in the development of the REMS program, it may request that the REMS program meet specific requirements prior to approval.

The iPledge program is one of the most common REMS programs used in pharmacies. As an example, acne medications that contain the active pharmaceutical ingredient isotretinoin are dispensed using the iPledge REMS program. The distribution of isotretinoin, marketed under several brand names including Claravis and Amnesteem, is restricted in the United States because it is likely to cause serious birth defects if a woman becomes pregnant while taking it. Each participant in the iPledge REMS program has a responsibility to ensure every childbearing-age female recipient of isotretinoin is not pregnant at the start of therapy and does not become pregnant while taking the medication.

The iPledge REMS program requires each prescriber, patient, and pharmacy to be registered with iPledge to participate. Prescribers registered with iPledge are required to identify and document the patient's gender as well as the patient's childbearing potential if female. In addition to being enrolled in the iPledge program, all patients who wish to be prescribed isotretinoin must be provided counsel regarding the risks associated with taking isotretinoin and sign an informed patient consent form acknowledging these potential risks. In addition, prior to being prescribed isotretinoin, female patients with the potential to become pregnant must have a pregnancy test to confirm that they are not pregnant, and they must receive contraceptive counseling.

The prescriber must then document two forms of contraception the patient has chosen to use while taking isotretinoin. After the initial pregnancy test, there is a mandatory waiting period of one month in which the patient must use the chosen contraception methods. At the end of the waiting period, the prescriber must conduct another pregnancy test to confirm the patient is still not pregnant. The prescriber will then document which two forms of contraception the patient is using, as well as the results from the pregnancy screenings, in the iPledge system. The patient will be required to complete a set of comprehension questions to ensure they fully understand all associated risks of becoming pregnant while taking the medication. Once all the required information is submitted to the iPledge system, the prescriber can issue a prescription for isotretinoin.

The pharmacy is required to verify that all iPledge requirements for isotretinoin prescriptions have been met by logging in to the iPledge verification system and submitting the patient's iPledge ID. After verification, the pharmacy is required to enter which drug name is dispensed including the product National Drug Code (NDC), the quantity of medication to be dispensed, and the day supply, which should not exceed thirty days. If all requirements are met, the iPledge system will issue a Risk Management Authorization (RMA) number and a date by which the patient must pick up the medication. The prescription's pickup window for a patient of childbearing potential is only seven days from the day the second pregnancy test was administered. The pickup date and the RMA number must be documented on the prescription as well as the placed on an iPledge label and affixed to the prescription bag. For male patients and female patients who are not of childbearing potential, the prescription pickup window is thirty days. If a patient fails to pick up the prescription by the required date, the pharmacy must log in to the iPledge system, reverse the RMA, and return the medication to stock.

Another example of a medication for which the FDA requires a REMS program is clozapine. Clozapine is indicated for, and highly effective at treating, treatment-resistant schizophrenia. Clozapine, however, can cause severe drug-induced neutropenia in a small percentage of patients. Neutropenia is a reduction in the number of infection-fighting white blood cells referred to as neutrophils, which can be life-threatening because it decreases the body's ability to fight infections. Monitoring of the patient's absolute neutrophil count (ANC) is therefore a required element of the Clozapine REMS program. The Clozapine REMS program is a shared program that requires prescribers as well as pharmacy representatives to undergo program training and obtain certification to participate.

Prescribers must first enroll the patient in the Clozapine REMS program and then monitor the patient's ANC while they are taking clozapine. The monitoring frequency depends on various factors including the patient's baseline ANC when starting the medication, the dose being administered, and how long they have been taking the medication. Lab work may be performed weekly, every two weeks, or once monthly. The prescriber must also enter the result of the patient's ANC test in the clozapine shared system before the pharmacy dispenses the medication. A certified pharmacy can dispense clozapine only to a patient whose ANC is current, whose ANC is within an acceptable range, and who is enrolled in the clozapine REMS program by a certified prescriber. If all these criteria are met, the pharmacy will be issued a Predispense Authorization (PDA) and can dispense enough medication to treat the patient until the next ANC is drawn.

Sublocade, another restricted access medication, is an extended-release injectable formulation of buprenorphine and is indicated for moderate to severe opioid addiction. A Sublocade REMS program was implemented due to the serious safety risks associated with self-administration of the injection. The Sublocade REMS program requires all prescribers and pharmacies to be certified in order to prescribe or dispense Sublocade. The main requirement of the Sublocade REMS program is that the medication cannot be dispensed directly to a patient; rather, it must be sent directly to the healthcare provider or picked up from the pharmacy by a representative of the healthcare provider.

## Restricted Access Medications

The Combat Methamphetamine Epidemic Act (CMEA), passed by Congress in 2005, is an amendment to the Controlled Substance Act (CSA). The CMEA allows the federal regulation of non-prescription medications that contain pseudoephedrine, ephedrine, and propanolamine. These chemical ingredients are considered listed chemicals in the CMEA legislation since they can be used in the illegal manufacturing of Schedule II medications such as methamphetamine and amphetamine. Therefore, the CMEA restricts the purchase of any OTC medications that contain the listed ingredients. The CMEA does this by limiting the quantity and frequency of purchase for these OTC medications. These CMEA regulations are overseen and enforced by the DEA to ensure compliance.

Although considered OTC medications, non-prescription products that contain pseudoephedrine, ephedrine, or propanolamine must be kept behind the pharmacy counter, according to CMEA regulations. Quantity restrictions permit a person to purchase up to 3.6 grams of the restricted chemical ingredients per day, but purchases cannot exceed 9 grams in thirty-day period. Per CMEA regulations, a state or federal photo ID must be presented to purchase any product that contains pseudoephedrine, ephedrine, or propanolamine. Pharmacies must keep a written or electronic logbook for two years detailing the sale of all products that contain these restricted chemical ingredients. Required information includes the purchaser's name and address, the purchaser's signature attesting that they will not use the product to manufacture illegal drugs, the date and time of the sale, which product was sold, and the quantity that was purchased.

## FDA Recall Requirements

The Food and Drug Administration (FDA) is responsible for the regulation of prescription medications, medical devices, medical supplies, and dietary supplements. Public safety concerns regarding an FDA-regulated product can, however, arise after a product is on the market, which can result in a recall of the product. A product recall is a system of procedures used to eliminate or correct products that are in violation of laws administered by the FDA. Such violations could provoke legal action by the FDA if not corrected. Recalled products may contain an unintentional or undeclared ingredient, the product may be misbranded or labeled improperly, the product may be altered or contaminated, or the product may be defective. The FDA can issue a public health alert regarding a product if it receives sufficient evidence that a product can cause an adverse effect, which is especially helpful if the product has been widely distributed.

Often it is a consumer or the manufacturer itself that discovers the potential problem and alerts the FDA. There are several approaches to reporting defective or unsafe products, depending on the type of product. For medications and medical devices, some patients may choose to report adverse effects to their physicians while others may choose to reach out to the manufacturer of the product directly. The FDA also maintains a reporting system called MedWatch that allows consumers and healthcare professionals to report adverse effects of medications, dietary supplements, medical devices, and medical supplies. Consumers and health professionals are both encouraged to report any adverse effects of a medication, supplement, medical supply, or medical device to the manufacturer or to MedWatch. The FDA compiles the reported data from adverse effects and can use the information to determine if a product poses a public health risk.

The FDA requires the manufacturer of a recalled product to develop a recall strategy that establishes the extent of the recall as well as how to reach the affected consumers. The manufacturer must contact consumers with pertinent product information including the name of the affected product, the package size, the affected lot number, and specific serial numbers or other identifying information. The manufacturer must also make the consumer aware of why the medication has been recalled, any harm associated with its use, and information on how to return or dispose of the product. Product manufacturers most often notify consumers via first-class mail. Product recall information is included in the FDA's Enforcement Report, which is published weekly.

In general, product recalls are voluntary acts initiated by the manufacturer to correct a problem. The FDA, however, can request the recall of a product if the manufacturer is made aware of a safety issue with one of its products and fails to respond or does not respond in an adequate manner. In addition to issuing a recall, the FDA can pursue legal action to force the manufacturer to cease production of the product and seize any current stock on the market.

## Classifications of Recalls

The FDA evaluates product recalls and classifies them according to their potential for harm. Class I recalls are those with the potential for significant adverse reactions, including death. Examples of a Class I recall might include an injectable medication that was exposed to contaminants during the manufacturing process, an improperly labeled emergency medication, or a defective medical device such as a pacemaker. Class I recalls require immediate action by the manufacturer and the FDA to remove unsafe products from the market. Class II recalls are recalls of products that can cause less severe or reversible adverse effects. A Class II recall may include a product that does not meet quality assurance specifications; for example, a common OTC product is found to contain less of an active ingredient than the manufacturer intended. A

Class III recall is one in which the defect is not likely to cause adverse effects. Class III recalls are typically a result of mislabeling, such as a missing lot number or missing expiration date.

Market withdrawals and medical device safety alerts are two other separate classifications of recalls. A market withdrawal is the voluntary correction or removal of a product initiated by the product manufacturer for a minor reason, such stock rotation or a slight issue created by maintenance or repairs at the manufacturing facility, or a minor violation that would not be subject to legal action by the FDA. A market withdrawal can be the result of an aftermarket safety concern such as product tampering. Once the safety concern has been identified, the manufacturer may cease the production and distribution of the affected product. The manufacturer is also responsible for removal of the affected product from the inventory of any retailers and distributors as well as from its own stock. Medical device notifications or safety alerts are disseminated either by the manufacturer or the FDA when a medical device is found to pose significant safety risks to patients.

## Medication and Dietary Supplement Recalls

When a recall notification for a medication or dietary supplement is issued by the manufacturer or the FDA, it is sent to the distributor or vendor of the product. In general, the distributor will notify pharmacies with a recall notification. If a pharmacy receives a recall notification for a medication or dietary supplement, the pharmacy should immediately cease dispensing the product and pull all the affected products or lots from the shelf. The recalled products should remain separated from unaffected products until they can be disposed of or sent back to the vendor for crediting. A pharmacy team member should be chosen to contact all customers that received the recalled medication. It is also best to notify prescribing physicians regarding the recalled medication. Prescribers may want to document the receipt of a recalled medication in the patient's chart in the event that any medical issues arise from it. In addition, when numerous lots of a product are affected by a recall, it may be appropriate to switch the patient to an alternative medication.

## Medical Device and Medical Supply Recalls

Medical device and medical supply safety alerts are notifications that are issued voluntarily by a product manufacturer or by request from the FDA. A safety alert is generally issued when a medical device or medical supply has been identified as having the potential to cause considerable harm to the public. Safety alerts can be issued for devices for a variety of reasons including malfunctions or ineffectiveness of the device. In the event of a recall, manufacturers are required to compile a list of vendors or distributors as well as issue public safety alerts that allow consumers of the affected products to return them for a refund. The product manufacturer is required to ensure it has done its due diligence to remove all the affected products from the market.

# Practice Quiz

1. A retail pharmacy is filling out an application for authorization to prepare and dispense controlled substances. Which form will the pharmacy use?
   a. DEA Form 225
   b. DEA Form 224
   c. DEA Form 363
   d. DEA Form 364

2. A physician sends an electronic prescription of oxycodone to a patient's pharmacy. The pharmacy's software system is not certified by a third-party auditor and cannot be used to fill the prescription electronically. What is required to fill the patient's prescription?
   a. A change in medication
   b. An authorization letter from the insurance
   c. The physician's manual signature
   d. The patient's identification card

3. A pharmacist is performing inventory on Schedule II controlled substances in the pharmacy. The pharmacist needs to order more stock from a distributor. Which form will the pharmacist fill out?
   a. DEA Form 222
   b. DEA Form 106
   c. DEA Form 107
   d. DEA Form 224

4. A bulk of controlled substances in the pharmacy have expired. The pharmacist selects to destroy the controlled substances in-house. In addition to filling out DEA Form 41, what other action is required by the pharmacist?
   a. Fill out a DEA Form 222 and store it for a period of 2 years
   b. Destroy the medication in the presence of another pharmacist
   c. Submit all of the completed paperwork to the DEA
   d. Contact the distributor for notification of the process

5. The Food and Drug Administration has recently recalled an over the counter medication that shows evidence of causing a temporary side effect and is deemed a slight threat to a patient's health. What recall classification corresponds to this description?
   a. Class IV
   b. Class III
   c. Class I
   d. Class II

# Answer Explanations

**1. B**: Choice *B* is correct because Drug Enforcement Agency (DEA) Form 224 is used to apply for a DEA registration number as a retail pharmacy. Other entities that use Form 224 are hospitals, clinics, teaching institutions, and practitioners. Choice *A* is incorrect because DEA Form 225 is used by manufacturers, distributors, and research facilities. Choice *C* is incorrect because DEA Form 363 is intended to be filled out by narcotic treatment programs. Choice *D* is incorrect because DEA Form 364 is not a form number used to fill out an application for a DEA registration number.

**2. C**: Choice *C* is correct because prescriptions for controlled substances that cannot be accepted electronically require a manual signature for dispensing. Choice *A* is incorrect because the prescription can still be filled, but it requires a manual signature by the ordering physician. Choice *B* is incorrect because an insurance company is not authorized to approve the electronic dispensing of controlled substances. Choice *D* is incorrect because a patient's identification card does not resolve a software certification issue.

**3. A**: Choice *A* is correct because DEA Form 222 is used for ordering and returning Schedule II controlled medications from and to another DEA registered entity. Only providers and distributors that have a DEA registration number may handle, order, and receive controlled substances. Choice *B* is incorrect because DEA Form 106 is used to report the theft or loss of controlled substances. Choice *C* is incorrect because DEA Form 107 is used to report the theft or loss of listed chemicals. Choice *D* is incorrect because DEA Form 224 is used to apply for a DEA registration number.

**4. B**: Choice *B* is correct because controlled substances that are destroyed in the pharmacy must be witnessed by another licensed personnel, such as a pharmacist, nurse, or practitioner, to avoid drug diversion or theft. Choice *A* is incorrect because DEA Form 222 is used when the controlled substances are returned to a distributor. If the CII substances are destroyed in the pharmacy, only DEA Form 41 is used. Choice *C* is incorrect because the paperwork does not need to be submitted unless requested by the DEA. Choice *D* is incorrect because the distributor does not need to know that the pharmacist has destroyed expired controlled substances.

**5. D**: Choice *D* is correct because Class II recalls are products that may cause temporary health problems or side effects and can pose a slight threat to a patient's health. Choice *A* is incorrect because Class IV is not a classification for an FDA product recall. Choice *B* is incorrect because Class III recalls are products that are not likely to cause any adverse effects but violate FDA manufacturing laws. Choice *C* is incorrect because Class I recalls are products that are defective and can cause serious adverse effects or death.

# Patient Safety and Quality Assurance

**High-Alert/Risk Medications and Look-Alike/Sound-Alike (LASA) Medications**

Medication errors can lead to preventable deaths in healthcare. Two causes of medication errors are look-alike/sound-alike drug names, commonly known as LASA medications, and high alert/risk medications.

## Look-Alike/Sound-Alike (LASA) Medications

The United States Food and Drug Administration (FDA) approves new medications each year, and a generic form of the medication is often also approved years later after the patent for the brand name drug expires. This results in many medications whose names sound the same or have similar spellings. These medications are called look-alike/sound-alike (LASA) medications, and they are often extremely easy to confuse when they are prescribed and/or dispensed. Entities such as the FDA and a nonprofit accreditation agency called the Joint Commission suggest strategies to reduce medication errors and prevent patient harm when dispensing LASA medications. One strategy is labeling medications with what is called "tall man lettering." Tall man lettering was established in 2001 through an FDA initiative and uses mixed-case letters—uppercase and lowercase—to help highlight the differences between medication names. As new medications are approved, the number of LASA medications added to the tall man lettering recommendation list increases.

For an example of the usefulness of tall man lettering, consider alprazolam, which is commonly confused with clonazepam and lorazepam. While all of these medications are benzodiazepines, they all have different indications, dosages, and routes of administration. To distinguish among these medications, tall man lettering is used on the labels. Alprazolam is labeled ALPRAZolam, clonazepam is labeled clonazePAM, and lorazepam is labeled LORazepam. Another example is the medication methylprednisolone, which is a steroid used to treat a variety of medical problems including arthritis, severe allergic reactions, and some cancers. Methylprednisolone is commonly confused with medroxyprogesterone, a type of the female hormone progestin, and methyltestosterone, an androgen. To distinguish these medications using tall man lettering, the name methylprednisolone is displayed as methylPREDNISolone, medroxyprogesterone is medroxyPROGESTERone, and methyltestosterone is methylTESTOSTERone. In practice, the labels will look like the image below:

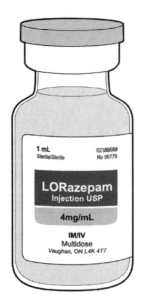

In addition to tall man lettering, LASA medications should be organized, stored, and dispensed according to pharmacy needs. Utilization patterns will help determine which LASA medications are commonly dispensed in the facility. The Institute for Safe Medication Practices (ISMP) also recommends using both a brand name and a generic name on the medication labels and including the purpose of the medication on prescriptions. A generic name differs significantly from the brand name and can be a tool to help distinguish LASA medications. For example, in the previous list, ALPRAZolam is the generic form for the brand Xanax, clonazePAM is the generic form of Klonopin, and LORazepam is the generic form of Ativan. In practice, including both the generic name and the brand name on the label further minimizes the risk of a medication error. The images below display a label with only the generic name and another with both the generic name and the brand name:

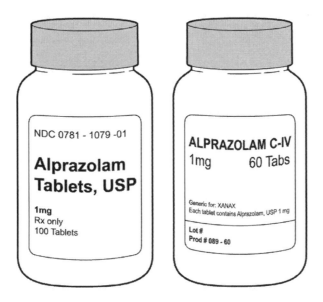

The Joint Commission also suggests labeling LASA medications with a sticker that identifies the potential for error. Each facility or pharmacy should determine which medications are high risk for being confused with one another. To remain current, pharmacies should review their list of LASA medications at least annually. Segregated areas or bins are useful in keeping LASA medications separated, thus reducing the risk of error. The LASA stickers may vary and can be unique to each facility. The images below are examples of LASA stickers used in various facilities.

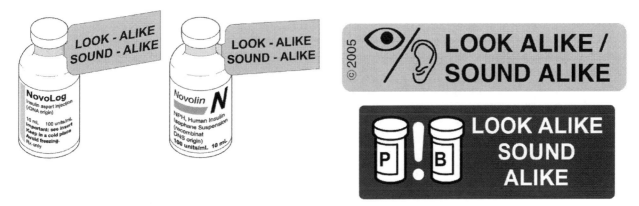

Pharmacy staff should be trained in the recognition of LASA medications and the necessary precautions to take when dispensing a prescription. Labels, tall man lettering, and stickers on medication containers should be used universally throughout the facility.

## High-Alert/Risk Medications

Pharmacy technicians are also responsible for recognizing high-alert (or high-risk) medications. High-alert medications are those that can potentially cause significant harm to the patient if prescribed, dispensed, or administered incorrectly. ISMP maintains a list of high-alert medications based on studies that identify medications most often involved in errors causing significant patient harm. Information is obtained via surveys from safety experts and clinicians to determine which medications require safeguards to reduce the risk of errors. The physical effects of wrongful administration of a high-alert medication can lead to acute emergent conditions, permanent disability, or death.

For example, all subcutaneous and intravenous forms of insulin are considered high-alert medications. Insulin is a hypoglycemic agent used in the treatment of diabetic conditions. Insulins vary in their peak, onset, and duration of action. Rapid-acting insulin such as insulin lispro has an onset of 15 minutes when administered subcutaneously. Alternatively, long-acting insulin such as insulin glargine has an onset of 3 to 4 hours and a duration of 24 hours when administered subcutaneously. The dosage of long-acting insulins will vary greatly when compared to rapid or short-acting insulins. For example, 40 units of insulin lispro will cause a rapid decrease in serum glucose levels, potentially causing a hypoglycemic coma or death.

In contrast, 40 units of insulin glargine are absorbed in constant concentrations over a period of 24 hours. Incorrectly prescribing, dispensing, and administering insulin dosages can have catastrophic effects. Another category of high-alert medication is neuromuscular blocking agents. These medications are used to paralyze and relax muscles during anesthesia for surgery or tracheal intubation. Because they paralyze the muscles necessary for breathing, improper usage or lack of adequate ventilation can result in catastrophic injury or death. The use of safeguards decreases the risk of error with these and other high-alert medications. Independent double-checks, pre-printed prescription orders, computerized alerts, and cautionary labels or containers are examples of safeguards to ensure high-alert medications are handled with caution. The images below display cautionary labels and containers used for high-alert medications:

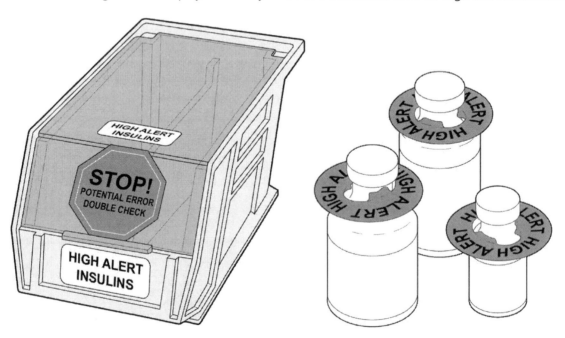

It is important to note that safeguards are required for high-alert medications not only because of the potential for confusion regarding which medication is dispensed, but also because these medications should be administered with caution regardless of the dosage. For example, opioid medications are commonly prescribed, dispensed, and administered in acute care settings and outpatient facilities. Opioids are primarily prescribed for pain relief and have several routes of administration including oral, sublingual, transdermal, and parenteral. Each route of administration has a different onset and duration of action. For example, 30 milligrams of morphine prescribed orally will have a significantly different onset than 30 milligrams of intravenous morphine. Large doses of intravenous morphine can lead to rapid respiratory depression, respiratory arrest, and death. Dosages among opioids also vary greatly, even for those with the same route of administration. For example, even though they are in the same category of opioids, hydromorphone (Dilaudid) is a potent analgesic that is approximately four to five times more powerful than morphine. To help bring the differences into perspective, 30 milligrams of oral morphine is equal to 7 milligrams of oral hydromorphone.

It is imperative that pharmacy technicians double-check prescription orders and follow the safeguards established within the facility to ensure accurate dosages of high-alert medications are prescribed and dispensed. Similar to LASA medications, a list of commonly used high-alert medications should be reviewed at least annually to ensure special precautions are taken when dispending these medications. Additionally, storing high-alert medications separately from other commonly used drugs prevents accidental selection by pharmacy staff. High-alert medications that tend to cause significant adverse effects such as insulin, opiates, and anticoagulants benefit from being stocked in smaller units, volume, or quantities. Verifying prescriptions with another licensed pharmaceutical staff member ensures that high-alert medications are checked twice before being dispensed. The image below shows an example of a cautionary label for a high-alert medication that should be counterchecked before dispensing:

## Error Prevention Strategies

There are many different types of medication errors that can potentially cause patient harm including errors of prescribing, omission, wrongful preparation, monitoring, and compliance. Error prevention is a high priority for pharmacists. Pharmacists must ensure the prescriptions have the correct patient information as well as the correct dosages, frequencies, indications, and routes of administration. Pharmacy technicians hold a key role in assisting the pharmacist by ensuring error prevention measures are in place and by using multiple checks throughout the medication dispensing process.

### Check 1: Drop Off
The first check occurs at the time the patient drops off the prescription. The prescription should be checked carefully for errors, inconsistencies, and illegibility. Missing information such as route, frequency, or dosage should be shared with the pharmacist and clarified promptly with the healthcare provider. Patient identification is crucial to ensure the correct medication will be dispensed to the correct patient. Pharmacy technicians should ensure the patient's name is spelled correctly and their date of birth is

included on the prescription as an additional patient identifier. Allergic reactions to medications can potentially cause adverse effects. Therefore, the pharmacy technician should verify any known allergies and note them on the prescription and in the computer system.

Other components to check on a prescription include error-prone abbreviations, symbols, and dose designations. The Joint Commission has developed a "Do Not Use" list that identifies common prescription errors that may lead to incorrect order entry and wrongful dispensing of medication. Similarly, the ISMP has compiled a list of error-prone components that have been reported through its National Medication Errors Reporting Program (ISMP MERP). For example, "cc" (cubic centimeters) is an abbreviated measurement that is commonly misinterpreted as a "unit." A unit is a dosage, whereas cc is a volume. Because an incorrect dose designation can cause considerable harm to a patient, cc should be displayed as milliliters (mL) on a prescription. Another example of a "Do Not Use" abbreviation is $MSO_4$, or magnesium sulfate, which is commonly confused with morphine sulfate.

Dosages are another common area where errors occur. As a general rule, leading zeros should be placed before the decimal point when the dose consists of less than one measurement unit. Additionally, the use of trailing zeros is not necessary and can increase the risk of error. For example, a dosage of .6 mg can easily be confused for 6 mg and .60 mg can easily be confused for 60 mg. Therefore, it is advised to include leading zeros and omit trailing zeros in the dosage, which would be correctly displayed as 0.6 mg. The pharmacy technician should check the prescription dose carefully, especially if the dosage information does not follow the format above.

## Check 2: Order Entry

After checking the prescription for accuracy, the pharmacy technician will perform the second check, the task of order entry. During order entry, the information found on the prescription is entered into a computer system to begin the process of dispensing. Pharmacy technicians must be vigilant when entering the information to ensure that high-alert medications and LASA medications are not mistakenly selected. For example, a patient may have dropped off a prescription for duloxetine, an antidepressant. A medication that is commonly selected in place of duloxetine is fluoxetine. Although fluoxetine is also an antidepressant, the medication has additional indications and drug interactions. Tall man lettering is extremely useful in avoiding confusion between LASA medications, but the pharmacy technician should still double check that they have entered the correct medication.

Computerized alerts also ensure that each prescription is double-checked when the information is entered for various issues such as medication duplications, allergies, interactions that can potentially harm the patient, and LASA medications. Creating patient profiles in the system that include their medical history and current prescriptions is particularly important because it ensures the detection of drug interactions and medical alerts during order entry. For example, if a patient with a prescription for duloxetine is also taking linezolid, the computer system would trigger a drug interaction alert during order entry because linezolid is a monoamine oxidase inhibitor and concurrent use with a medication such as duloxetine can cause potentially fatal reactions. Computerized warnings should be acknowledged and reported to the pharmacist promptly. The image below is an example of a computerized warning during order entry:

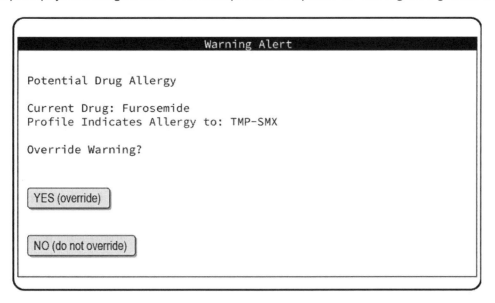

## Check 3: Dispensing Process

The dispensing process is the third check for pharmacy technicians and yet another area where errors can occur. Dispensing medications involves gathering the correct medication, strength, and formulation. During this step, pharmacy technicians should verify the prescription label against the prescription hard copy. Medications are often arranged alphabetically or by drug class. However, some medications are available in multiple forms such as tablets, capsules, oral liquids, parenteral fluids, and suppositories. Selecting the correct form of medication will ensure the patient safely administers the medication via the correct route. For example, acetaminophen is a common anti-pyretic/analgesic medication that is supplied in various forms. Although the dosage strength may be the same, dispensing the incorrect formulation can lead to adverse effects. For example, if a patient's profile indicates that they have history of dysphagia, or trouble swallowing, a large capsule or tablet may lead to aspiration, so the prescription should indicate that the medication must be dispensed in liquid form. The pharmacy technician must be sure to check for this type of information when dispensing medications.

## Check 4: Pharmacist Verification

The fourth check is the pharmacist verification process. With this process, the pharmacist (rather than the pharmacy technician) uses the National Drug Code (NDC), a unique, three-segment number assigned to each medication by the FDA, to identify the correct medication to be dispensed. All medications that are manufactured are required to be reported to the FDA. The FDA then identifies and assigns an NDC to each medication. The number is published in a directory that is updated daily. The directory is sorted using information such as the proprietary name, dosage form, route, labeler, and substance name. The unique NDC will identify all properties of the medication that is being dispensed. The pharmacist must check the NDC number against the stock bottle, ensure the drug being dispensed matches the illustration image, and check the prescription label against the hard copy of the prescription for accuracy. Any discrepancy must be promptly addressed and corrected. Additionally, at this point the pharmacist ensures that all other checks have been accurately completed.

## Check 5: Point-of-Sale

The fifth and final check component is conducted at the check-out counter, known as the point-of-sale check. During this stage, the pharmacy technician must once again verify that the correct medication is being handed to the correct patient. Requesting an additional identifier such as an address, telephone number, or date of birth ensures that the right patient receives the right medication.

## Bar Codes

In addition to the multiple checks outlined above, one of the most common error prevention strategies is the use of a bar code system that stores, identifies, and tracks prescription and medication activity. Bar codes may include information such as expiration dates, NDC numbers, and current storage information. The visual appearance of a barcode is important to note. One-dimensional linear barcodes contain the NDC number in order to reduce medication errors. Two-dimensional data matrix barcodes identify and trace prescription drugs during distribution throughout the country. This type of barcode includes serial numbers, lot numbers, expiration dates, and NDC identification.

Two-dimensional quick response barcodes, also known as QR codes, are informational labels. These QR codes are not required by the FDA but may be beneficial for patients, who thereby receive additional information about the medication. Universal Product Codes (UPCs) are used to keep track of sales and inventory within a facility. In acute care facilities, bar codes are also matched to patient wristbands to ensure the correct medication is administered to the correct patient. Pharmacy technicians should ensure they receive proper training on the use of a bar code system and report any discrepancies identified during scanning. The image below displays the different types of barcodes used on medications:

| Criteria | 1D Linear | 2D Data Matrix | 2D Quick Response (QR) | UPC Code |
|---|---|---|---|---|
| **Visual Appearance** | | | | 3 00450 12230 8 |

## FMEA

All error prevention strategies should include education and training of pharmaceutical staff. Many healthcare organizations implement a Failure Mode and Effects Analysis (FMEA) improvement process to identify the possibility of error and the effects errors can have on patients. FMEA is a five-step process that attempts to avoid errors before the medication is dispensed to the patient. Step one includes the determination of how a medication is prepared and stored in the pharmacy. High-alert medications and LASA medications should ideally be stored in separate areas to decrease the risk of accidental selection. Step two discusses how the medication is to be used and determines the probability of the packaging or label being confused with another active medication. The main focus of step two is process failures. Step three analyzes the magnitude of a possible error. For example, if an anticoagulant medication is accidentally dispensed at a higher dose, what adverse effects will the patient experience? Anticoagulant medications can lead to excessive blood thinning, internal bleeding, and death.

Medications identified as high alert may require numerous safeguards to ensure that multiple checks are performed during the prescription filling process. Step four identifies any pre-existing processes that would minimize the severity of an error. Each medication should be evaluated for the need to implement additional safeguards such as computer alerts, warning labels, and storage accommodations. Step five is the actual development of the actions needed to detect and prevent errors before they occur.

## Issues that Require Pharmacist Intervention

Many of the tasks performed by the pharmacy technician will require pharmacist verification and intervention. The end goal is to ensure that all safeguards have been followed and that the patient receives the intended product and any necessary follow-up care.

## Drug Utilization Review (DUR)

Drug utilization review (DUR) is a quality assurance program that aims to improve the prescribing, dispensing, and use of medications. A DUR is classified as either a prospective, concurrent, or retrospective process. A prospective category evaluates the patient's drug therapy before the medication is dispensed. During this process, the pharmacist must identify problems such as therapeutic duplications, interactions, incorrect dosages, duration of treatment, allergies, or drug misuse. These discrepancies must be addressed before dispensing the medication to the patient. For example, a patient drops off a prescription for morphine. Upon order entry, the pharmacy technician notes that the patient's profile indicates a recent prescription for oxycodone and another for Tylenol with codeine. All these medications are controlled substances with a high risk of misuse. The pharmacy technician would have to promptly report this information to the pharmacist. The pharmacist would then verify the therapeutic use of the medications and clarify the prescription with the healthcare provider.

Another DUR classification is the concurrent category. This process focuses on the ongoing monitoring of drug therapy by a pharmacist during the patient's treatment. Concurrent DUR is common in inpatient facilities where patients are constantly being evaluated for their treatment. Laboratory values and clinical manifestations alert the healthcare team of any issues with drug therapy. For example, a patient is prescribed 10 units of a short-acting insulin before meals and 30 units of a long-acting insulin before bedtime. Upon review of the patient's laboratory results, it is noted that the patient's serum glucose levels have consistently been below 70 mg/dL. This would indicate that the dosages need to be adjusted to prevent hypoglycemic episodes.

The last DUR classification is the retrospective category. During this process, drug therapy is reviewed by a pharmacist after the patient has received the medication. The goal of a retrospective DUR is to detect patterns of medication prescription, dispensing, and administration. Evaluating the goals of therapy helps identify whether a medication had the intended effect or not. For example, a patient is prescribed a beta-blocker as a first-line therapy for high blood pressure. After initiation of treatment, the patient's hypertension does not improve. The pharmacist may collaborate with the healthcare provider to select an alternate medication, such as a diuretic, to control the patient's blood pressure.

## Adverse Drug Event (ADE)

An adverse drug event (ADE) is any type of injury that is caused after administration of a medication. ADEs can be in the form of allergic reactions, overdoses, or significant side effects of a drug. Medication errors can also lead to an ADE. ADEs can occur in a variety of healthcare settings; fortunately, the majority of ADEs are preventable. The most common drugs associated with ADEs are anticoagulants, opioids, and insulin. Pharmacy technicians must recognize high-alert medications and refer the patient to the pharmacist for consultation on a new prescription. Pharmacists will counsel and educate patients on drug interactions, side effects, special precautions, and recognition of adverse effects.

## OTC Recommendation

Pharmacists may also intervene when a medication can be purchased over the counter (OTC) rather than as a higher-cost prescription. Many patients are unaware that some OTC medications contain the same active ingredient as medications that are prescribed by a healthcare provider. The pharmacist may counsel the patient on alternative options to address financial concerns. For example, Pepcid is a medication sold both as a prescription and OTC that is used in the treatment of gastric ulcers, gastro-esophageal reflux disease (GERD), and heartburn, among other things. On average, as of 2022, 30 tablets of 20mg Pepcid cost more than $300 without insurance. The OTC version of Pepcid, Pepcid AC, has an average price less than $25 for the same dosage and quantity as the prescription drug. A generic OTC version of famotidine may be even cheaper than the brand name Pepcid. The images below display the prescription-only version of Pepcid and an OTC medication label for famotidine. Both medications contain the same active ingredient.

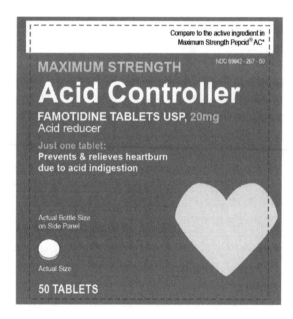

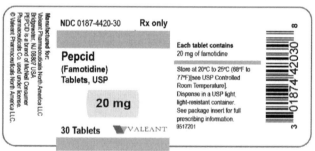

## Therapeutic Substitution

A therapeutic substitution occurs when a pharmacist changes a patient's medication to one with a different active pharmaceutical ingredient. In general, substitutions provide the same desired outcome for the patient. Although outcomes are equivalent, a substitution may be needed due to reasons such as patient allergy, poor tolerance of side effects, poor medication adherence, or because of some other adverse outcome from the originally prescribed medication. Therapeutic substitution can also occur if the substitute provides cost-savings for the patient, provider, health plan, or pharmacy network. Occasionally, a medication may be substituted with a more expensive medication for patient-specific reasons (e.g., the patient prefers a monthly injectable versus a daily oral dose). Best practices recommend that pharmacists collaborate with the patient, the prescribing physician, and any other health care providers involved in the patient's care before ordering a substitution. This reduces the risk of an unintended outcome from the substitution.

## Misuse

Pharmacist intervention can help mitigate the risk of medication misuse. Misuse can occur innocuously if a patient does not understand the correct dosing schedule of their prescription, or it can be more serious, such as if a patient develops an addiction to a prescribed medication. Patient education and counseling is an important part of supporting patients in taking their medications correctly. During this time, pharmacists work privately with the patients to ensure, firstly, that the correct medication is being dispensed to the intended patient. Then, the pharmacist and patient should come to an understanding about why the medication was prescribed, what outcomes and side effects are expected, and what the correct dosing schedule is.

The pharmacist should use active listening skills to facilitate responses from the patient that confirm understanding and collaboration in each of these areas, and they should also provide the patient with an opportunity to share personal concerns about the prescription. For example, if a patient shares that they have a recovering addict in their household, the pharmacist may work with the patient to provide a unique medication storage and administration plan. Having pharmacy staff check in with patients, especially those with chronic conditions, about their medication adherence can also help ensure that medications are being used properly. Finally, pharmacy staff should continuously monitor patients' refill history for medications and the healthcare facility's auto-renewal processes for medications. These can help flag if medications are being dispensed at a rate that seems inappropriate for the desired outcomes.

## Adherence and Medication Therapy Management (MTM)

Pharmacists are also tasked with reviewing a patient's adherence to their medication regimen. This service is known as medication therapy management (MTM). Adherence to a prescribed drug regimen improves health outcomes and lowers healthcare costs. Noncompliance can be due to obstacles such as the inability to pay for treatment or the inaccessibility of medical care. It is important for pharmacy technicians to recognize these obstacles and promptly refer the patient to a pharmacist for counseling. For example, a patient is prescribed Lopressor 50mg for hypertension. The average cost for 100 tablets of Lopressor 50mg is $270.

The patient may not have the financial means to purchase the medication and therefore stops taking the medication or splits the tablets in half to extend the doses. Abrupt discontinuation of the medication or taking an incorrect dosage may lead to adverse events. Referral of this issue to a pharmacist can improve compliance. The pharmacist may recommend a generic form of the medication (metoprolol), which is less expensive. The average cost for 100 tablets of metoprolol 50mg is $25. The difference in cost is significant and may improve patient compliance. Other strategies to improve compliance include requesting 90-day supplies for maintenance medications from providers, enrolling the patients in mail-order and delivery options, and sending refill alerts when applicable. There are also mobile device applications available to remind patients when their refills are due. Encouraging patients to download these applications prevents delays in drug therapy and improves compliance. Below are images of mobile device applications that help manage a patient's medication regimen:

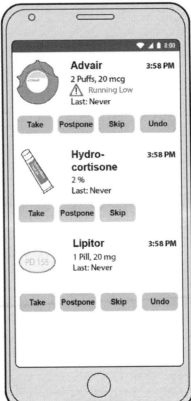

## Immunizations and Post-Immunization Follow-Up

Immunizations are commonly administered in pharmacies. In many states, however, pharmacy technicians are not allowed to administer vaccinations. Pharmacy technicians must make sure they are aware of the vaccination policies in their state. To start the vaccination process, patients are informed of their eligibility for a vaccine based on their medical history, age, or infection risk. Once identified as eligible, patients should be screened, counseled, and educated on immunizations and vaccine-preventable diseases. For example, patients with newly diagnosed chronic illnesses such as diabetes or heart disease will benefit from a yearly influenza vaccine or a pneumococcal vaccine due to their increased risk of illness. After the patient consents to being immunized and the vaccine is administered, documentation is crucial to avoid revaccinations. The pharmacist must record data such as the name of the vaccine, manufacturer, lot number, and the vaccinator's identifying information. Promotion of vaccinations helps to decrease the incidence of respiratory infections and disease-causing illnesses.

Pharmacists and pharmacy staff play an important role in providing follow-up care after administering immunizations. These providers are well-versed in routine vaccine requirements, recommended dosing schedules, possible side effects, and managing patient care for those who have adverse reactions to an immunization. While vaccines undergo rigorous trials for safety before becoming available to the public, risk is never zero. Pharmacists should observe patients for a minimum of 15 minutes after administering an immunization to look for local or systemic reactions. These can vary from mild symptoms that are expected to self-resolve (e.g., redness or pain at the vaccination site) to more serious reactions that may require emergency intervention (e.g., anaphylaxis).

During the immediate follow-up period, pharmacists should ensure they have access to emergency supplies (such as a blood pressure cuff and an epinephrine pen) to help stabilize a patient if needed. Each facility should also have clear, documented emergency plans and roles in place for these situations. In the longer follow-up period, lasting several days after a vaccine is administered, pharmacists should be available for patients to contact if adverse events suddenly occur or if mild effects linger. Finally, having systems in place for initiating follow-up with the patient is also helpful for quality and public health outcomes. Following up with patients is recommended for patients who decline a routine vaccination, patients who delay a routine vaccination due to a personal or medical issue, or patients who have had a history of significant side effects with other types of immunizations.

## Patient Profiles – Allergies, Drug Interactions, Drug Duplications, Special Considerations

Creating a patient profile in pharmacy computer systems assists with the recognition of allergies, drug interactions, drug duplications, and special considerations. Pharmacy technicians can complete a patient profile when the patient drops off a prescription for the first time. Subsequent visits to the pharmacy require the technician to verify or update the profile with any changes. Pharmacists should be informed when a medication interacts with other drugs currently on the patient's profile or when a medication is flagged as an allergy. Unintended drug interactions and allergic reactions can cause significant patient harm if not addressed promptly.

Record all medications a patient is taking and, when recording allergies, make sure to include medications, food, or environmental substances. As the pharmacy technician performs an order entry for a prescription, computerized warning systems should be referred to the pharmacist for further review. For example, if a patient's profile indicates a severe allergy to codeine and the patient drops off a prescription for Tylenol #3, the patient may be unaware that one of the main active ingredients in Tylenol #3 is codeine. The patient's healthcare provider must be contacted for an alternate prescription. Computerized allergy warnings require an override and should be carefully evaluated by the pharmacist. The images below are examples of allergy warnings requiring attention when a medication is entered into the computer system:

```
┌──────────────────────────────────────────────────────────────┐
│                    Drug-Allergy Alerts                         │
│ YOU ARE WRITING FOR:                                           │
│ ATORVASTATIN PO                                                │
│                                                                │
│                   Cancel Current Order                         │
│ To keep current order, you must respond to the interaction     │
│ alerts below.                                                  │
│                                                                │
│ Drug-Allergy Interaction Alerts      Reasons for override:     │
│ ┌──────────────────────────────┐   ┌─────────────────────┐    │
│ │ Pt. has a PROBABLE allergy to │   │                     │    │
│ │ Statins-Hmg-Coa Reductase     │   │                     │    │
│ │ Inhibitors;                   │   │                     │    │
│ │ reaction is GI Upset.         │   │                     │    │
│ │                               │   └─────────────────────┘    │
│ │                               │    Previous override:        │
│ │                               │   ┌─────────────────────┐    │
│ │      Keep Current Order       │   │                     │    │
│ │                               │   │                     │    │
│ └──────────────────────────────┘   └─────────────────────┘    │
│ Select Alt R to enter reason for override and then Alt K to    │
│ keep current order                                             │
└──────────────────────────────────────────────────────────────┘
```

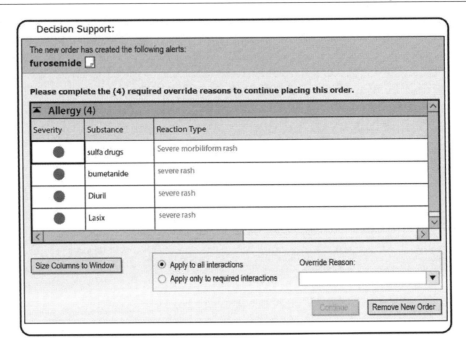

## Event Reporting Procedures

Pharmacy technicians sometimes come across situations that are not ideal and may potentially cause an adverse event. Adverse events may be preventable, such as medication errors and visible lack of product integrity; ameliorable, such as dispensing the correct medication but not ensuring proper follow-up care; or nonpreventable, such as patient-reported adverse effects despite the correct use of the medication and appropriate follow-up care. It is important for the pharmacy technician to be aware of the event reporting procedures of the facility to ensure these occurrences are properly reported, documented, and investigated if needed. Reporting can help address systemic flaws and improve work processes that may have led to the event. A culture of safety is essential in a facility to encourage staff to report adverse events; many actual or near-miss adverse events are not reported for fear of punitive action against the person reporting them.

### Medication Errors and Near-Miss Events

Some of the most commonly reported adverse events are medication errors. Medication errors may occur at any stage of the multiple check system and can be due to environmental or personal factors. Some errors will be caught before they can cause the patients any adverse effects, while others may cause chronic disability, impairment, or death. Regardless of the extent of the error, occurrences must be reported. Medication errors may still occur despite training, education, policies, and procedures, but reporting errors helps to improve processes and correct any factors that led to the error and is a personal responsibility for every pharmacy professional. As an example of how a medication error might occur, a pharmacy technician arrives to work to find that the pharmacy is short staffed and he will have to perform multiple work duties.

Additionally, the area where order entry is usually performed has been relocated to a busy area of the pharmacy due to construction within the facility. The pharmacy technician is tasked with doing order entry, taking incoming calls to the pharmacy, and dispensing medications to patients. The pharmacy technician begins an order entry for a sulfasalazine prescription. During the order entry, the phone rings and the technician answers the call while still performing the order entry. In the background, the pharmacy technician can hear a patient arguing with a pharmacist about a missing refill. During these events, the pharmacy technician bypasses the LASA alert on the computer, selects sulfadiazine, and confirms the prescription order. During the pharmacist verification check, the pharmacist sees that the original prescription was for sulfasalazine, not sulfadiazine, a LASA medication commonly confused with the ordered drug. The error was committed by the pharmacy technician during the order entry. This near-miss event would have to be reported according to facility policy, despite no harm coming to the patient.

There are several methods for reporting and investigating a near-miss event. As a supervisor, the pharmacist would have to report the error. As the one who committed the error, the pharmacy technician would have to openly discuss the factors that contributed to the event. There are various forms used to report near-miss events. Facilities create documents as part of their policies and procedures to ensure such events are documented in detail.

The majority of incident reports require a description of the incident, personnel involved, and suggestions on how these types of events can be prevented. It is important to be as detailed as possible and include all factors that may have contributed to the event. In the example given, many factors contributed to the error. The pharmacy technician was tasked with performing several duties due to short staffing, a situation that should have been addressed with management prior to assuming responsibility for multiple duties. Additionally, the work environment was not conducive to safety. Interruptions and excessive noise levels were distractors. Furthermore, the pharmacy technician bypassed a safeguard for LASA medications. All these factors are taken into consideration when a near-miss event is reviewed.

Below is an example of a near-miss reporting form:

**Safety Meetings for Health Care Workers**

Appendix
9025

# Near Miss Reporting Form

Date: ......................................................................................................

Department: ..............................................................................................

Supervisor: ...............................................................................................

Physical Location: .....................................................................................

Personnel Involved: ..................................................................................

Witnesses: ................................................................................................

Description of incident (what happened, how it happened, any objects or substances involved, results of incident) .......................................................................................................

How future incidents can be prevented (changes or improvements in equipment, procedures, personal protective equipment, training, etc.) .......................................................................

Date and type of corrective action initiated: ..............................................

Date of planned completion for corrective action: ......................................

Comments ...............................................................................................

Supervisor's signature ..............................................................................

Route this form to  ☐  Safety Manager
                    ☐  Other (.........................)

9025-1

## Root Cause Analysis (RCA)

Once an event is reported, methodologies such as a root cause analysis (RCA) and a failure mode and effect analysis (FMEA) can be conducted. As stated above, FMEA is a five-step process that attempts to avoid errors before the medication is dispensed to the patient. An RCA focuses on systemic processes rather than individual performance. RCAs examine which safeguards are currently in place and which factors contributed to the near miss or actual event. Pharmacy technicians should be aware that an RCA is designed to examine the conditions of the pharmacy that led to the error as opposed to placing blame on the person who committed the error. While personal responsibility is still a major factor in error prevention, it is important to emphasize that investigations of adverse events are not meant to be punitive. An RCA of the example above would determine that factors such as short staffing, multiple duties, and an undesirable environment were all contributors to the error.

## Continuous Quality Improvement (CQI) and FOCUS-PDSA

In addition to the processes above, pharmacies should have a continuous quality improvement (CQI) process to help identify and alleviate areas where mistakes have occurred. CQIs are supportive of shared accountability, or ensuring that pharmacies are held accountable for the processes set in place and that the staff is held accountable for implementing such processes. The overall objective of CQI is for all team members to feel comfortable reporting adverse events with the goal of improving quality care and service. This ensures that each member of the work team has an opportunity to voice issues that need to be addressed.

One quality improvement approach is the use of a procedure called a FOCUS-PDSA. This change model focuses on understanding the problems that contribute to near misses or adverse events. Each letter of the acronym FOCUS-PDSA stands for the steps required to recognize, analyze, and address issues that contribute to errors. The actions for each step are as follows:

F – find a problem. In the case of the order entry error, the problem is the near-miss event related to incorrectly entering a medication in the system.

O – organize a team. For a near-miss event, the person who made the error, the supervisor, and the management team need to collaborate to solve the contributing factors.

C – clarify the problem. It is important to analyze all of the factors that led to a near-miss event. Initially, the pharmacy technician may have omitted some contributing factors.

U – understand the problem. Near miss events should be outliers. If they happen frequently, there is clearly an area for improvement in the current processes.

S – select an intervention. After collaborating, changes in the systemic process or addressing short-term contributing factors is key (short staffing, relocating the workstation).

The rest of the steps outline the implementation of an action plan: P stands for *plan*, D for *do*, S for *study*, and A for *act*. The action plan may be continuously revised to ensure adverse events are minimized. The image below demonstrates the pathway of a FOCUS-PDSA:

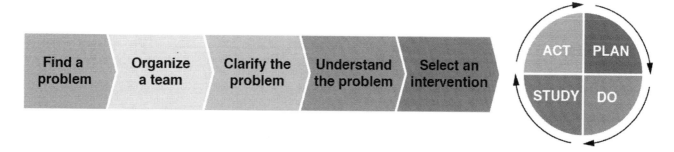

## Reporting Adverse Effects and MedWatch

Patients who experience adverse effects to medications will often report these events to the pharmacy staff. Adverse effects are any unwanted effects or dangerous reactions to a medication. It is important to properly refer any concerns from the patient to the pharmacist on duty. The same adverse effect may occur in several patients, or it can be due to a patient's individual outliers. For example, a patient who purchased an OTC bottle of aspirin develops a rash shortly after taking a pill. The patient reports the reaction to the pharmacy staff and the event is documented accordingly. Several days later, another

patient reports getting a rash after purchasing the same product within the same timeframe. These adverse reactions would require immediate reporting as they can necessitate a consumer safety alert.

The FDA has developed a medical product safety reporting program known as MedWatch. MedWatch compiles data from health care personnel and patients who report adverse reactions to medications or medical products. Each MedWatch report should include a description of the event, the problem it caused, and the product or medication that was used. Any other relevant data, such as date of the event, outcome, and relevant medical history should be included. Product information will also be entered to aid in data collection. Information received through MedWatch is monitored, analyzed, and published as safety alerts when appropriate.

MedWatch should also be used to report any problems with product quality. Pharmacy technicians are responsible for assessing the integrity of medications and performing the advanced task of compounding medications. During these processes, the pharmacy technician must carefully inspect each product for any defects. Discolored medications, cloudy solutions that should be clear, or additional components that should not be present require reporting. The image below shows the precipitate that can form when a medication solution is defective or incompatible:

Types of Prescription Errors

Medication errors can occur throughout the various systems in healthcare. However, almost half of all medication errors occur during the prescribing stage. Healthcare providers prescribe a large number of medications daily. There are thousands of medications available for prescription. Healthcare providers are responsible for prescribing a medication that is appropriate for the patient based on their medical history, allergies, and therapeutic goals. Pharmacists are responsible for verifying that the prescription information is safe and accurate based on the medication's intended use. Pharmacy technicians are responsible for checking a prescription to ensure that all necessary components are present including the patient's name, dosage of the medication, frequency, route, duration, refill count, and any special indications. With the volume of prescriptions filled on a daily basis, the responsibility of pharmacy staff to ensure prescription errors do not occur is substantial.

## Incorrect Patient

There are many components within a prescription where an error can occur. One of those errors is prescribing a medication to the incorrect patient. Healthcare providers write prescriptions in various healthcare settings. The patient may have a prescription that was ordered in an acute care facility, an urgent care center, or an outpatient clinic. Some facilities have similar patient populations with frequently seen diagnoses and commonly ordered medications. In an effort to decrease healthcare errors, the Joint Commission has developed national patient safety goals. One of those goals is improving the accuracy of patient identification by using at least two patient identifiers used prior to providing care. This goal is applied to patient care, treatment, and services, including dispensing medications in a pharmacy. During the prescription drop-off, the pharmacy technician must verify two patient identifiers to ensure the prescription is written for the correct patient.

## Incorrect Dose

One of the most significant medication errors is prescribing the incorrect dose. Incorrect doses can cause significant patient harm. A patient who takes a higher dose of a medication may experience adverse effects or develop toxicity from the medication. A dose that is lower than indicated may not adequately manage a medical condition and the patient may develop complications from their disease process. Although the healthcare provider is responsible for prescribing the medication dose, the pharmacist must verify that the dose is safe according to therapeutic recommendations. For example, pramipexole is an anti-Parkinson medication with a recommended starting dose of 0.125mg TID. A patient with newly diagnosed Parkinson has been prescribed 1.5mg TID. Although the safe upper dosing limit of the medication is 4.5mg daily, the medication should be gradually increased every 5 to 7 days. Large doses of the medication can cause sudden sleep attacks and sedation. Any abnormal doses should be clarified with the healthcare provider during the pharmacist verification process.

## Leading and Trailing Zeros

Another aspect of incorrect doses includes the use of trailing zeros or the omission of leading zeros. A fractional dosage may be incorrectly interpreted if a leading zero is omitted. Likewise, a whole number may be mistaken for a larger dose if a trailing zero is used. For example, digoxin is an antiarrhythmic medication used in the treatment of atrial fibrillation and heart failure. A common dose for this medication is 0.5 mg. A leading zero is crucial for this medication. Prescribing the dose as .5 mg can be confused with 5 mg. If the dose is incorrectly interpreted, the patient may receive a dose that is 10 times higher than recommended. Likewise, prescribing the dose as .50 mg can easily be mistaken for 50 mg. Any prescription with a decimal point that lacks a leading zero or has a trailing zero should be referred to the pharmacist for verification. Below is an example of a prescription with a leading zero in the dosage (correct) and a prescription missing the leading zero (incorrect):

Digoxin 0.125 mg
tablets do no.7
S 1 do 1 tablet          Digoxin 5 mg IV X now

## Incorrect Route of Administration

Another form of incorrect dosing is the route of administration. The route indicates how the medication should be taken. There are various routes of administration including oral, parenteral, and intravenous.

Prescribed routes are commonly seen in acute care facilities. Incorrect prescribing, dispensing, and administration of medications can have catastrophic effects. Pharmacy technicians must verify that each prescription contains a route of administration for the medication. Missing routes should be promptly reported to the pharmacist. As an example, magnesium hydroxide is an antiulcer medication that should only be administered orally. In addition to being available as a tablet and a chewable tablet, it is available as an oral suspension or a liquid.

In hospital settings, oral liquids and suspensions are often dispensed in a syringe. Because nurses frequently administer medications intravenously with a syringe, there is a significant chance of confusion between the two types of syringes, with potentially catastrophic effects. Administration of medications intravenously that are meant to be given orally may lead to blood incompatibility, organ failure, and death. Interventions used to decrease these errors include verification of the correct route on the prescription and distinctive syringe colors that are clearly labeled for oral/enteral use only. Below are images of syringes meant to administer medications orally (Oral/Enteral Only, often orange in color, no place for a needle) or intravenously (IV syringe, often clear in color, tip can accept a needle):

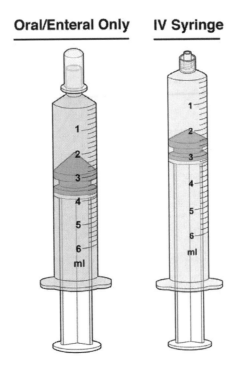

**Oral/Enteral Only**      **IV Syringe**

## Incorrect Quantity

Another common prescription error is the incorrect quantity of medication. A prescription should indicate how many tablets, capsules, or milliliters should be dispensed. Patients often take medication as maintenance therapy, requiring ongoing prescription refills. Large quantities will commonly be seen for maintenance medications. Other patients require prescription medications to treat an acute illness. Medications that are used for short-term medical conditions require a specific quantity to fulfill the length of treatment. For example, glipizide is an antidiabetic medication used in the long-term treatment of type 2 diabetes mellitus. A patient taking this medication is likely to be prescribed large quantities of the medication (for example, 90 tablets or #90) to fulfill daily doses. Another patient may have a prescription for ciprofloxacin to treat a urinary tract infection. The usual duration of treatment for ciprofloxacin is 7 to 14 days, taken twice daily. Therefore, the quantity on a ciprofloxacin prescription will be low (#14 or #28).

Knowledge of therapeutic indication is important during the process of filling a prescription. Missing quantities on a prescription should be promptly referred to the pharmacist and clarified with the healthcare provider.

## Number of Refills

In addition to quantity, a prescription should include the number of refills for the medication. One factor affecting quantity and refill amounts is insurance plan coverage. Some insurance plans will cover monthly refills only while others will authorize only a 90-day supply of medications. Quantities and refill limits are also set by the FDA in an attempt to prevent misuse and control healthcare costs. The refill limits set by the FDA are dependent on the medication classification. Medications that are used to treat a chronic condition may be authorized for a larger number of refills. Controlled substances are limited to a single prescription, a six-month wait time on refills, or a limit on how many times a medication can be refilled.

For example, a healthcare provider prescribes a patient 30 tablets of Tylenol with codeine, a Schedule III controlled substance. According to Title 21 of the FDA's code of federal regulations, the refill limit for this medication is five. Additionally, the refill quantity should be equal to or less than the originally prescribed amount (#30). The prescription should also be refilled within six months of the original prescription. A subsequent need for the medication would require a new prescription. Pharmacists have the responsibility to verify the frequency of prescribed controlled substances. A patient may drop off prescriptions for controlled substances from different providers. Due to the risk of misuse, it is not uncommon for controlled substances to have zero refills ordered.

## Early Refills

Patients will sometimes request an early refill for their medication. Limitations on early refills are set in place to prevent misuse. The refill timeframe is dependent on the frequency listed on the original prescription. There are often factors that can influence the need for an early refill such as lost medication, extended vacations, or weather emergencies. Each patient's circumstance should be carefully examined. After reviewing the patient's individual need for an early refill, a pharmacist can request an override from the patient's insurer. Insurance plans will review the patient's history, type of medication, and reason for the request. If approved, the pharmacist may refill the medication early. Early refill authorizations are carefully monitored and authorized in limited quantities.

## Hygiene and Cleaning Standards

Infection control is an essential component of maintaining safety in every medical workplace. Pharmacy technicians work directly with medications that are ingested by patients. Lack of infection control practices may lead to contaminated products. Safety and infection control regulations within the pharmacy are outlined by the Occupational Safety and Health Administration (OSHA). OSHA is part of the U.S. Department of Labor and is responsible for establishing mandatory guidelines and monitoring their implementation. Each pharmacy should also have policies and procedures in place to guide the staff on performing adequate hygiene, aseptic handling of products, and proper cleaning of pharmaceutical equipment.

## Hand Hygiene

Hands and fingertips are the main reservoir for infectious microorganisms. Pharmacy technicians prepare and often compound medications. Lack of hand hygiene leads to contamination and possible transfer of microorganisms to the patient. Handwashing is a universal precaution that should be followed consistently to decrease the risk of contamination. Handwashing should occur at various stages. Hands should be washed before and after coming into contact with a patient or their environment. Cross contamination can easily occur during prescription drop-off or pickup. If the hands are not visibly soiled, an alcohol-based formulation can be used to clean them. Soap and water should be used when the hands are visibly soiled and before and after handling medications. Proper handwashing includes several steps. The hands must be thoroughly wetted with water, and then enough soap is applied to cover all hand surfaces. The soap should be rubbed into the hands, ensuring the palms, fingertips, wrists, and spaces between the fingers are washed. This technique should be performed for at least 20 seconds to ensure all surfaces are cleaned. The entire handwashing procedure takes between 40 and 60 seconds. The image below outlines the steps of handwashing as recommended by the World Health Organization:

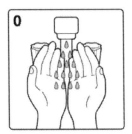

Wet hands with water

Apply enough soap to cover all hand surfaces

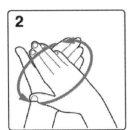

Rub hands palm to palm

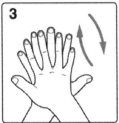

Right palm over left dorsum with interlaced fingers and vice versa

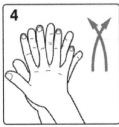

Palm to palm with fingers interlaced

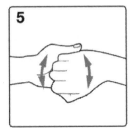

Back of fingers to opposing palm with fingers interlocked

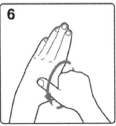

Rotational rubbing of left thumb clasped in right palm and vice versa

Rotational rubbing, backwards and forwards with clasped fingers of right hand in left palm and vice versa

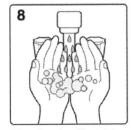

Rinse hands with water

Dry hands thoroughly with a single use towel

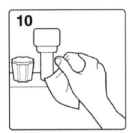

Use towel to turn off faucet

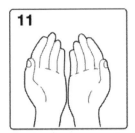

Your hands are now safe

## Personal Protective Equipment (PPE) and Clean Air Environments

Personal protective equipment (PPE) is used when handling medications and pharmaceutical equipment. PPE includes gloves; masks; goggles; lab suits and gowns; and hair, shoe, and beard covers. Gloves are the most commonly used PPE in pharmacies. Gloves protect the hands and prevent the transmission of microorganisms. Glove material should be made of vinyl, latex, or nitrile. Gloves should be used when touching medications or pharmaceutical equipment used to prepare medications. Gloves should be exchanged for a new pair between medications and when they are visibly torn or punctured. Sterile compounding will require application of sterile gloves, which should be handled carefully to avoid contaminating surfaces. Gloves should cover the wrist area and be tight enough to remain on the hands but loose enough to be able to perform hand movements. Below is an image of how gloves should fit on the hands:

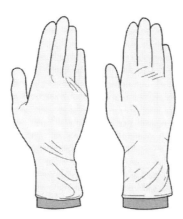

Lab suits or gowns are meant to protect the skin from exposure to toxic chemicals and solutions. Suits should have long sleeves with cuffs covering the wrists and be long enough to cover the lower extremities. Below are images of the various types of lab suits and gowns used as part of PPE:

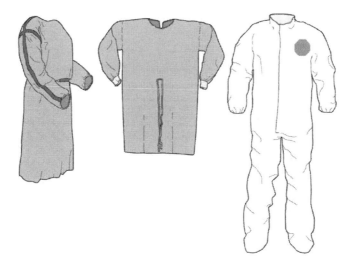

Masks should be worn when preparing or compounding sterile medications. Pharmacy technicians should also be self-aware of their health status. Coughing and sneezing can cause transmission of microorganisms through saliva particles. Masks should fit tightly on the face, ensuring that it fully covers the nose and mouth area. Below is an image of how a mask should fit on the face:

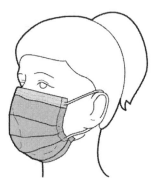

Bouffant caps, shoe, and beard covers should be applied prior to preparing sterile medications. Hair and beard covers specifically prevent contamination of the area by hair particles. The bouffant cap should fully cover the hair and the shoe covers should be placed prior to entering a clean or sterile room. Goggles protect the eyes from irritants found in solutions or suspensions. Below are images of shoe covers, hair covers, and goggles used in pharmaceutical settings:

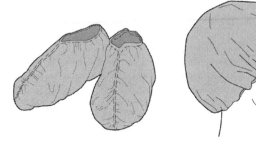

Donning, or garbing, PPE should follow a specific order. PPE should always be applied from the dirtiest to the cleanest areas. If all PPE is to be used, shoe covers and bouffant caps should be donned first. Hand hygiene should be performed next, followed by application of the gown and mask. All of these steps should be performed in the anteroom. In this context, an anteroom is a place to prepare for medication compounding. Handwashing, labeling, PPE storage, and order entry take place in the anteroom. A clean room is where medications are compounded. The clean room should be free from contaminants and dust. Once the clean room is entered, the hands should be cleansed with an alcohol-based solution and then allowed to dry, and then gloves are donned as the last step of donning PPE.

The use of PPE equipment is dependent on the preparation of medications. For example, counting tablets and placing them in a container should be performed using aseptic technique, or clean technique. The pharmacy technician would perform hand hygiene and wear gloves to perform this procedure. Medications that are formulated to enter the bloodstream, such as those given via injection, require sterile technique when handled. Some medications can be hazardous, such as chemotherapy or radioactive drugs. The environment in which these medications are prepared must be carefully controlled. Fumes and particulates produced by hazardous medications must be prepared in a clean air environment with a negative air flow and filtering system. A vertical laminar airflow hood is a piece of equipment used in environments where room air is filtered and pushed away from the person preparing the medications.

High efficiency particulate abstractor (HEPA) filters are also used to remove the majority of particulates from the air in the clean room. Below is an image of the functionality of a vertical laminar flow hood:

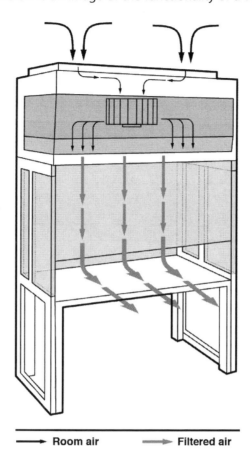

⟶ **Room air**　⟹ **Filtered air**

## United States Pharmacopeia and National Formulary (USP-NF) Standards

The United States Pharmacopeia (USP), along with the National Formulary (NF), is a compendium of established standards of practice for all pharmacy settings. Together they are referred to as USP-NF. The USP is published annually by the United States Pharmacopeial Convention, often simply referred to as USP as well. USP Chapter <797> lays out the requirements for sterile compounding and for the facilities that prepare, store, and dispense compound sterile preparations to ensure the protection and safety of both patients who are using sterile compounds and healthcare workers who are making sterile compounds. USP <797> discusses three main areas needed for compliance and safety: staff training and guidance, risk category determination, and implementation of policies and procedures. State pharmacy boards and the FDA are tasked with enforcing compliance with USP <797>; the Joint Commission may conduct surveys to verify compliance. Any pharmacy staff members, such as pharmacy technicians, who are involved in compounding sterile medications require regular training on sterile procedures. Pharmacy staff responsible for supervising the sterile technique of pharmacy technicians should review competencies every six to twelve months. Annual review is required for low and medium-risk preparations and semi-annual reviews should be performed for high-risk compounding.

Risk levels are determined by the possibility of contaminating a compounded sterile preparation (CSP) with endotoxins, spores, microorganisms, or any other foreign material. The risk levels are categorized as either low-risk, medium-risk, or high-risk. Low-risk conditions are characterized by manual mixing of up to three manufactured products to create a CSP. The transfer of sterile liquids from sealed ampules or vials to other sterile devices with the use of needles and syringes is also classified as a low-risk condition. Medium-risk conditions entail compounding multiple doses of sterile products that will be administered to multiple patients or to one patient several times. Compounding processes that take a long time or involve more than a single volume transfer are classified as medium risk. High-risk conditions include making a sterile solution from non-sterile bulk powders or mixing sterile ingredients in a device that is non-sterile prior to developing a sterile product. Pharmacy technicians should be aware of risk level conditions and follow proper protocol when compounding medications in a clean room. Regardless of risk level, appropriate PPE gear should be used.

Areas that are used for compounding medications should be cleaned and disinfected according to policy in line with USP <797> standards. Sink and work surfaces, pass-throughs, and floors should be cleaned on a daily basis. Primary engineering controls (PECs) and the equipment used inside the PECs should be cleaned at the beginning and end of the shift, when spills occur, and if surface contamination is suspected. Surfaces should be cleaned prior to being disinfected. A cleaning agent should be able to remove residue such as dirt, debris, residual drugs, chemicals, and microbes. Disinfecting agents, such as 70% isopropyl alcohol, should be able to destroy viruses, bacteria, and fungi. Bacterial endospores require sporicidal disinfectants such as peracetic acid. The type of solutions used to clean and disinfect should follow Environmental Protection Agency (EPA) standards.

## Spill Kits

Spill kits should be available in every pharmacy setting. Spill kits are used when hazardous agents are accidentally spilled on surfaces. The spill should be safely contained to avoid causing health hazards. Spill kits include several items such as gloves, warning signs indicating a hazard in the immediate area, alkali detergent solution, a mat to absorb liquids, and a plastic broom and dustpan. Pharmacy technicians should be aware of the type of spill and don additional PPE as needed. Cleaning should occur gradually from the edge of the spill towards the center. Below is an example of the items included in a drug spill kit:

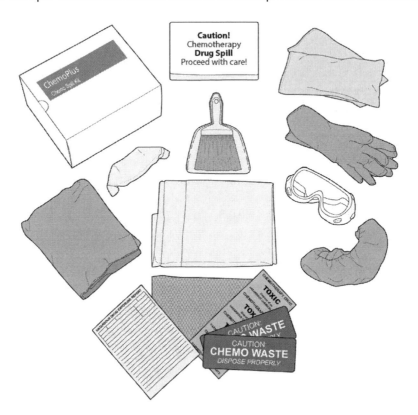

# *Practice Quiz*

1. A pharmacist is reviewing an electronic order that reads: MSO₄ 1g q6hr IV. What action does the pharmacist perform next?
    a. Clarifies the drug name
    b. Approves the electronic order
    c. Requests a change in frequency
    d. Rejects the route of administration

2. A pharmacy technician is updating a patient's medical record. The patient confirms history of liver disease and hypertension. Which prescription should be clarified if noted on the patient's medication list?
    a. Ibuprofen
    b. Furosemide
    c. Acetaminophen
    d. Atenolol

3. A pharmacist is developing interventions to decrease the number of near miss events in the pharmacy. The pharmacist wants to use a change model to help implement the action plan. What tool will the pharmacist use to accomplish this goal?
    a. RCA
    b. DUR
    c. FMEA
    d. PDSA

4. A system warning is triggered when the pharmacy technician enters a patient prescription for sulfasalazine. The warning is most likely due to which of the following?
    a. The medication can cause respiratory depression
    b. It is a look-alike/sound-alike medication
    c. The dose is usually overprescribed
    d. It was ordered for the incorrect patient

5. A pharmacy technician will be compounding medications. Donning of personal protective equipment will occur in which location?
    a. The anteroom
    b. The isolation room
    c. The clean room
    d. The biohazard room

# Answer Explanations

**1. A**: Choice *A* is correct because MSO4 is a "Do Not Use" abbreviation as determined by The Joint Commission. MSO4, or magnesium sulfate, is commonly confused with morphine sulfate. The pharmacist should clarify the drug name. Choice *B* is incorrect because the drug name is an unapproved abbreviation and must be clarified. Choice *C* is incorrect because the frequency is written appropriately. Choice *D* is incorrect because intravenous is an approved route of administration for magnesium sulfate.

**2. C**: Choice *C* is correct because acetaminophen (Tylenol) is highly metabolized by the liver. Acetaminophen is contraindicated in patients with active liver disease. Choice *A* is incorrect because ibuprofen is a nonsteroidal anti-inflammatory drug used in the treatment of mild to moderate pain. Liver disease is not contraindicated with this medication. Choice *B* is incorrect because furosemide is a diuretic used in the treatment of fluid overload and hypertension. Liver disease is not a contraindication for furosemide. Choice *D* is incorrect because atenolol is a beta blocker used in the treatment of hypertension. Liver disease is not a contraindication for atenolol.

**3. D**: Choice *D* is correct because a PDSA (plan, do, study, act) is a quality improvement tool that helps to implement an action plan after a problem is identified and analyzed. Choice *A* is incorrect because an RCA (root cause analysis) is an investigative tool used to identify systemic problems that lead to adverse events. Choice *B* is incorrect because a DUR (drug utilization review) is patient-specific and focuses on the effectiveness of medication therapy. Choice *C* is incorrect because an FMEA (failure mode and effect analysis) is a tool that helps to identify possible errors and their effects on patients' health.

**4. B**: Choice *B* is correct because sulfasalazine is a look-alike/sound-alike medication. Sulfasalazine, an anti-rheumatic/anti-inflammatory, is commonly confused with sulfadiazine, an antibiotic. Choice *A* is incorrect because sulfasalazine does not cause significant respiratory side effects. Choice *C* is incorrect because the dose for sulfasalazine is not known to be incorrectly prescribed. Choice *D* is incorrect because there is no indication that the prescription was entered incorrectly.

**5. A**: Choice *A* is correct because the anteroom is separated from the clean room but is the closest location to the compounding stations. The anteroom is used to don personal protective equipment (PPE) and perform other tasks such as handwashing and medication labeling. Choice *B* is incorrect because PPE should already be donned prior to entering an isolation room. Choice *C* is incorrect because the clean room requires PPE to already be donned. The clean room is where medication compounding occurs. Choice *D* is incorrect because the biohazard room is contaminated. PPE that contains bodily fluids or waste products that may cause health problems are discarded in the biohazard room.

# Order Entry and Processing

## Procedures to Compound Non-Sterile Products

Extemporaneous compounding is the preparation of a medication to meet a patient's specific needs when a commercial product does not. Infusions, medications that will be injected, and medications that will be applied to the eye require sterile compounding. Non-sterile compounding involves the non-sterile preparation of various dosage formulations including ointments, creams, emulsions, suspensions, capsules, enemas, and suppositories. Compounded preparations are regulated by state boards of pharmacy and the FDA. USP-NF, a combination of the United States Pharmacopeia (USP) and the National Formulary (NF), contains the published standards for over 5,000 medications, compounds, and other pharmaceutical preparations. Non-sterile compounding regulations are detailed in USP Chapter <795> while USP Chapters <797> and <800> cover sterile formulations and handling hazardous drugs, respectively. Extemporaneous compounding requires a knowledge of compounding equipment, compounding procedures, good math skills, and a basic understanding of the physical and chemical properties of the raw materials. In addition, technicians must also possess excellent record-keeping skills and demonstrate great attention to detail.

Things to consider before compounding:

- Evaluate and interpret the prescription to ensure the medication must be compounded.

- Determine whether the appropriate drugs, materials, and equipment are available.

- Determine whether there is a formula available with study literature to support it.

- Determine the compounding steps, procedures, and quality control information.

## Procedures for Compounding Non-Sterile Mixtures

Non-sterile compounded mixtures include topicals such as ointments, powder mixtures for filling capsules, and oral liquids such as suspensions. Procedures for compounding non-sterile preparations may vary depending on the type of mixture being made. Topical ointments and creams in which two or more topicals are combined to form one are the simplest non-sterile preparations that may be compounded. An example of a simple non-sterile topical compound would be adding the OTC steroid hydrocortisone 1% ointment to Aquaphor, a base that facilitates absorption.

The first step in preparing such a compound would be to weigh the required amount of each ingredient using an appropriate calibrated scale and weigh paper.

The second step would be to mix the ingredients together using either an ointment slab or an electronic mortar and pestle (EMP). An ointment slab is a thick, non-absorbent piece of glass or porcelain with a smooth surface that allows incorporating, which is the mixing of one ingredient into another to form one homogenous preparation. A simple preparation such as this can be mixed on an ointment slab using a spatula. An EMP is a vertical mixing machine with a rotating blade that can thoroughly combine topicals in minutes. With the EMP, the ingredients are weighed on a scale in the actual mixing jar prior to mixing.

To incorporate an active pharmaceutical ingredient (API) that is in a solid form, such as a powder, a technique called levigation may be used to ensure the powder is sufficiently combined with the base vehicle to produce a smooth, grit-free product. Levigation is the addition of an appropriate levigating agent, often referred to as a wetting agent, to the solid or semi-solid API to reduce particle size. When using an ointment slab, the solid should be weighed and placed in the center of the ointment slab; the levigating agent is then slowly worked into the solid using two spatulas. Once levigated, the ointment base can be incorporated using geometric dilution principles. Geometric dilution is a mixing technique in which two or more ingredients of unequal quantities are blended, starting with the ingredient that has the smallest volume (S) and combining it with an equal amount of the ingredient with the larger volume (L).

This process continues until the ingredient with the larger volume has been completely combined and a uniform mixture is achieved. For instance, 240 grams of a topical diaper rash ointment consists of 30 grams of nystatin ointment and 210 grams of zinc oxide ointment. For this preparation, the nystatin is the ingredient with the smaller volume and the zinc oxide the larger; therefore, 30 grams of the nystatin ointment should be combined with the 30 grams of the zinc oxide ointment first for a combined total of 60 grams. Another 60 grams of zinc oxide is then added to the 60 grams of the already combined nystatin and zinc oxide for a total of 120 grams. This process of adding the remaining zinc oxide continues until the final volume is reached.

The third step to preparing a topical is to place the preparation in an appropriate airtight dispensing container such as an ointment jar or, for medications requiring specific doses, a metered-dose pump dispenser. Any air pockets within the preparation must be removed by tamping the ointment jar on a countertop until they come to the surface or by pushing them out with a spatula. There are mixers on the market today with deaeration features that can be used to degas or remove air from topicals. This is especially useful for metered-dose pump dispensers. If necessary, ointments and creams can be run through a device called an ointment mill to remove any grittiness and create a smoother preparation. For topical bioidentical hormone replacement therapy (BHRT) and arthritic pain medications that require a patient to use a specific dose, it is important to ensure accurate dosing. Preparations of this type are therefore best dispensed in metered-dose pump bottles, pens, and applicators to ensure precise doses are administered.

The last steps include performing and documenting quality assurance checks and affixing the patient label as well as any auxiliary labels to the dispensing container.

## Procedures for Compounding Non-Sterile Liquids

Non-sterile compounded liquid preparations include syrups, emulsions, suspensions, elixirs, and tinctures. Each one of these formulations is unique in its preparation and requires specific compounding procedures. Compounded non-sterile solutions can be either aqueous or non-aqueous solutions. Aqueous solutions are preparations in which a solute is dissolved into purified water or another water-based delivery vehicle, while non-aqueous solutions require the dissolution of the active pharmaceutical ingredient into a variety of non-water-based solvents.

A cleansing enema is an example of a non-sterile aqueous solution in which the active ingredient is dissolved completely into purified water. Procedures to compound non-sterile enema preparations require the use of a scale to weigh out the active pharmaceutical ingredient or ingredients (API) and a graduated cylinder to accurately measure the aqueous base. A large beaker, magnetic stir plate, and magnetic stir bar will be needed to ensure the API is completely dissolved. Smaller particles will dissolve more easily; therefore, a mortar and pestle can be used to triturate the solute or API into smaller particles if necessary. Trituration is the process of blending and grinding the dry ingredients into a fine powder. It can also be used to indicate the thorough mixing of two or more components.

In general, the API is added to a percentage of the preparation's final volume to allow necessary pH adjustments to be made. For example, the entire quantity of the API would be slowly added to approximately 70% of the solution's final volume. The preparation's pH is then checked to be sure it is in range with the formula's specific recommendations before bringing it to the final volume. The pH of the final product is then checked at final volume to ensure it meets specifications.

Suspensions are unstable non-sterile liquid preparations in which the active ingredient is suspended (not dissolved) in a liquid delivery vehicle. When compounding a suspension, all powders, including the API and any sweeteners, are weighed using a calibrated scale. The powders are then triturated with a mortar and pestle to reduce the size of the particles. After the powders have been triturated, a levigation agent or a small amount of the suspension vehicle is added to create a paste. At this point, flavoring and flocculating or thickening agents may be added. The flocculating agent should help to loosen the paste slightly and aid in the overall dispersion of the particles in the suspension vehicle when brought to full volume. The ingredients are then transferred to an appropriate dispensing container, generally an amber bottle. The mortar and pestle should then be rinsed with the suspension vehicle a few times, and the mortar scraped with a rubber spatula until all the material has been transferred to the bottle. Then the preparation is brought to its final volume with the remaining suspension vehicle and shaken until the suspension is adequately distributed.

Emulsions are a type of non-sterile liquid preparation referred to as a two-phase system, internal and external, which is thermodynamically unstable. This instability is the effect of combining two liquids that are immiscible, or not easily mixed, such as oil and water. Procedures for compounding emulsions include the English or wet gum method, the continental or dry gum method, and the beaker method. The English/wet gum and continental/dry methods follow the 4:2:1 ratio of combining four parts oil, two parts water, and one part emulsifying agent or gum such as acacia, but the order in which they are combined is different for each method. The wet gum or English method requires the formation of a mucilage by triturating or mixing the two parts water with one part gum. Once the mucilage is formed, the four parts oil are added gradually while the mixture is triturated. This forms the primary emulsion. Any remaining ingredients should be added to the primary emulsion after the addition of the oil and thoroughly incorporated.

The dry gum or continental method requires triturating the four parts oil with the one part gum and then adding the two parts water and triturating to make the primary emulsion. Then the remaining ingredients can be added to the primary emulsion. The bottle method is a variation on the dry gum method in which the one part gum is placed in a bottle and the four parts oil are added. The bottle is capped and shaken until the ingredients are completely mixed, after which the two parts water are added and the bottle is shaken again to form the primary emulsion The beaker method is a little different in that it requires dissolving all oil soluble ingredients in the oil in one beaker and dissolving all water soluble ingredients in the water in a separate beaker. Both mixtures are then heated to approximately 70°C (158°F) and then the internal phase is added to the external phase and cooled to room temperature while being continuously stirred with a magnetic stir bar and stir plate.

## Procedures for Compounding Non-sterile Solid Dosage Forms

Non-sterile compounded solid dosage preparations include suppositories, troches, chewable treats, and capsules. Suppositories are solid dosage formulations that are typically composed of a fatty acid base, a suspension agent such as silica gel, and the active pharmaceutical ingredients. The basic process requires the active ingredient and suspending agent to be added to a melted base and then poured into a mold to solidify, a process referred to as fusion molding. Rectal and vaginal suppositories typically use a fatty acid base that is a solid at room temperature but dissolves at body temperature. When making suppository preparations, it is important to choose the correct mold and base. Molds can vary and must be calibrated to account for the amount of base that will be displaced by adding the API.

To calibrate a mold, a blank is made by melting the base, pouring the base into the mold, and allowing it to congeal. Once the blank has solidified, it should be weighed to determine how many grams of base the mold holds. From this information, the amount of base needed per suppository can be calculated. For example, a metal mold is determined to produce blanks that weigh 1.8 grams. The amount of base needed to prepare thirty-five suppositories containing a total of 50mg of a medication and 0.70 grams of the suspending agent silica gel, with a displacement value of 70%, in a mold that produces blanks of 1.8 grams, can be calculated as follows.

Begin by determining how much API and suspending agent is needed per suppository. First, convert the number of milligrams of API needed per suppository to grams. Therefore:

$$50 \text{ mg} \times \frac{1 \text{ g}}{1,000 \text{ mg}} = 0.05 \text{ g of API per suppository}$$

The amount of suspending agent per suppository can be calculated by dividing the total grams needed by the number of suppositories being made. Therefore:

$$\frac{\text{Total grams of suspending agent}}{\text{Number of suppositories}} = \frac{0.70 \text{ grams (silica gel)}}{35 \text{ suppositories}} = 0.02 \text{ g per suppository}$$

The next step in determining how much base is needed is to add the weight of the API needed per suppository (0.05 grams) and the weight of the suspending agent needed per suppository (0.02 grams), for a total of 0.07 grams, and then multiplying that total by the displacement value, which was noted above as 70%. Therefore,

$$\text{Total weight of powders} \times \text{Displacement value of base} = \text{Amount of displaced base}$$

$$0.07 \text{ grams} \times 70\% = 0.049 \text{ g}$$

The next step is to subtract the amount of displaced base calculated above from the weight of the blank to determine the weight of base needed per suppository. Therefore:

$$\text{Weight of blank} - \text{Weight of displaced base} = \text{Amount of base needed per suppository}$$

$$1.8 \text{ grams} - 0.049 \text{ grams} = 1.751 \text{ grams of base per suppository}$$

Next, multiply the base needed per suppository (1.751 grams) by the total number of suppositories needed (35). This will yield the amount of base required to make the preparation. Therefore:

$$\text{Number of suppositories} \times \text{Grams of base per suppository} = \text{Total amount of base needed}$$

$$35 \text{ suppositories} \times 1.751 \text{ grams of base} = 61.285 \text{ grams}$$

Therefore, with rounding, 61.29 grams of the base will be needed to compound the 35 suppositories.

To compound suppository preparations, the API, suspending agent, and base should be weighed using a calibrated scale. The base should be placed in a beaker and melted on a hot plate at a low temperature. Melting at too high a temperature can result in brittle suppositories. While the base is melting, the API and the suspending agent are triturated with a mortar and pestle to decrease the particle size as well ensure adequate mixing. Once the base is completely melted, the heat can be discontinued. The powders can then be sifted into the melted base and mixed using a magnetic stir bar and stir plate. Once thoroughly combined, the liquid can be poured into the suppository mold, slightly overfilling it. The excess can be removed using a hot spatula after the suppositories have cooled slightly. After the suppositories have set, they are removed from the mold and weighed for quality assurance. Spraying the inside of the mold's suppository cavities with a non-stick spray can aid in their removal. Each suppository should be smooth and uniform, and they should be within (+/-) 10% of the calculated weight range, using the following formula:

$$\text{Average suppository weight (gm)} = \frac{\text{Total Weight of Base } + \text{ Total Weight of Powders}}{\text{Total Number of Suppositories Made}}$$

To continue the example above, a batch of thirty-five suppositories with 61.29 grams of base and 2.45 grams of powder (0.05 grams API x 35 suppositories plus 0.70 grams suspending agent) would have an average weight of 1.82 grams and can be calculated as follows:

$$\text{Average suppository weight (gm)} = \frac{61.29g + 2.45g}{35 \text{ suppositories}} = 1.82 \text{ g}$$

To find the margin of error of (+/-) 10%, the average weight in grams calculated above is multiplied by 90% and 110%. The acceptable weight range should not exceed 10% above or below the average suppository weight of 1.82 grams and is calculated below:

$$-10\%: 1.82 \text{ g} \times 90\% = 1.64 \text{ g}$$

and

$$+10\%: 1.82 \text{ g} \times 110\% = 2.00 \text{ g}$$

Each suppository should therefore weigh between 1.64 grams and 2.00 grams. This process is also used to determine the margin of error of other solid dosage preparations such as capsules. However, capsules must be within (+/-) 5% of the target weight to be considered acceptable.

## Basic Formulas, Conversions, and Calculations

It is important for pharmacy technicians to understand the basic formulas, conversions, and calculations used in pharmacy. Calculations may be as simple as calculating the day's supply on a prescription order or as complex as calculating packing statistics for compounded capsules.

## Conversions

Common conversions are shown in the chart below:

| Common Measurements and Conversions | | | |
|---|---|---|---|
| Unit/Symbol | Conversion | Unit/Symbol | Conversion |
| Microgram (mcg, μg) | 1 mcg = 0.001 mg = 0.000001 g | Milliliter (ml) | 1 ml = 0.001 L |
| Milligram (mg) | 1 mg = 0.001g = 1,000 mcg | Liter (L) | 1 L = 1,000 ml |
| Grams (g) | 1 g = 0.001 kg = 1,000 mg | Teaspoon (tsp) | 1 tsp = 5 ml |
| Kilogram (kg) | 1 kg = 1,000 g = 2.2 lb | Tablespoon (tbsp) | 1 tbsp = 3 tsp = 15 ml |
| Pound (lb) | 1 lb = 16 oz = 454 g | Pint (pt) | 1 pt = 473 ml |
| Ounces (oz) | 1 oz = 30 ml | Grain (gr.) | 1 gr = 64.8 mg |

## Roman Numerals

Roman numerals are letters that stand for numbers; this system was used by ancient Romans and is still used in pharmacy today, often to indicate numeric quantities on prescriptions. Roman numerals may be written as uppercase or lowercase letters. The table below shows the basic system.

| Roman Numerals | |
|---|---|
| $ss = \dfrac{1}{2}$ | L = 50 |
| I = 1 | C = 100 |
| V = 5 | D = 500 |
| X = 10 | M = 1,000 |

The Roman numeral system uses an additive and subtractive method when combining letters to form various numbers. To do so, there are a few rules to consider. First, the same letter must not be used in succession more than three times. For example:

$$II = (1 + 1) = 2$$

or

$$III = (1 + 1 + 1) = 3$$

BUT

$$IIII \neq (1 + 1 + 1 + 1) \neq 4$$

Instead, use the next largest number and put smaller numerals in front of it, subtracting so the total adds up to the number you want, which leads to the second rule. The second rule states that when placing a smaller Roman numeral before a larger one, use the subtractive method as follows:

$$IV = (5 - 1) = 4$$

or

$$IX = (10 - 1) = 9$$

The third rule requires the use of the additive method when placing a smaller Roman numeral after a larger one. For example,

$$VI = (5 + 1) = 6$$

or

$$XV = (10 + 5) = 15$$

Lastly, use the subtractive method first when a smaller Roman numeral is placed between two larger Roman numerals. For example,

$$XIV = 10 + (5 - 1) = 14$$

or

$$XXIX = 10 + 10 + (10 - 1) = 29$$

## Ratios and Proportions

A ratio is a fraction that shows the relationship between two quantities. For instance, if you have four bananas and two apples, the ratio of bananas to apples is 4:2. A proportion is a statement of equality between two ratios. If two given ratios are equivalent, one ratio is said to be proportional to the other. Proportions and ratios can be helpful when trying to determine an unknown quantity. To correctly set up ratio and proportion equations, three of the four variables must be known, the numerator units must be the same, and the denominator units must be the same. To find the unknown variable $x$, create a proportion:

$$\frac{x}{a} = \frac{b}{c}$$

If three of the four terms are known, $x$ can be solved for by multiplying both sides of the equation by $a$.

$$a\left(\frac{x}{a}\right) = \left(\frac{b}{c}\right)a$$

$$x = a\left(\frac{b}{c}\right)$$

The variable $a$ therefore cancels out on the left side of the equation. Then it is a matter of plugging in the known values to solve for $x$. For instance, a prescription for clarithromycin suspension is written as follows:

> Clarithromycin suspension
>
> #QS
>
> Give 100 mg PO Q12H x 7 days

The pharmacy has a 100 ml bottle of clarithromycin 125 mg/5 ml suspension in stock that can be used to fill the order. The dose is 100 mg, but liquids are dosed in milliliters. The first step is to determine the unknown variable, $x$ (the number of milliliters to be given), and the ratios.

Variable = $x$, where $x$ is equal to the number of milliliters per dose

Known ratio = 125 mg/5 ml, also written $\frac{5 \text{ ml}}{125 \text{ mg}}$

Unknown ratio = 100 mg/$x$, also written $\frac{x}{100 \text{ mg}}$

The final step is to create a proportion or set each ratio equal to each other and solve for $x$ by multiplying each side of the equation by 100 mg.

$$\cancel{100\text{ mg}}\left(\frac{x}{\cancel{100\text{ mg}}}\right) = \left(\frac{5\text{ ml}}{125\text{ mg}}\right)100\text{ mg}$$

The milligrams on the right side of the proportion cancel out, leaving

$$x = 100\left(\frac{5\text{ ml}}{125}\right) = 100\,(0.04\text{ ml}) = 4\text{ ml}$$

Following the basic order of operations to solve, $x = 4$ **milliliters**. The patient will therefore need to take 4 ml of the medication to obtain the 100 mg dose prescribed. To check your answer, multiply the now-known variable $x$ (4 ml) by the concentration being dispensed (125mg/5ml). This will give the number of milligrams prescribed, or 100 mg.

$$4\text{ ml}\left(\frac{125\text{ mg}}{5\text{ ml}}\right) = 100\text{ mg}$$

Understanding ratios and proportions is important since they can be applied in many aspects of pharmacy including calculating IV drip rates, determining the quantity of a drug to dispense, and converting between concentrations.

## Gravity, Specific Gravity, and Clark's Rule

Several types of ratios and proportions commonly used in pharmaceuticals are gravity, specific gravity, and Clark's rule.

The gravity of a substance, in pharmaceuticals, refers to the ratio between the density of a substance to the density of water. The formula is written as:

$$\frac{\text{Density of the Substance}}{\text{Density of Water}} = \text{Gravity of the Substance}$$

If the substance has a gravity higher than 1, it will sink in water; if it is less than 1, it will float or suspend in the water.

Finding the specific gravity of a substance enables the pharmacy technician to convert between weight and volume. The formula is written as:

$$\frac{\text{Weight (in grams)}}{\text{Volume (in milliliters)}} = \text{Specific Gravity of the Substance}$$

This formula allows the pharmacy technician to determine the desired amount of the pharmaceutical in either measurement used in the formula.

Clark's rule is used to convert an adult dose of a medication to a pediatric dose. The formula is written as:

$$\frac{\text{Weight of the pediatric patient in pounds}}{150\text{ pounds}} \times \text{Dose of medication for an adult}$$

$$= \text{Dose for pediatric patient}$$

For example, if a single adult dosage of acetaminophen is 10 mL, a pediatric patient who weighs 60 pounds should receive the following dose:

$$\frac{60 \text{ pounds}}{150 \text{ pounds}} \times 10 \text{ mL} = 4 \text{ mL}$$

In recent years, Clarke's rule has been reconsidered within the context of increasing pediatric obesity rates. Higher weights in pediatric patients may be resulting in incorrect dosing, and some researchers recommend incorporating the variables of age, developmental growth, and other factors when considering pediatric doses for individual patients.

## Percentages and Proportions (Percent-Solution Formula)

Percent is a word derived from the Latin phrase "per centum," meaning for each one hundred. Percentages are parts of a whole or of one hundred; therefore, 25 parts of one hundred are equal to 25%, 50 parts of 100 are equal to 50%, 100 parts of 100 are equal to 100%, and so on. Percentages can also be written as fractions or decimals and are often used to indicate the concentration of a medication. The concentration of a solution can be expressed in terms of either their weight per volume, for example, grams per 100 milliliters (g/100 ml), or volume per volume, ml per 100 milliliters (ml/100 ml). For example, normal saline, which is a concentration of 0.9%, is expressed in terms of its weight (in grams) per volume (in milliliters) since there are 0.9 grams of NaCl in 100 ml of aqueous solution. The concentration is obtained by dividing the weight of the NaCl by the volume of solution; therefore:

$$\frac{0.9 \text{ g}}{100 \text{ ml}} = 0.9\%$$

When converting concentrations or performing dilutions, a proportion equation, referred to as a percent-solution formula, can be used. The percent-solution formula can be set up as follows:

$$\frac{\text{volume needed } (x)}{\% \text{ wanted concentration}} = \frac{\text{prescribed volume}}{\% \text{ concentration on hand}}$$

A percent-solution formula requires that three of these four variables be known. For example, an order is written for 1,000 ml of 5% dextrose solution, also referred to as D5W; however, the pharmacy has 1,000 ml of 50% dextrose solution. The 50% dextrose solution will therefore need to be diluted to obtain the lower concentration. To determine the volume of the 50% dextrose solution needed, $x$, set up the proportion equation with the known variables:

$$\frac{x}{5\% \text{ dextrose solution}} = \frac{1,000 \text{ ml}}{50\% \text{ dextrose solution}}$$

To solve for the needed volume, $x$, multiply both sides by 5% dextrose solution. This cancels the units in the denominators, leaving the following equation:

$$\text{5\% dextrose solution} \left(\frac{x}{\text{5\% dextrose solution}}\right) = \left(\frac{1,000 \text{ ml}}{\text{50\% dextrose solution}}\right) \text{5\% dextrose solution}$$

$$x = 5\left(\frac{1,000 \text{ ml}}{50}\right)$$

$$x = 100 \text{ ml}$$

Therefore 100 ml of 50% dextrose solution will need to be diluted. To find out how much diluent is needed, subtract the volume of 50% dextrose solution from the total volume ordered. Since the order is written for 1,000 ml of total volume, the 100 ml of 50% dextrose solution will need to be diluted by adding 900 ml of sterile water for a final concentration of 5%.

## Alligations

The alligation method can be used when mixing preparations whose components are of different concentrations. Generally, one of the preparation's components is of a higher strength or concentration than desired and one is of a lower concentration than the desired strength. The alligation method involves creating a box or grid of three columns and three rows, like a tic-tac-toe board, and placing the concentrations in specific sections within the grid to solve for how many parts of each strength are needed to obtain the desired concentration. To set up the alligation grid, the desired concentration, (D), is placed in the center square of the grid. The component with the lower concentration is placed in the lower left corner of the grid, while the component with the higher concentration (H) is placed in the upper left corner.

% higher
strength (H)

% desired
strength (D)

% lower
strength (L)

Working diagonally, determine the value of the lower right corner of the grid by calculating the difference between the desired strength D and the higher strength H, placing the result in the bottom right corner. Then find the difference between the desired strength D and the lower strength L, placing the result in the top right corner. The calculated values in the top and bottom right portion of the grid give the number of parts of each component needed to prepare the desired concentration D.

| % higher strength (H) | | D – L = amount of H needed to prepare D |
|---|---|---|
| | % of desired strength (D) | |
| % lower strength (L) | | H – D = amount of L needed to prepare D |

These values will then be used to set up the proportion equations. For example, a physician writes an order for 480 ml of half-strength Dakin's solution, which is 0.25%; however, the pharmacy only has quarter-strength (0.125%) and full-strength (0.5%) Dakin's solution stocked. To determine how many milliliters of each strength is needed to prepare the order make an alligation grid using the information provided:

H = Higher concentration = 0.5%

L = Lower concentration = 0.125%

D = Desired concentration = 0.25%

Desired quantity = 480 ml

| Dakin's 0.5% solution (H) | | 0.125 |
|---|---|---|
| | Dakin's 0.25% solution (D) | |
| Dakin's 0.125% solution (L) | | 0.25 |

Here the difference between H and D is 0.25 parts, while the difference between D and L is 0.125 parts. To set up the proportion, add the parts in the top right corner of the grid to the parts in the bottom right corner of the grid to fine the total number of parts needed (0.375 parts). Reading the alligation grid from left to right, the proportions can be set up as follows:

$$\frac{\text{Parts needed}}{\text{Total parts}}$$

Dakin's 0.5% solution (H):

$$\frac{0.125 \text{ parts}}{0.375 \text{ parts}} = \frac{0.125}{0.375}$$

Dakin's 0.125% solution (L):

$$\frac{0.25 \text{ parts}}{0.375 \text{ parts}} = \frac{0.25}{0.375}$$

Next, multiply the proportions by the total volume ordered, 480 ml.

Dakin's 0.5% solution (H):

$$\frac{480 \text{ ml} \times 0.125}{0.375} = 160 \text{ ml}$$

Dakin's 0.125% solution (L):

$$\frac{480 \text{ ml} \times 0.25}{0.375} = 320 \text{ ml}$$

It will therefore require 160 ml of Dakin's 0.5 % solution and 320 ml of Dakin's 0.125 % solution to prepare 480 ml of Dakin's 0.25% solution.

## Sig Codes, Symbols, Abbreviations, and Medical Terminology

Sig codes and symbols comprise a shorthand method of expressing important health information in the medical and pharmacy fields. Not all sig codes and symbols are universal; therefore, it is important to understand and recognize instances in which variations may occur. For example, human medicine uses the sig code "QD" to represent once daily; however, in veterinary medicine once daily is notated with "SID." Sig codes can be used to express the dose, frequency, duration, route of administration, and so on. Technicians are required to interpret prescription orders to ensure accurate order entry. To do this, technicians must be able recognize and understand the many sig codes, abbreviations, and terminology used by prescribers.

Below is a table of sig codes and medical terminology commonly used in pharmacy.

## Common Sig Codes

| Sig Code | Meaning | Sig Code | Meaning |
|---|---|---|---|
| **Dosage Forms** | | | |
| CAP, C, c | Capsule | LIQ | Liquid |
| ODT | Orally disintegrating tablet | SOL | Solution |
| TAB, T, t | Tablet | SUSP | Suspension |
| SUPP | Suppository | SYR | Syrup |
| SR, XR, XL, ER, CR | Sustained/Extended/Controlled Release | UNG/OINT | Ointment |
| **Frequency and Timing of Administration** | | | |
| QD | Once daily | QW | Once weekly |
| BID | Twice daily | BIW | Twice weekly |
| TID | Three times daily | Q_H | Every ___ hours |
| QID | Four times daily | WM | With meals |
| QOD | Every other day | AC | Before meals |
| QAM | Every morning | PC | After meals |
| QPM | Every afternoon (evening) | PRN | As needed |
| QHS | Every day at bedtime | STAT | Immediately |
| Q8H | Every 8 hours | ATC | Around the clock |
| Q12H | Every 12 hours | WA | While awake |
| **Routes of Administration** | | | |
| PO | By mouth | EN | Each nostril |
| SL | Sublingual (under tongue) | IV | Intravenous |
| BU | Buccal (inside cheek) | IVP | Intravenous push |
| OS | Left eye | IVPB | Intravenous piggyback |
| OD | Right eye | IM | Intramuscular |
| OU | Each eye | SC/SQ | Subcutaneous |
| AS | Left ear | PR | Per rectum/rectally |
| AD | Right ear | PV | Per vagina/vaginally |
| AU | Each ear | TOP | Topically |
| **Measurements and Miscellaneous Sig Codes** | | | |
| mL, ml | Milliliter | mEq | Milliequivalent |
| cc | Cubic centimeter | gtt | Drop |
| l, L | Liter | qs | Quantity sufficient |
| **Measurements and Miscellaneous Sig Codes (cont.)** | | | |
| fl. oz | Fluid ounce | uad, utd | Use as directed, as directed |
| mcg, µg | Microgram | Ī, ĪĪ or T, TT | 1 tab, 2 tabs, etc. |
| mg | Milligram | s̄s, SS | ½, single strength |
| g | Gram | DS | Double strength |
| kg | Kilogram | AAA | Apply to affected area(s) |
| Tsp | Teaspoon | c, w | With |
| Tbsp | Tablespoon | s̄, w/o | Without |
| gr | Grain | NR, ø | No refill |

It is important to understand basic medical terminology and abbreviations prescribers use to communicate medical information. Medical terminology generally consists of a root word that refers to the affected part of the body, some combining vowels, and a prefix or suffix to provide clarity. The most basic root words may indicate a body part such as the stomach; however, they can also refer to tissues, limbs, and so on. Root words may also be used to describe characteristics such as color or size as well as medical processes. Not all root words, however, will have both a prefix and a suffix. Often, a combining vowel is used to connect the root word with the prefix or suffix.

The table below is a list of common root words.

| Root | Meaning | Root | Meaning | Root | Meaning |
|---|---|---|---|---|---|
| aden | Gland | gast | Stomach | ot | Ear |
| adip | Fat | glyc | Sugar | ovari | Ovary |
| adrena | Adrenal | gynec | Woman | ox/oxy | Oxygen |
| aer | Air | hemat/hemo | Blood | patell | Kneecap |
| aero | Gas | hepat | Liver | pector | Chest |
| andr | Male | hist | Tissue | ped/pod | Foot |
| angi | Vessel | humer | Bone of upper arm | pelv | Pelvis |
| aort | Aorta | hyster | Uterus | phalang | Finger bones and toe bones |
| arteri | Artery | kerat | Hard | phas | Speech |
| arthr | Joint | lacrim | Tear duct | phleb | Vein |
| blephar | Eyelid | lact | Milk | pneum | Lung |
| bronch | Bronchus | lapar | Abdomen | prostat | Prostate gland |
| card | Heart | laryng | Larynx | pulmon | Lung |
| carp | Wrist | lingu | Tongue | rachi | Vertebrae |
| cerebr | Cerebrum | lipid | Fat | ren | Kidney |
| chol | Bile | lymph | Lymph | retin | Retina |
| chondr | Cartilage | mamm/mast | Breast | rhin | Nose |
| col | Colon | men | Menstruation | sinus | Sinus |
| crani | Skull | mens | Mind | somat | Body |
| cutane | Skin | mening | Meninges | splens | Spleen |
| cyst | Bladder | metr | Uterus | spondyl | Vertebrae |
| cyt | Cell | my | Muscle | stern | Sternum |
| dactyl | Finger or toe | myel | Spinal Cord | stenosis | Narrowing |
| derma | Skin | nas | Nose | tendin | Tendon |
| dudoen | Duodenum | necr | Death (of cells) | thromb | Clot |
| encephal | Brain | nephr | Kidney | thym | Thymus |
| enter | Intestine | neur | Nerve | thyr | Thyroid |
| esthesi | Sensation | ocul | Eye | tibi | Large bone of lower leg |
| **Root** | **Meaning** | **Root** | **Meaning** | **Root** | **Meaning** |
| esophag | Esophagus | onych | Nail | toc | Birth |
| femor | Thigh bone | or | Mouth | tympan | Eardrum |
| fibr | Fiber | orexia | Appetite | uter | Uterine |
| fibul | Small bone of lower leg | oste | Bone | vas | Vessel or duct |

Prefixes are modifiers that can be added to the root word to provide emphasis or further clarify the meaning of the root word. Prefixes, when necessary, are added to the beginning of the root word; they are used less frequently than suffixes. Below is a table of commonly used prefixes.

## Common Prefixes

| Prefix | Meaning | Prefix | Meaning | Prefix | Meaning |
|---|---|---|---|---|---|
| A-/An | Without | Epi- | Upon | Neo- | New |
| Ab- | Away from | Erythr- | Red | Onco- | Tumor |
| Acro- | Top of (tip-end) | Eu- | Normal (good) | Pan- | All |
| Acu- | Sharp | Extra-/Extro | Beyond/outside of | Para- | Abnormal or alongside of |
| Ad- | Toward | Hemi- | Half | Peri- | Around |
| Ambi- | Both | Heter- | Different | Poly- | Many |
| Ante- | Before | Hyper- | Above or excessive | Post- | After or following |
| Anti-/Anter- | Against/opposing | Hypo- | Below or deficient | Pre-/Pro- | Before |
| Bi- | Two | Im-/In- | Not | Pseudo- | False |
| Brachio- | Arm | Immun- | Safe or protected | Purpur- | Purple |
| Brady- | Slow | Infra- | Below or under | Quadri- | Four |
| Chemo- | Chemical | Inter- | Between | Re- | Again or back |
| Circum- | Around | Intra- | Within | Retro- | Behind |
| Cirrh- | Yellow | Iso- | Equal | Rube- | Red |
| Co-/Con-/Com- | Together/with | Leuk- | White | Semi- | Half |
| Contra- | Against | Macro- | Large | Sub- | Below under |
| Cyan- | Blue | Medi-/Meso | Middle | Super-/Supra- | Above or excessive |
| Dia-/Trans- | Across or through | Melan- | Black | Sym-/Syn- | With |
| Di- | Twice or two | Meta- | Beyond, after, or changing | Tachy- | Fast |
| Dis- | Separate from/Apart | Micr-/Micro | Tiny/Small | Tri- | Three |
| Dys- | Difficult/painful | Mid- | Middle | Ultra- | Beyond or excessive |
| Ec- | Away/out | Mono- | One | Uni- | One |
| Ecto-/Exo | Outside | Multi- | Many | Xanth- | Yellow |
| Endo- | Within | Morto- | Death | Xer- | Dry |

Suffixes are modifiers that are added to the end of the root word. For example, the word "neuralgia" is a combination of the root word "neur," meaning nerve, and the suffix "algia," meaning pain. Neuralgia, therefore, is a condition in which the patient experiences intense pain along a nerve.

## Common Suffixes

| Suffix | Meaning | Suffix | Meaning | Suffix | Meaning |
|---|---|---|---|---|---|
| -ac/-al | Pertaining to | -itis | Swelling or inflammation | -philia | Attraction to |
| -algia | Pain | -ium | Structure or tissue | -phoby | Fear of |
| -ar/-ary | Pertaining to | -lith | Calculus or stone | -phylaxis | Protection |
| -asthenia | Without strength | -lysis | Breakdown or deteriorate | -plasia/ -poesis | Formation |
| -cele | Hernia or pouching | -malacia | Softening | -plegia | Paralysis |
| -clasis | To break | -megaly | Enlargement | -pnea | Breathing |
| -constriction | Narrowing | -meter | Measuring instrument | -rrhage | To burst forth |
| -cyesis | Pregnancy | -metry | Process of measuring | -rrhea | Discharge |
| -cynia | Pain | -mortem | Death | -schisis | To split |
| -dilation | Expansion or stretch | -mycosis | Fungal infection | -sclerosis | Constriction or narrowing |
| -eal | Pertaining to | -oid | Resembling | -scope | Examination instrument |
| -ectasis | Expansion or dilation | -ole | Small | -scopy | Examination |
| -ectomy | Removal | -oma | Tumor | -spasm | Involuntary contraction |
| -edema | Swelling or inflammation | -opia/ -opsia | Vision | -stasis | To control or stop |
| -emia | Blood condition | -opsy | Display of | -stoma/ -stomy | To create a new opening |
| -genic | Origin or production | -osis | Abnormal condition, increase | -tic | Pertaining to |
| -gram | Record | -osmia | Smell | -tocia | Childbirth labor |
| -graph | Recording instrument | -ostosis | Condition of bone | -tomy | Incision |
| -graphy | Process of recording | -ous | Pertaining to | -toxic | Poison |
| -ia | Condition of | -paresis | Partial paralysis | -tresia | Opening |
| -iasis | Condition or formation of | -partum | Birth | -tropia | To turn |
| -iatry | Treatment | -pathy | Disease | -tropic | Stimulate |
| -ic | Pertaining to | -penia | Decrease | -tropin | To trigger |
| -icle | Small | -phagia | Swallowing | -ula/-ule | Small |
| -ism | Condition of | -phasia | Speech | -uria | Urine |

An example that combines all three modifying components is the word "tachycardia," which means the condition of having a fast heart rate. In this example, the prefix "tachy" means fast, the root word "card" refers to the heart, and the suffix "ia" means a condition of. Not all root words require the addition of all three modifying components, and often a combining vowel is necessary to make the word easier to pronounce. Dry mouth or xerostomia, for example, combines the prefix "xer" or dry, the combining vowel "o," the root word "stom" or mouth, and the suffix "ia" or condition of.

While knowing the full medical terms is vitally important, members of the medical community use a wide variety of abbreviations to save time and space. Common abbreviations for medical terms are listed in the chart below.

## Common Medical Terminology Abbreviations

| | | | |
|---|---|---|---|
| ADD | Attention deficit disorder | LDL | Low density lipoprotein |
| ADR | Adverse drug reaction | MI | Myocardial infarction |
| AMI | Acute myocardial infarction | MRI | Magnetic resonance imaging |
| BM | Bowel movement | NKA | No known allergies |
| BP | Blood pressure | NKDA | No known drug allergies |
| BPH | Benign prostatic hyperplasia | NPO | Nothing by mouth |
| BS | Blood sugar | NS | Normal saline |
| CAD | Coronary artery disease | NVD | Nausea, vomiting, diarrhea |
| CF | Cardiac failure | OR | Operating room |
| CHF | Congestive heart failure | PAH | Pulmonary arterial hypertension |
| CMV | Cytomegalovirus | PMH | Past medical history |
| CNS | Central nervous system | PVD | Peripheral vascular disease |
| COPD | Chronic obstructive pulmonary disease | RA | Rheumatoid arthritis |
| CVA | Cerebrovascular accident, stroke | RBC | Red blood count (red blood cell) |
| D/C | Discontinue | SBP | Systolic blood pressure |
| DM | Diabetes mellitus | SOB | Shortness of breath |
| DOB | Date of birth | STD | Sexually transmitted disease |
| DUR | Drug utilization review | Sx | Surgery |
| Dx | Diagnosis | TB | Tuberculosis |
| EC | Enteric coated | TEDS | Thrombo-embolic disease stockings |
| EKG (ECG) | Electrocardiogram | TPN | Total parenteral nutrition |
| ENT | Ear, nose, throat | Tx | Treatment |
| GERD | Gastroesophageal reflux disease | U | Units |
| GI | Gastrointestinal | U/A | Urinalysis |
| HA | Headache | URI | Upper respiratory infection |
| HDL | High density lipoprotein | UTI | Urinary tract infection |
| Hx | History | VS | Vital signs |
| HR | Heart rate | WBC | White blood count (white blood cell) |
| IV | Intravenous | WT | Weight |

## Equipment/Supplies Required for Drug Administration

### Package Size

The package size in which prescription medications are provided to a patient plays an important role in medication adherence and mitigating risks associated with misuse. They also play a role in billing and insurance reimbursement. Package size is regulated for a variety of drugs that tend to be misused, as misuse can cause additional health problems for the patient. Package size parameters vary based on whether the medication is a liquid, a liquid suspension, or tablets. Parameters may include the total volume of a bottle, the total concentration of a suspension, and the total number of tablets in a blister package. The size of a package may also take into account the target patient populations and any user needs. For example, children's medications may be in larger containers with child-safety caps, while pharmacists may create tailored daily blister packs for patients who are managing chronic conditions and need many different types of medications.

## Diabetic Supplies

Diabetic patients require a multitude of supplies for blood glucose testing and monitoring and insulin administration. To test blood glucose levels, diabetic patients are required to obtain a blood sample through a finger prick. For supplies they will need test strips, a glucometer, alcohol swabs or soap and running water, a lancing device (optional), and a lancet. The patient first inserts a new test strip into the glucometer and then cleans the area of their skin (usually a fingertip) with alcohol swabs or with soap and running water. Then, if using a lancing device, they insert a lancet, a small, single-use needle, into the lancing device, which uses a spring mechanism to quickly puncture the finger, allowing the blood sample to be drawn. If the patient is not using a lancing device, they can simply prick their finger with the lancet. The tip of the test strip is dipped into the blood and the glucometer automatically takes the blood glucose level reading. It is important to note that not all lancets are compatible with all lancing devices, nor are all test strips compatible across all glucometers; therefore, it is imperative to ensure compatibility.

The insulin-dependent diabetic patient will also need medical supplies to administer insulin. Administering insulin injections requires alcohol swabs to clean the injection site, insulin syringes or pen needles for injecting insulin, and a sharps container for disposing of used needles and lancets. Insulin syringes are available in a variety of sizes and needle lengths. The most common insulin concentration is U100 insulin, which means one milliliter of insulin is equivalent to 100 units of insulin. Therefore, insulin syringes are dosed in units and come in several sizes, which can deliver anywhere from 0.3 ml or 30 units to 1 ml or 100 units of insulin. Insulin is delivered subcutaneously, so needle lengths on insulin syringes may range from 6 mm to 12.7 mm, while the gauge or needle thickness can range from 28 G to 31 G. Lastly, pen needles are small, single-use needles that are used to administer insulin from dosing pens.

## Inhalant Devices and Equipment

Inhaled medications can be used to treat various respiratory ailments including asthma and chronic obstructive pulmonary disease (COPD). Inhaled formulations are available as metered-dose inhalers (MDIs), dry powder inhalers (DPIs), and nebulizing solutions, and they may require specialized equipment to aid in their administration. An MDI consists of a medication canister that is inserted into an adapter with a mouthpiece. The adapter, which may be referred to as an actuator, includes a metering valve. When depressed, the metering valve delivers the pressurized liquid medication as an aerosol through the mouthpiece.

Some MDI actuators have a counter that displays the number of actuations or puffs remaining. MDIs can be used with another device called a holding chamber or spacer to ensure optimal delivery of the medication by coordinating actuations with inspiration, or inhaling. A spacer is a long tube or chamber that the MDI aerosol is released into. One end of the spacer has a mouthpiece for administration, while the other end is attached to the mouthpiece of the MDI. For patients that find it difficult to maintain contact with the mouthpiece during treatment, a mask may be attached to the end of the spacer. Masks are especially helpful with pediatric patients.

DPIs are specialized devices that allow the release of a dry powder medication upon inspiration by the patient. These devices are breath activated and require the patient to take a short, deep breath from the device's mouthpiece, drawing the powdered dose of medication out of the inhaler. DPIs may be packaged as individual doses, such as blisters or capsules that are punctured prior to inspiration by being inserted into the inhaler itself, or as multidose cartridges. The Spiriva Handihaler is an example of a DPI that uses individual capsules that must be inserted into the inhaler's capsule chamber before use.

A nebulizer is a medical device used to administer inhaled formulations such as albuterol sulfate solution. A nebulizer device consists of a small compressor unit, rubber tubing, and a mouthpiece or mask. The nebulizer atomizes nebulizing solutions into a fine mist that is then inhaled by the patient. DuoNeb is an example of an inhaled liquid medication that is added to the chamber of the nebulizer. Nebulizer units are extremely helpful when administering inhaled formulations to pediatric patients.

## Oral Administration Supplies

There are several types of dosing devices for administering oral liquid formulations including oral syringes, medication spoons, dosing cups, and medication droppers. It is important to use the most appropriate administration device when dispensing liquid oral medications to ensure that the patient can accurately measure their dose. Oral syringes are most frequently given when dispensing liquid medications, and they tend to be the most accurate dosing device. Oral syringes come in a variety of sizes, but the most frequently used sizes range from one milliliter to ten milliliters.

Oral syringes consist of a clear or amber colored cylindrical barrel with a small tip at the end and a plunger with a rubber-tipped stopper that is inserted into the barrel. Markings or lines are placed along the barrel in 0.1 ml increments to indicate the dosage. Oral syringes are often used with press-in bottle adapters, or PIBAs. PIBAs are small plastic stoppers that are inserted into the neck of the medication bottle. PIBAs have a hole in the center that is the diameter of most oral syringes. The oral syringe is inserted into the PIBA and the bottle is inverted, allowing the medication to be drawn from the bottle into the syringe while preventing leakage.

Dosing or medication spoons, dosing cups, and medication droppers may also be used to administer oral liquid medications. Dosing spoons are a close ended clear barrel lined with dosage markings with a spoon or scoop on the other end, most frequently used to administer medication to children. Dosing cups are small, shallow measuring cups, often made of clear plastic, with dosage marks along the side. Medication droppers are clear plastic or glass tubes with dosage markings along the side that are tapered at one end and have a rubber bulb at the other end. To use a medication dropper, draw the medication up into the dropper by squeezing and releasing the rubber bulb.

Orally administered liquid medications including syrups, solutions, and suspensions are typically dosed in milliliters (mL) or cubic centimeters (cc). However, it is also not unusual to see liquid medications dosed in teaspoons (tsp) and tablespoons (Tbsp). The dosage markings on these devices may include one or more of these dosing units, with milliliters being most common. To ensure the most precise dosing, it is best to use devices that can measure to the nearest tenth of a milliliter.

## Injectable Syringes

Injectable syringes are chosen based on the type of injection as well as the type of medication being administered. Injectable syringes consist of a cylindrical barrel, usually clear, with a plunger with a rubber-tipped stopper that is inserted into the barrel on one end and a needle on the other end. Markings or lines are placed along the barrel to indicate the dosage. Syringes for injection come in various sizes that are defined by the syringe's needle length and gauge. Needle lengths can range from as short as 3/8 of an inch to 3 ½ inches, with some specialty syringes having even longer needles. The gauge is the diameter of the needle's lumen, or the opening of the needle that penetrates the skin. Gauges generally range from 18G to 30G. The higher the gauge, the smaller the needle's diameter; therefore, a 25G needle would be smaller than a 22G.

Factors that must be taken into consideration when choosing an appropriate size syringe for injection include the type of injection being administered, the location of the injection, and the material or medication being administered. Medications that are injected into the muscle are called intramuscular (IM) injections, while those injected under the skin are referred to as subcutaneous (SQ) injections. Medications that are delivered IM, such as testosterone injections, will require a longer needle than an SQ medication such as insulin since the injection needs to penetrate into the muscle rather than just penetrating the skin.

An example of a medication delivered IM is the Depo-Provera injectable contraceptive. The viscosity or thickness of the medication being injected must also be considered since more viscous medications may have difficulty passing through a small needle. Therefore, it is necessary to use a smaller-gauge (larger size) needle for more viscous medications to allow the solution being injected to flow more easily. The injectable steroid medication Depo-Testosterone, for example, is delivered IM and is formulated in a cottonseed oil delivery vehicle which may have difficulty passing through a needle with a small opening; therefore, a smaller-gauge needle would make it easier to draw up and administer.

## Lot Numbers, Expiration Dates, and National Drug Code (NDC) Numbers

Prescription medication label requirements are regulated by the Federal Drug Administration (FDA) in the U.S. Code of Federal Regulations (CFR). Prescription drug information that must be printed on the label includes information about the drug including the brand and generic name of the medication, the active ingredients, the medication's strength and dosage formulation, and the quantity of medication in the package. If applicable, the prescription medication label must also include a controlled substance stamp and a statement regarding its abuse or habit-forming potential. In addition to containing important drug information, the medication label must also include manufacturer-specific information such as the National Drug Code (NDC), the manufacturer's name and address, the lot number, and the expiration date. Lastly, the medication label must also contain the proper storage requirements regarding temperature, allowable temperature excursions, and the recommended containers for dispensing. Of these label requirements, the medication's lot number, expiration date, and NDC number are perhaps the most important because these identifiers are used to track and trace medications in the supply chain in the case of safety issues such as a medication recall.

### Lot Numbers

A lot number is a unique sequence of identifying characters, typically composed of numbers, letters, or a combination of both, which are assigned to a product during the manufacturing process. In pharmaceutical manufacturing, a lot number is assigned to the finished products of a specific batch as a quality control measure. For each batch, the manufacturer must also record the lot numbers and expiration dates of all the ingredients that were used to produce the drug. This process ensures the manufacturer can easily trace issues with products and the raw materials used to make them if a concern should arise. Lot numbers are the most effective method of tracing a pharmaceutical product in the drug supply chain in the event of a recall. Pharmaceutical manufacturers are required to keep accurate inventory records that detail which lots of medication have been shipped and which distributor received them.

The distributor is then responsible for maintaining their own inventory records. These records should document the drug lot numbers received and the pharmacies to which they were sold. Individual pharmacies must also maintain their own purchase records, which will have the lot numbers that they received from their distributor. A medication's lot number is incredibly important in the event a drug recall is issued. This is especially true if there is a known patient safety concern such as product contamination. Knowing the recalled lot numbers allows all parties in the drug supply chain to trace, identify, and remove any affected medications from the market as well as notify consumers that received the recalled medication.

## Expiration Dates

The expiration date for prescription and OTC medication is defined as the length of time a medication retains its potency and quality under proper storage conditions. The shelf life can vary significantly depending on the drug's formulation, active ingredients, and so on. A medication's shelf life is thoroughly evaluated during the early stages of drug development through rigorous stability testing. Aside from determining a product's expiration date, stability testing also yields important information such as the proper storage requirements and the type of container the drug should be dispensed in, as the type of dispensing container can affect the stability of the medication over time. In general, when pharmacies repackage medications or dispense them outside their original container, the pharmacies give drugs an expiration date of one year although the stock bottle may have a longer expiration date.

Some prescription medications, such as reconstituted antibiotics and insulins, will have two different expiration dates that depend on whether the drugs have been dispensed. Drugs in dry powder forms have a long shelf life; however, the expiration can change once they drugs are reconstituted. For example, azithromycin suspension in its dry powder form may be stable for up to three years when unopened on the shelf and under proper storage conditions. However, once the seal is broken and water is added for reconstitution, the expiration date decreases to ten days.

While medications may still be potent past the established expiration date, the manufacturer cannot guarantee the potency at that point, and therefore it is best to discard the expired drug. The active ingredients in medications can begin to degrade after they expire. This loss of stability can result in the decreased effectiveness of the medication as well as the potential for development of toxic degradation byproducts. It is therefore best to remove and properly discard of or process expired medications.

## NDC Numbers

The FDA requires that drug manufacturers keep current records of all finished and unfinished drugs produced in their facilities. Each of these drugs and drug products is assigned a unique identifier called a National Drug Code (NDC); this is true whether or not the drug or drug product has received FDA approval. National Drug Codes are published in the FDA's NDC directory, which includes prescription and OTC medications. An NDC is numerical, generally made up of ten digits, and composed of three segments with one of the following numerical formats: 5-4-1, 5-3-2, or 4-4-2. The first segment is composed of four or five numbers and is referred to as the labeler code because it is specific to the manufacturer. For example, the labeler code 00378-xxxx-xx means the product is manufactured by Mylan Pharmaceuticals, while the labeler code 00093-xxxx-xx is used by the manufacturer Teva. The second segment, which is composed of three or four numbers, is called the product code and refers to the drug's strength and dosage formulation.

The third segment, or package code, identifies the medication's package size and is generally composed of two digits, although some may only have one. While the FDA's directory requires NDC numbers be composed of ten digits, some insurance processors use an eleven-digit format, which can lead to confusion when converting for billing purposes. The eleven-digit NDC format used for insurance billing is a 5-4-2 configuration. Since the FDA's standard ten-digit NDC does not follow this 5-4-2 format, a leading zero can be added to any of the three segments to convert the NDC to an eleven-digit code for insurance billing purposes. For example, a 4-4-2 NDC such as xxxx-xxxx-xx can be changed to the 5-4-2 format by adding a 0 at the beginning of first segment of the code: 0xxxx-xxxx-xx. Additionally, a 5-3-2 code such as xxxxx-xxx-xx can be changed to the 5-4-2 format by adding a 0 at the beginning of the second segment:

xxxxx-0xxx-xx. Or, a 5-4-1 code such as xxxxx-xxxx-x can be changed to the 5-4-2- format by adding a 0 at the beginning of the third segment: xxxxx-xxxx-0x

## Medication and Supplies Returns

### Inventory Management

Many pharmacies today operate using a perpetual first-in, first-out approach to inventory management, also known as FIFO; this term means that older inventory is dispensed before newer. Pharmacies should have inventory management procedures in place to ensure the movement of their oldest inventory. The point of dispensing older or short-dated medications first is to prevent medications from expiring on the shelf and having to be destroyed. The first-in, first-out approach is therefore an overall cost-effective method of ensuring dispensable medications are used and not wasted. Inevitably, there will be some medications that are not picked up for a variety of reasons. These medications are generally returned to stock after approximately fourteen days.

Pharmacies are legally required to reverse insurance claims on medications not picked up; this task, often managed by technicians, should be performed daily. When returning medications to stock, the insurance claim must be reversed through the computer's online system. This process reverses any paid insurance claim and returns the dispensed quantity or fill back to the original prescription. If the returned medication was dispensed in its original packaging, all patient-identifying information should be removed and the medication should be returned to the shelf. If the medication was dispensed in a prescription vial, the patient information should be removed and a return-to-stock label should be affixed to the vial. Often the return-to-stock label will retain the one-year expiration date from which it was originally filled and therefore these vials should be utilized first when dispensing to another patient.

### Non-Dispensable Medications and Reverse Distributors

Pharmacy inventory should be regularly checked for expiring medications and supplies to ensure they are not dispensed in error. In addition, medications that have been damaged in transit and those under recall notices should also be pulled from inventory. Expired, recalled, and damaged medications are considered non-dispensable medications. Non-dispensable medications and supplies cannot be dispensed or sold; therefore, they are processed as pharmaceutical waste. In most retail pharmacies, it is the responsibility of the pharmacist and pharmacy technicians to pull non-dispensable prescription medications from the inventory and prepare them for return to an approved pharmaceutical waste processor, also called a reverse distributor. A reverse distributor is a federally licensed and regulated processer of both non-saleable pharmacy waste and saleable prescription medications.

The purpose of a reverse distributor is to remove unwanted or unsafe medications from the market, helping to create a safer drug supply chain. Often a reverse distributor can negotiate credit on both non-dispensable and dispensable prescription medications from the wholesaler or manufacturer. The reverse distributor will determine if the item is returnable; if so, it will be sent back to the wholesaler or manufacturer and a credit will be issued. If the medication is still dispensable, it can be redistributed to other hospitals, pharmacies, and clinics. If credit cannot be given on an item, the reverse distributor will destroy the item according to any federal and state laws. This is especially important regarding controlled substances. For controlled substances, reverse distributors must be registered with the DEA to process scheduled medications, whether dispensable or non-dispensable.

# *Practice Quiz*

1. A pharmacy technician is compounding a hazardous drug. The medication has been labeled as hazardous because it meets which criteria?
    a. Chemical instability
    b. Carcinogenicity
    c. Complexity
    d. High potency

2. A pharmacy technician needs to determine the specific gravity of a substance. The solid weighs 60 grams. The volume of the solvent is 750 milliliters. What is the specific gravity of the substance?
    a. 8.0 g/mL
    b. 0.08 g/mL
    c. 12.5 g/mL
    d. 0.125 g/mL

3. A healthcare provider recommends prescribing vancomycin for a child with a systemic infection who weighs 35 kg. The usual adult dose is 500 mg q6hr. Using Clark's rule, what pediatric dose should be prescribed?
    a. 257 mg
    b. 140 mg
    c. 250 mg
    d. 170 mg

4. Every medication has a unique numeric identifier known as a National Drug Code (NDC). An NDC identifies a medication by its product code, package code, and which other segment?
    a. Dosage
    b. Formula
    c. Quantity
    d. Labeler

5. A healthcare provider prescribes Lexapro for a patient and indicates that the brand name is medically necessary. Which dispense as written (DAW) code will the pharmacy technician enter in the system?
    a. DAW 8
    b. DAW 1
    c. DAW 4
    d. DAW 2

# Answer Explanations

**1. B**: Choice *B* is correct because carcinogenicity is one of the six criteria used to label a drug as hazardous. Carcinogenic drugs have the potential to cause cancer. Choice *A* is incorrect because chemically unstable drugs are not a type of hazardous classification as outlined in USP <795>. Choice *C* is incorrect because complexity does not indicate that a medication will be hazardous. Choice *D* is incorrect because the potency of a medication does not indicate it is hazardous while being compounded.

**2. C**: Choice *B* is correct because the specific gravity of the substance is 0.08 g/mL. The formula used to determine the specific gravity is weight (in grams) divided by volume (in milliliters).

$$\frac{60 \text{ grams}}{750 \text{ milliliters}} = 0.08 \text{ g/mL}$$

Choices *A, C,* and *D* are incorrect because 8.0, 12.5, and 0.125 g/mL are not the correct numerical solution when the specific gravity formula is used.

**3. A**: Choice *A* is correct because 257 mg is the recommended pediatric dose according to Clark's rule. The formula for Clark's rule is:

$$\frac{pediatric \; weight \; (in \; pounds)}{150} \times adult \; dose$$

The child's weight must first be converted to pounds. 35 kg = 77 lbs. (35 × 2.2 = 77). The formula is as follows:

$$\left(\frac{77}{150}\right) \times 500 = 256.6$$

The result is rounded to the nearest whole number. 256.6 = 257 mg. Choice *B* is incorrect because 140mg is the result obtained by not converting the weight into pounds first. Choices *C* and *D* are incorrect because 250 mg and 170 mg are not numerical solutions when using Clark's rule.

**4. D**: Choice *D* is correct because the first segment in the National Drug Code (NDC) is the labeler. The labeler is the medication's manufacturer, marketer, or distributor. Choices *A* and *B*, dosage and formula, are incorrect because they are part of the product code. Choice *C* is incorrect because the quantity of the medication is part of the package code segment of the NDC.

**5. B**: Choice *B* is correct because dispense as written 1 (DAW 1) is the code used when a substitution for a medication is not allowed by the prescriber and the brand name version has been determined to be medically necessary. Choice *A* is incorrect because DAW 8 is the code used when the generic version of the medication is not available. Choice *C* is incorrect because DAW 4 is the code used when the generic version of the medication is not in stock at the pharmacy. Choice *D* is incorrect because DAW 2 is the code used when the patient requests the brand name of the medication even though the prescriber did not deem the brand name to be medically necessary.

# Practice Test

1. Which of the following concepts of medication therapy management (MTM) can a pharmacy technician perform?
   I.   Creating a patient profile
   II.  Setting up medication review appointments
   III. Providing medication counseling to patients
   IV.  Collecting patient data

   a. Choices I, II, and IV
   b. Choices II, III, and IV
   c. Choices I, II, and III
   d. All of the above

2. Assuming all the following prescription medications were stored under proper recommended conditions after dispensing, which medication would expire first?
   a. Crestor tablets
   b. Augmentin suspension
   c. Tussionex suspension
   d. Cephalexin capsules

3. Which of the following antibiotics is an example of a first-generation cephalosporin?
   a. Ceftin
   b. Keflex
   c. Omnicef
   d. Suprax

4. Which of the following is NOT something a reverse distributor can do?
   a. Remove unwanted prescription medications from the drug supply chain
   b. Destroy recalled, expired, or damaged medications
   c. Redistribute overstocked medications from a pharmacy directly to patients
   d. Help pharmacies obtain monetary credit from manufactures for returned prescription medications

5. Toprol XL is an example of which class of medication?
   a. Beta blocker
   b. Angiotensin-converting enzyme (ACE) inhibitor
   c. Angiotensin receptor blocker (ARB)
   d. Calcium channel blocker (CCB)

6. The transporting of hazardous waste products is overseen by which federal organization?
   a. EPA
   b. DOT
   c. OSHA
   d. DEA

7. A pharmacy supervisor is researching an adverse event as a result of a pharmacy technician's error. The supervisor is focusing on improving the current processes as opposed to reprimanding the pharmacy technician. Which methodology is the supervisor implementing?

    a. DUR

    b. FMEA

    c. CQI

    d. RCA

8. If a prescription is written for the generic proton pump inhibitor (PPI) Protonix, which medication would be dispensed?

    a. Lansoprazole

    b. Esomeprazole

    c. Pantoprazole

    d. Omeprazole

9. Which antibiotic medication is the generic equivalent to Augmentin?

    a. Azithromycin

    b. Ciprofloxacin

    c. Clarithromycin

    d. Amoxicillin/clavulanate

10. For the antibiotic amoxicillin 400 mg/5 ml, a patient is to administer 2 TSP PO BID x10 days. How many milliliters will be needed to complete the entire course of therapy?

    a. 40 milliliters

    b. 200 milliliters

    c. 100 milliliters

    d. 300 milliliters

11. Which statement about therapeutically equivalent medications is correct?

    a. Therapeutically equivalent medications lack bioequivalence.

    b. Therapeutically equivalent medications have identical efficacy.

    c. Therapeutically equivalent medications lack pharmaceutical equivalence.

    d. Therapeutically equivalent medications have different dosage forms.

12. Which medication is considered a maintenance medication?

    a. Metformin

    b. Levofloxacin

    c. Diphenhydramine

    d. Oxycodone

13. Which statement about a medication recall is NOT accurate?

    a. Current recall information can be obtained from the FDA's weekly Enforcement Report.

    b. Product safety concerns can be reported via MedWatch, the FDA's reporting system.

    c. Product recalls are issued for medications with minor violations of FDA regulations.

    d. Product recalls are in general voluntarily initiated by the manufacturer.

14. Which pair of medications contains two pharmaceutical alternatives that have the same uses?
   a. Monodox and Doryx
   b. Fortamet and Glumetza
   c. Haldol and Haloperidol
   d. Lovenox and Enoxaparin

15. A patient is dropping off a prescription at a pharmacy. Which of the following could the pharmacy technician use to verify the patient's identity?
   I.   Allergies
   II.  Telephone number
   III. Home address
   IV.  First name
   V.   Date of birth

   a. I, III, and IV
   b. III, IV, and V
   c. II, III, and V
   d. I, II, and V

16. Which DAW product selection code must a physician include on a prescription to prevent generic substitution of a medication?
   a. DAW 4
   b. DAW 2
   c. DAW 0
   d. DAW 1

17. Which DEA form would be used to report the loss of a controlled substance?
   a. DEA Form 222
   b. DEA Form 41
   c. DEA Form 106
   d. DEA Form 107

18. Which anti-infective medication is contraindicated with alcohol use?
   a. Macrobid
   b. Flagyl
   c. Amoxicillin
   d. Keflex

19. Tall man lettering is a strategy recommended to reduce medication errors for which kind of medications?
   a. Look-alike/sound-alike medications
   b. High-alert medications
   c. Narcotic medications
   d. Commonly dispensed medications

20. Excessive bleeding that can occur with concomitant use of an NSAID and an anticoagulant such as Coumadin is a life-threatening condition caused by which type of interaction?
    a. Drug-drug interaction
    b. Drug-disease interaction
    c. Drug-nutrient interaction
    d. Drug-dietary supplement interaction

21. Which of the following is NOT considered a common side effect of antibiotic medications?
    a. Nausea
    b. Hives
    c. Diarrhea
    d. Abdominal pain

22. Which type of barcode is used to trace prescription medications as they are distributed throughout the country?
    a. One-dimensional linear
    b. Two-dimensional data matrix
    c. Universal Product Code
    d. Two-dimensional quick response

23. Patients with hypertension should avoid which cold and allergy medication due to a drug-disease interaction that raises blood pressure?
    a. Claritin-D
    b. Allegra
    c. Mucinex DM
    d. Coricidin HBP

24. Which OTC product is restricted under the Combat Methamphetamine Epidemic Act?
    a. Bronkaid
    b. Sudafed PE
    c. Alavert
    d. Mucinex

25. When a medication is assigned a National Drug Code (NDC), what is confirmed?
    a. The medication has been assigned FDA approval.
    b. The medication has been defined as a drug by federal law.
    c. The medication is eligible for Medicare reimbursement.
    d. The medication has been assigned a unique product identifier.

26. How many milliliters of 60% alcohol solution and 80% alcohol solution would a technician need to prepare 480 ml of 75% alcohol solution?
    a. 120 ml of 60% alcohol solution and 360 ml of 80 % alcohol solution
    b. 60 ml of 60% alcohol solution and 420 ml of 80 % alcohol solution
    c. 400 ml of 60% alcohol solution and 80 ml of 80 % alcohol solution
    d. 360 ml of 60% alcohol solution and 120 ml of 80 % alcohol solution

27. Women who are pregnant or of childbearing age should use personal protective equipment (PPE) such as gloves when handling which medication?
    a. Flomax
    b. Cardura
    c. Finasteride
    d. Prazosin

28. Which piece of specialized medical equipment would be needed to administer DuoNeb solution?
    a. MDI
    b. Nebulizer
    c. DPI
    d. Actuator

29. Which drug category includes high-alert medications?
    a. Proton pump inhibitors
    b. Anticonvulsants
    c. Neuromuscular blocking agents
    d. Intravenous antibiotics

30. A pharmacy technician reports laboratory data to a pharmacist for a patient receiving antibiotic therapy. Which process of a drug utilization review (DUR) would the pharmacist perform?
    a. Retrospective
    b. Concurrent
    c. Prospective
    d. Historical

31. What are the correct Tamiflu 75 mg capsule dosing directions for influenza prophylaxis?
    a. Take one capsule by mouth once daily for ten days.
    b. Take two capsules by mouth on day one, and then take one capsule daily on days two through five.
    c. Take one capsule by mouth twice daily for five days.
    d. Take one capsule by mouth once daily for one day (a single dose).

32. Which statement about ophthalmic dosage formulations is NOT true?
    a. Ophthalmic dosage formulations can be instilled in the eye.
    b. Ophthalmic dosage formulations include solutions, suspensions, ointments, and inserts.
    c. Ophthalmic dosage formulations can be instilled in the ear.
    d. Ophthalmic dosage formulations must be non-sterile.

33. Which statement about ratio and proportion is NOT correct?
    a. The numerators units must be different.
    b. To solve a proportion, three of the four terms must be known.
    c. The denominators units must be the same.
    d. Two equal ratios compose a proportion equation.

34. What type of information should be reported to the U.S. Food and Drug Administration MedWatch program?

    I.   Unexpected medication side effects
    II.  Product quality issues
    III. Expired medications
    IV. Therapeutic failures
    V.  Medication errors

    a. Choices I, II, III, and V
    b. Choices I, III, IV, and V
    c. All of the above
    d. Choices I, II, IV, and V

35. If an insulin prescription is written to inject 0.3 milliliters of U-100 insulin, how many units of insulin will be administered?
    a. 150 units of insulin
    b. 30 units of insulin
    c. 60 units of insulin
    d. 90 units of insulin

36. Which type of waste is excluded from the RCRA regulations?
    a. F-listed waste
    b. P-listed waste
    c. Household waste
    d. U-listed waste

37. Which medication should NOT be dispensed to a patient with a severe allergy to the antibiotic Levaquin?
    a. Duricef
    b. Cleocin
    c. Vigamox
    d. Zyvox

38. What is a common side effect of the urinary analgesic Pyridium?
    a. Rhinorrhea
    b. Diarrhea
    c. Vomiting
    d. Urine discoloration

39. Which piece of information is required when attempting to identify recalled medications?
    a. NDC number
    b. Expiration date
    c. Manufacturer
    d. Lot number

40. A pharmacy technician is entering a new patient prescription into the system. A computerized alert indicates the medication interacts with another drug on the patient's profile. Which action should the technician take?
   a. Revise the patient's profile
   b. Inform the pharmacist
   c. Override the warning
   d. Contact the patient's healthcare provider

41. Which statement about anaphylactic reactions to medications is true?
   a. Anaphylactic reactions are almost always fatal.
   b. Anaphylactic reactions are common allergic reactions.
   c. Anaphylactic reactions include constricted airways and swelling of the tongue.
   d. Anaphylactic reactions typically occur hours after administration.

42. Which medication is commonly associated with adverse drug events (ADEs)?
   a. Carvedilol
   b. Acetaminophen
   c. Levothyroxine
   d. Rivaroxaban

43. Which medication is dispensable or saleable?
   a. A medication that is returned to stock after a waiting bin audit
   b. A medication that has expired
   c. A medication that was damaged upon delivery to the pharmacy
   d. A medication that was dispensed in error and returned to the pharmacy

44. Adverse reactions to medications should be reported to which entity?
   a. CDER
   b. MedWatch
   c. FAERS
   d. FDA

45. Which generic medication is indicated for the treatment of hypertension?
   a. Rosuvastatin
   b. Glyburide
   c. Pioglitazone
   d. Olmesartan

46. Which statement about controlled substance take-back programs is true?
   a. Collection kiosks may be placed in any public location for medication disposal.
   b. Collectors must be registered with the DEA to oversee the return of controlled substances.
   c. Mail-back envelopes should be identifiable as controlled substance returns.
   d. Receptacle liners should be clear so that the contents are visible prior to disposal.

47. An order is written for a patient to administer 60 units of U-100 insulin such as Humalog. How many milliliters does the patient need to draw up to obtain 60 units of insulin?
   a. 0.6 milliliters
   b. 0.4 milliliters
   c. 0.3 milliliters
   d. 0.2 milliliters

48. A patient is informed by the healthcare provider that they will require 100 mcg of levothyroxine daily to treat their hypothyroidism. The provider prescribes the dose in milligrams. How should the dose be written on the prescription?
    a. 1 mg
    b. 0.1 mg
    c. .1 mg
    d. 1.0 mg

49. Which statement about the off-label use of OTC and prescription medications is correct?
    a. Indications for off-label use are FDA-approved.
    b. Off-label drug usage is common practice.
    c. Indications for off-label use can be included in marketing material.
    d. Off-label drug indications can be included on the drug label.

50. Which statement about a medication's National Drug Code (NDC) is true?
    a. An NDC code is composed of two segments indicating the package size and manufacturer.
    b. The FDA's NDC registry lists finished drug products only.
    c. Only FDA approved drug products are required to have an NDC.
    d. The labeler code indicates the manufacturer of the drug.

51. A patient drops off a prescription that reads: Coumadin 1.0 mg, take 1 tablet PO daily, #30. Which part of the prescription requires clarification?
    a. Take 1 tablet.
    b. PO daily
    c. 1.0 mg
    d. #30

52. Which dietary supplement is recommended to maintain proper bone health?
    a. Fish oil
    b. Vitamin D
    c. Iron
    d. Echinacea

53. Which brand name medication is indicated for the treatment of fibromyalgia?
    a. Lyrica
    b. Horizant
    c. Amrix
    d. Relafen

54. How many tablets is the following Methotrexate prescription written for?

> Methotrexate 2.5 mg tablet
> # XVI
> Take 4T PO QW for RA

    a. 13 tablets
    b. 14 tablets
    c. 26 tablets
    d. 16 tablets

55. After opening, which brand of insulin remains stable refrigerated or at room temperature for up to twenty-eight days?
   a. Tresiba FlexTouch
   b. Levemir
   c. Lantus
   d. Toujeo

56. Which statement about the stability of medications is true?
   a. Reconstituted medications require refrigeration to maintain stability.
   b. Diluents do not affect a drug's stability.
   c. Multiple doses can be drawn from reconstituted SDV vials without compromising stability.
   d. Reconstitution of a medication significantly decreases drug stability.

57. A pharmacy technician is compounding multiple sterile products that will be administered to several patients. Which risk level would be assigned to this process?
   a. Low
   b. High
   c. Medium
   d. Severe

58. Which of the following is NOT a label requirement when dispensing a controlled substance to a patient?
   a. The prescription number
   b. The name of the patient
   c. The DEA schedule of the drug
   d. The name of the prescriber

59. A pharmacy technician is performing an order entry for prescribed Tylenol #3. The pharmacy technician notes that the patient was dispensed the same prescription one week ago. The current prescription was ordered by a different healthcare provider. Which action should the pharmacy technician take?
   a. Tell the patient the medication cannot be filled
   b. Continue entering the prescription into the system
   c. Inform the pharmacist of the findings
   d. Call the healthcare provider to clarify the current prescription

60. A prescription order is written to dispense 100 mg progesterone vaginal suppositories using a 2.3 g metal mold. How many grams of progesterone will need to be weighed to make thirty-five suppositories?
   a. 3.5 grams
   b. 350 grams
   c. 35 grams
   d. 3,500 grams

61. Which statement about the non-sterile preparation of an emulsion is correct?
   a. Non-sterile emulsions are thermodynamically stable liquid preparations.
   b. The mucilage formed in the wet method consists of two parts water and one part gum.
   c. Both the wet and dry methods follow the 4:2:1 ratio of 4 parts water, 2 parts oil, and 1 part gum.
   d. The primary emulsion formed in the dry method should be heated to 70°C.

62. Who is NOT responsible for ensuring an effective vaccine cold chain system is maintained?
   a. Vaccine administrators
   b. Vaccine manufacturers
   c. Vaccine recipients
   d. Vaccine distributors

63. A pharmacy technician is donning personal protective equipment (PPE) prior to entering a clean room. After donning shoe covers, which item does the pharmacy technician don next?
   a. Bouffant cap
   b. Gown
   c. Mask
   d. Sterile gloves

64. Which statement about the transfer of a controlled substance prescription is NOT correct?
   a. Schedule II prescriptions can be transferred between pharmacies one time only.
   b. Schedule V prescriptions can be transferred between pharmacies one time only unless the pharmacies share the same real-time database.
   c. Schedule III prescriptions can only be transferred between two DEA-registered pharmacies.
   d. Schedule IV prescription transfers must be communicated between two licensed pharmacists.

65. A pharmacy technician selects the incorrect medication during order entry. The error is caught as the label is placed on the medication container. Which action should the pharmacy technician take?
   a. Inform another pharmacy technician of the error
   b. Do nothing since the error was caught
   c. Document the error on an incident report
   d. Report the error to the healthcare provider

66. Below are examples of needle gauges. Which one has the smallest lumen?
   a. 18 G
   b. 25 G
   c. 30 G
   d. 28 G

67. What is a visually observable indicator that an oral suspension has lost stability?
   a. A change in color
   b. Loss of therapeutic potency
   c. A change in pH
   d. The presence of degradation byproducts

68. The anticoagulant Coumadin is available in multiple strengths. Which strength is NOT one of Coumadin's strengths?
   a. 1 mg
   b. 7.5 mg
   c. 4.5 mg
   d. 5 mg

69. Which of the following devices is most accurate for dosing oral liquid medications?
    a. Dosing cup
    b. Oral syringe
    c. Medicine dropper
    d. Dosing spoon

70. Which of the following is an example of a Class III medication recall?
    a. A stock bottle of Atorvastatin 20 mg tablets is found to contain some 40 mg tablets.
    b. The presence of particulates found in a vial of ceftriaxone injection.
    c. Gabapentin capsules found to not meet weight specifications during a QA check.
    d. A vial of insulin is found to be missing the lot number.

71. A pharmacist is verifying the accuracy of a dispensed medication. The pharmacist notes that the hard copy prescription stated a frequency of BID. The medication label reads "daily." What is this error classified as?
    a. Near-miss event
    b. Adverse effect
    c. Sentinel event
    d. Side effect

72. Which narrow therapeutic index (NTI) medication is used to treat thyroid conditions?
    a. Carbamazepine
    b. Synthroid
    c. Phenobarbital
    d. Vancomycin

73. A patient with an INR value greater than three is at risk for which condition or symptom?
    a. DVT
    b. Stroke
    c. Pulmonary embolism
    d. Hemorrhage

74. What is another name for an electrolyte substance that can be used to slow the rate of sedimentation in a compounded oral suspension?
    a. Levigating agent
    b. Viscosity enhancer
    c. Wetting agent
    d. Flocculating agent

75. Convert the following NDC from its standard FDA format to one that can be processed through an insurance provider: 54321-987-60.
    a. 54321-9870-60
    b. 054321-987-60
    c. 54321-0987-60
    d. 54321-987-060

76. Chapter <797> regulates and monitors facilities that handle compound sterile preparations. Which organization developed Chapter <797>?
    a. The Food and Drug Administration
    b. United States Pharmacopeial Convention
    c. Environmental Protection Agency
    d. Occupational Safety and Health Administration

77. Which statement about refilling prescriptions for controlled substances is correct?
    a. Schedule V controlled substances are refillable for six months from the date written.
    b. Schedule IV controlled substances are refillable for one year from the date written.
    c. Schedule III controlled substances are refillable for one year from the date written.
    d. Schedule II controlled substances cannot be refilled.

78. Which statement about coalescence of an emulsion is correct?
    a. Coalescence is a disruption of interfacial tension between internal and external phases of an emulsion.
    b. An emulsion that has coalesced will still retain therapeutic efficacy.
    c. Coalescence causes the complete separation of the internal and external phases.
    d. Coalescence is a reversible process.

79 A batch of compounded progesterone SR 175-mg capsules should have an average weight of 0.287 g. If the margin of error is within 5%, which weight would be acceptable?
    a. 0.316 g
    b. 0.331g
    c. 0.301g
    d. 0.258g

80. Which of the following is NOT a potentially fatal consequence of precipitate formation resulting from chemically incompatible intravenous solutions?
    a. Administration of inactivated medication
    b. A lethal overdose of the active ingredient
    c. Administration of toxic compounds
    d. Particulate embolism

81. Which DEA schedule is for controlled substances that have no legitimate medical purpose?
    a. Schedule I
    b. Schedule II
    c. Schedule III
    d. Schedule IV

82. A patient arrives to the pharmacy to pick up a medication. Before handing the medication to the patient, the pharmacy technician compares the prescription label to the original healthcare provider order. The pharmacy technician has performed which check in the medication dispensing process?
    a. Dispensing process
    b. Verification process
    c. Point-of-sale
    d. Prescription drop-off

83. Which statement about the storage of light-sensitive medications is accurate?
    a. Photodegradation of light-sensitive medications requires repeated or prolonged exposure to light.
    b. Artificial lighting does not affect light-sensitive medications.
    c. Light-sensitive medications should be stored or packaged in amber vials or other materials that block light.
    d. Drug excipients are unaffected by exposure to light.

84. Which of the following safeguard strategies are recommended for high-alert medications?
    I.    Independent double-checks
    II.   Stocking large quantities of the medications
    III.  Cautionary labeling
    IV.   Computerized alerts

    a. All of the above
    b. Choices I, III, and IV
    c. Choices I, II, and IV
    d. Choices II, III, and IV

85. The Federal Combat Methamphetamine Epidemic Act (CMEA) restricts the purchase quantity on which OTC medication?
    a. Phenylephrine
    b. Dextromethorphan
    c. Guaifenesin
    d. Pseudoephedrine

86. A pharmacy technician is receiving training on infection control measures when handling medications. Which of the following is true about hand hygiene?
    a. It only needs to be performed when hands are visibly soiled.
    b. Alcohol-based rubs are used to remove bacterial spores.
    c. Washing hands with soap and water should last at least 10 seconds.
    d. Hands should be thoroughly wet before applying soap.

87. Which statement about the temperature requirements of stored medications is true?
    a. The medication storage temperature can be found on the drug label.
    b. The controlled room temperature range is between 59°F and 86°F.
    c. Temperature excursions between 68°F and 77°F are permitted.
    d. Refrigerated medications are stored at 20°C to 25°C.

88. In general, what would be the maximum supply of clozapine dispensed to a patient who is in the clozapine registry and receives ANC monitoring every two weeks?
    a. 7-day supply
    b. 14-day supply
    c. 30-day supply
    d. 90-day supply

89. For which medication name should tall man lettering be used?
    a. Morphine
    b. Pregabalin
    c. Bupropion
    d. Furosemide

90. Which sig code indicates a sublingual route of administration?
    a. PO
    b. OS
    c. AU
    d. SL

# Answer Explanations

**1. A:** Choice *A* is correct because a pharmacy technician can assist a pharmacist with creating a patient profile, setting up medication review appointments, and collecting patient data. All these aspects are important parts of medication therapy management (MTM). The main goal is to ensure patient compliance and safe administration of medications. Choices *B*, *C*, and *D* are not correct because providing medication counseling to patients is a pharmacist's duty.

**2. B:** Choice *B* is the correct choice. Choice *B*, Augmentin suspension, is a dry powder that is shelf stable at room temperature; however, that stability decreases considerably once it is dispensed because it is a drug that must be reconstituted. Once mixed, it must be refrigerated and is only stable for seven days. Choice *A*, Crestor tablets, and Choice *D*, Cephalexin capsules, are incorrect because they are both solid dosage formulations that generally have a lengthy shelf life when stored properly. These formulations can often remain shelf stable for at least a year or longer even after being dispensed. Choice *C* is also incorrect because oral suspensions such as Tussionex are shelf stable as non-refrigerated liquids and can remain stable under those same conditions after being dispensed.

**3. B:** Choice *B*, Keflex (cephalexin) is the correct choice. Keflex is a first-generation cephalosporin that is used in both human and veterinary medicine to treat various skin infections, ear infections, strep throat, and pneumonia. Choice *A* is incorrect since Ceftin (cefuroxime) is a second-generation cephalosporin. Choices *C* and *D* are incorrect because Omnicef (cefdinir) and Suprax (cefixime) are both third-generation cephalosporins.

**4. C:** Choice *C* is the correct choice. Reverse distributors can and do help redistribute saleable medications throughout the supply chain, but they cannot dispense medications directly to patients. Choice *A* is incorrect because reverse distributors do remove unwanted prescription medications from the supply chain. Choice *B* is also incorrect because reverse distributors do safely destroy recalled, expired, or damaged medications. Choice *D* is incorrect because reverse distributors can help pharmacies receive credit from manufacturers for returned medications.

**5. A:** Choice *A* is the correct choice. Toprol XL is an extended-release cardiovascular medication that is used to treat hypertension, and it belongs to a class of medications known as beta blockers. Toprol XL acts to selectively block beta-1 adrenergic receptors and beta-2 adrenoreceptors. This mechanism relaxes the heart muscle, reducing overall cardiac output, which ultimately results in a reduction in blood pressure. Choices *B* and *C*, angiotensin-converting enzyme (ACE) inhibitors and angiotensin receptor blockers (ARBs), are incorrect. ACEs and ARBs are both cardiovascular medications used to treat hypertension; however, their mechanisms are different. In the body, the enzyme angiotensin I is converted to angiotensin II, a substance that causes narrowing of the blood vessels. ACEs reduce this narrowing by inhibiting the conversion of angiotensin I to angiotensin II while ARBs prevent angiotensin II from working to narrow the blood vessels. Choice *D* is incorrect because CCBs relax the heart muscle by inhibiting calcium ion conduction by the smooth vascular heart muscle, which reduces the contractive force of the heart.

**6. B:** Choice *B* is the correct choice. Hazardous waste transporters move waste using various transportation routes including public roads, highways, and waterways. The Department of Transportation (DOT) is responsible for ensuring that transporters of hazardous materials comply with all guidelines and protocols for the movement of hazardous waste products among these routes. When transporting hazardous waste between locations, transporters must comply with all DOT requirements regarding transport containers, labeling, manifests, and protocols in case of a hazardous waste spill. Choice *A*, the

EPA, is incorrect because the EPA does not oversee the actual movement of hazardous waste. The EPA works in conjunction with the DOT regarding environmental concerns, for example, hazardous waste spills that occur while waste is in transport. The Occupational Safety and Health Administration (OSHA), Choice *C*, is incorrect because OSHA regulates the safety of employees in the workplace, not the transport process itself. The DEA, Choice *D*, is also incorrect because the DEA regulates the movement and custody of controlled substances rather than hazardous waste.

**7. D:** Choice *D* is correct because a root cause analysis (RCA) focuses on identifying systemic factors that led to an adverse event. An RCA is aimed at improving a process as opposed to punitive action against an individual. Choice *A* is not correct because a drug utilization review (DUR) is a quality assurance program that aims to improve the overall prescribing, dispensing, and use of medications. Choice *B* is not correct because a failure mode and effect analysis (FMEA) identifies the possibility of error and the effect that errors can have on patients. Choice *C* is not correct because continuous quality improvement (CQI) is an ongoing process in team-based environments that helps to emphasize shared accountability.

**8. C:** Choice *C*, pantoprazole is the correct choice because it is the generic name for the PPI Protonix. Choices *A*, *B*, and *D* are incorrect since lansoprazole is the generic name for the PPI Prevacid, esomeprazole is the generic name for the PPI Nexium, and omeprazole is the generic name for the PPI Prilosec.

**9. D:** Choice *D*, amoxicillin/clavulanate, is the correct choice because this combination penicillin-derived antibiotic is the generic for Augmentin. The macrolide antibiotic azithromycin, Choice *A*, is incorrect because it is the generic name for Zithromax. The fluoroquinolone antibiotic ciprofloxacin, Choice *B*, is also incorrect because this is the generic for Cipro. Choice *C*, the macrolide antibiotic known as clarithromycin, is also incorrect because it is the generic for Biaxin.

**10. B:** Choice *B* is the correct choice. One teaspoon or 1 TSP is equivalent to 5 milliliters. The sig code BID indicates twice daily, and it is to be given for 10 days. The amount of medication needed to complete the ten-day course of therapy can be calculated as follows:

$$2 \text{ TSP} = 10 \text{ ml}; 10 \text{ ml} \times 2 \text{ times daily} \times 10 \text{ days} = 200 \text{ milliliters}$$

Since Choice *B* is the correct choice, Choices *A*, *C*, and *D* are incorrect.

**11. B:** Choice *B* is the correct answer because therapeutically equivalent medications must have identical safety, therapeutic, and efficacy profiles. Choice *A* is incorrect because the medications must be bioequivalent to one another. Choice *C* is incorrect since therapeutically equivalent medications are also required to be pharmaceutically equivalent. To be pharmaceutically equivalent, they must be the same strength, have the same route of administration, and have the same dosage formulation. Choice *D* is incorrect since bioavailability, the amount of medication delivered, and the site of administration are not the same in all dosage forms.

**12. A:** Choice *A* is correct because metformin is an antidiabetic medication used to treat type 2 diabetes mellitus, a chronic illness. Maintenance medications are prescribed to treat long-term conditions. Choice *B* is not correct because levofloxacin is an antibiotic used to treat acute infections. This medication is prescribed short-term. Choice *C* is not correct because diphenhydramine is used to treat acute allergic reactions. This medication is not intended for long-term use. Choice *D* is not correct because oxycodone is a controlled substance that is heavily regulated. This medication is not considered a maintenance medication and has refill restrictions.

13. C: Choice *C* is the correct choice. Product recalls are issued by the FDA or the manufacturer to eliminate or correct products that are in violation of laws administered by the FDA. Such violations could provoke legal action by the FDA if not corrected. Market withdrawals, in contrast, are issued by the manufacturer to correct or remove products with relatively insignificant concerns that are in violation of FDA regulations but are not likely to result in litigation. Choice *A* is incorrect because the FDA does issue a weekly recall report called the Enforcement Report which contains any product recall information as well as updates on previously issued recalls. Choice *B* is incorrect because MedWatch is a method consumers and healthcare professionals can use to report safety concerns about any FDA-regulated product. Choice *D* is incorrect because 1) most manufacturers do issue product recalls voluntarily and 2) manufacturers are responsible for issuing product recalls even if it is at the suggestion of the FDA. The FDA will, however, step in if the manufacturer blatantly ignores reported concerns.

14. A: Choice *A*, is the correct choice because Monodox and Doryx are pharmaceutical alternatives of each other. They have the same active ingredient, doxycycline; however, they are different salt formulations, monohydrate and hyclate, respectively. Choice *B* is incorrect since both Fortamet and Glumetza are therapeutically equivalent medications. They are both extended-release formulations of metformin and are available in the same strengths. Choices *C* and *D* are both incorrect as well. Haloperidol is the generic for Haldol and enoxaparin is the generic for Lovenox; therefore, both pairs are therapeutic equivalent medications.

15. C: Choice *C* is correct because a telephone number, home address, and date of birth are acceptable forms of identification. If a patient's address or telephone number has changed, the pharmacy technician should ensure the patient profile is updated. Choices *A*, *B*, and *D* are not correct because an allergy is not unique to a particular patient and the patient's first and last name are both required. The first name by itself is not sufficient to identify a patient.

16. D: Choice *D*, DAW (dispense as written) 1, is the correct choice since it prohibits the pharmacy from substitution per the physician's wishes. Choice *A* is incorrect because the DAW 4 product selection code is used in situations where the generic drug is not in stock, allowing substitution of the brand medication in place of the generic. Choice *B*, DAW 2, is incorrect because this is the product selection code that is used when the patient requests the dispensing of a brand medication. Choice *C* is also incorrect because the DAW 0 product selection code is used most often and permits generic substitution since neither the prescriber, patient, nor insurance have declared a preference.

17. C: Choice *C* is the correct choice. DEA Form 106 is the DEA form used to report the loss or theft of any controlled substances. Choice *A* is incorrect because DEA Form 222 is the requisition form used to order Schedule I and II controlled substances. Choice *B* is incorrect because DEA Form 41 is the form used to document the surrender and destruction of controlled substances by a reverse distributor. Choice *D* is also incorrect because DEA Form 107 is used to report the theft or loss of listed chemical substances that are used to make controlled medications.

18. B: Choice *B* is the correct answer. Flagyl is an antibiotic/antiprotozoal that can have severe side effects if taken with alcohol. In addition to severe abdominal cramping, nausea, and vomiting, mixing Flagyl with alcohol can lower an individual's seizure threshold. Choices *A*, *C*, and *D* are incorrect because Macrobid, amoxicillin, and Keflex are all antibiotics; however, they are not contraindicated with alcohol.

19. A: Choice *A* is correct because tall man lettering is a strategy that was developed to distinguish look-alike/sound-alike (LASA) medication names. Tall man lettering uses mixed-case letters (uppercase and lowercase) to emphasize differences in medication names. Choice *B* is not correct because high-alert medications are those that have the potential to cause significant harm if prescribed, dispensed, or

administered incorrectly. Tall man lettering is not intended specifically for this purpose. Choice *C* is not correct because narcotic medications are categorized by their potential for misuse. Tall man lettering does not serve this purpose. Choice *D* is not correct because the fact that a medication is commonly dispensed does not automatically meant that it is a LASA medication that would utilize tall man lettering.

**20. A:** Choice *A* is the correct choice since the use of an NSAID such as the drug ibuprofen with an anticoagulant drug like Coumadin is an example of a drug-drug interaction. Choices *B, C,* and *D* consequently are incorrect since NSAIDs and anticoagulants are not disease states, nutrients, or dietary supplements.

**21. B:** Choice *B* is the correct choice. Hives are the result of an adverse effect caused by an allergic reaction or sensitivity to the medication. Choices *A, C,* and *D* are incorrect because many antibiotic medications can cause gastrointestinal side effects since they can disrupt the natural flora present in the digestive tract. Antibiotics do not distinguish between the bad bacteria they are intended to treat and the good bacteria that live in the intestinal tract. Therefore, common side effects of antibiotic mediations are GI upset including indigestion, nausea, vomiting, diarrhea, abdominal pain, and cramping. These side effects can be lessened by adding a probiotic to the diet while taking a course of antibiotics.

**22. B:** Choice *B* is correct because a two-dimensional data matrix barcode has the primary purpose of identifying and tracking prescription medications as they are distributed throughout the United States. Two-dimensional data matrix bar codes must contain the national drug code (NDC), serial number, expiration date, and lot number of the medication. Choice *A* is not correct because the one-dimensional linear barcode has the primary purpose of reducing medication errors. It contains the NDC for each product. Choice *C* is not correct because the Universal Product Code (UPC) is used to keep track of inventory and sales of retail products sold within the country. The UPC is a 12-digit number that identifies the product. Choice *D* is not correct because the two-dimensional quick response (QR) code is a barcode that provides informational data only. This barcode is not an FDA requirement.

**23. A:** Choice *A* is the correct choice since Claritin-D is a combination of the allergy medication loratadine and the decongestant pseudoephedrine. Pseudoephedrine medications relieve congestion in the nasal passages by constricting blood vessels, which opens the airway. This constriction of the blood vessels is potentially dangerous in individuals with hypertension, especially if it is uncontrolled, because the constriction can cause the heart rate and blood pressure to increase. Choice *B*, Allegra, is incorrect. Allegra is an antihistamine used to treat allergy symptoms. Choice *C* is also incorrect; Mucinex DM is a combination OTC medication that contains the expectorant guaifenesin and the cough suppressant dextromethorphan, both of which are safe to use in patients with hypertension. Choice *D*, Coricidin HBP, is an OTC combination of an antihistamine chlorpheniramine and dextromethorphan. Coricidin HBP is used to treat cough and cold symptoms in patients with hypertension; therefore, Choice *D* is incorrect.

**24. A:** Choice *A* is the correct choice. Bronkaid is an OTC medication indicated for the treatment of asthma symptoms. Bronkaid contains the expectorant guaifenesin and the bronchodilator ephedrine. Ephedrine is a regulated ingredient under the CMEA, which mandates purchase limitations and requires that the product be kept behind the pharmacy counter. Choice *B* is incorrect because Sudafed PE is a decongestant that contains phenylephrine. Phenylephrine is an alternative to the CMEA-regulated pseudoephedrine; however, phenylephrine itself is not subject to CMEA restrictions. Choice *C* is incorrect because Alavert is an antihistamine whose active ingredient is loratadine and is not subject to CMEA regulations. Choice *D* is incorrect because Mucinex contains the expectorant guaifenesin, which is also not covered under CMEA regulations.

**25. D:** Choice *D* is correct because the purpose of an NDC is to identify medications based on their unique manufacturing properties. An NDC provides information such as the proprietary name, labeler, and marketing start date. Choice *A* is not correct because an NDC does not imply that the drug has been approved by the FDA. The process for FDA approval is not related to the assignment of an NDC. Choice *B* is not correct because assignment of an NDC number does not mean the drug product has been defined as a drug by federal law. Choice *C* is not correct because inclusion in the NDC directory does not confirm eligibility for reimbursement by Medicare, Medicaid, or third-party payers.

**26. D:** Choice *D* is the correct choice. An alligation grid should be used to set up the ratios and proportions as follows:

H = Higher concentration = 80%
L = Lower concentration = 60%
D = Desired concentration = 75%

| 80% | | $(75\%-60\%) = 15$ parts |
|---|---|---|
| | 75% | |
| 60% | | $(80\%-75\%) = 5$ parts |

Add the two values in the right-hand column to get the total number of parts needed (15 + 5 = 20) and then set up the proportions for each solution by placing the number of parts needed over the total number of parts.

80% alcohol solution (H):

$$\frac{15 \text{ parts}}{20 \text{ parts}}$$

60% alcohol solution (L):

$$\frac{5 \text{ parts}}{20 \text{ parts}}$$

Next, multiply the proportions by the total volume ordered, 480 ml.

80% solution (H):

$$\frac{480 \text{ ml} \times 15}{20} = 120 \text{ ml}$$

60% solution (L):

$$\frac{480 \text{ ml} \times 5}{20} = 360 \text{ ml}$$

The technician will therefore need 120 milliliters of the 80% alcohol solution and 360 milliliters of the 60% alcohol solution to prepare 480 milliliters of 75% alcohol solution. Since Choice *D* is the correct choice, Choices *A*, *B*, and *C* are incorrect.

**27. C:** Choice *C* is the correct choice since Finasteride is currently listed on the CDC's NIOSH list of hazardous medications. Finasteride is an FDA Category X medication, which means it is proven to affect the development of the male fetus of women who are or may become pregnant. Choices *A*, *B*, and *D* are incorrect because they are not on the NIOSH hazardous medication list.

**28. B:** Choice *B* is the correct choice. DuoNeb solution must be administered via a nebulizer machine. DuoNeb is an inhaled liquid medication that is added to the chamber of the nebulizer. The nebulizer atomizes the liquid solution into a mist that is slowly breathed in over time by the patient. Choice *A*, MDI, and Choice *C*, DPI, are types of inhaled medications, not administration devices; therefore, Choices *A* and *C* are incorrect. Choice *D* is also incorrect because an actuator is a device used to administer compressed liquid medications such as MDIs, not liquid nebulizing solutions such as DuoNeb.

**29. C:** Choice *C* is correct because neuromuscular blocking agents such as rocuronium, vecuronium, and succinylcholine are high-alert medications. Neuromuscular agents can cause significant respiratory depression, malignant hyperthermia, and hyperkalemia if not administered and monitored appropriately. Choices *A*, *B*, and *D* are not correct because proton pump inhibitors, anticonvulsants, and intravenous antibiotics are not medications that have been determined to be high-alert medications.

**30. B:** Choice *B* is correct because a concurrent drug utilization review (DUR) monitors the patient's ongoing therapy. This process allows for changes in therapy based on clinical manifestations and the patient's response to the medication. Choice *A* is not correct because a retrospective DUR is performed after the patient has received the medication and completed therapy. Choice *C* is not correct because a prospective DUR evaluates the patient's planned therapy and is performed before the patient receives the medication. Choice *D* is not correct because "historical" is not a type of DUR.

**31. A:** Choice *A* is the correct choice since the dosing instructions for Tamiflu for the prophylactic treatment of influenza exposure are to take one capsule once daily for ten days. Choice *C* is incorrect because the dosing instructions for Tamiflu for an individual that has tested positive for the influenza virus is one capsule taken twice daily for five days. Choices *B* and *D* are not dosing instructions for Tamiflu and are therefore incorrect.

**32. D:** Choice *D* is the correct choice; because ophthalmic medications are intended to be administered in the eye, which is susceptible to infections, the medications must be sterile. The statement that the medications must be non-sterile is false. Choice *A* is incorrect because ophthalmic medications are intended to be instilled in the eye (the statement is true). Choice *B* is incorrect because ophthalmic medications are available in multiple dosage formulations that include solutions, suspensions, ointments, and inserts (the statement is true). Choice *C* is incorrect because routes of administration of ophthalmic medications include the eye and sometimes the ear (the statement is true).

**33. A:** Choice *A* is the correct choice. A ratio shows the relationship between two quantities. For two ratios to be equal, the units of each numerator must be the same; therefore, Choice *A* is the correct choice. Choice *B* is incorrect because it is a true statement; to solve a proportion equation composed of 4 terms, three of those terms must be known. Choice *C* is incorrect because it is a true statement; the units of each denominator must be the same. Choice *D* is incorrect because it is a true statement; a proportion equation is essentially a statement of equality; therefore, the two ratios composing the proportion must be equal.

**34. D:** Choice *D* is correct because the information that should be reported to the MedWatch program includes unexpected side effects of medications; product quality issues such as defects, precipitates, or unexpected colors and odors; therapeutic failures that can occur when medications are switched from one generic brand to another; and medication errors due to look-alike/sound-alike packaging. Choices *A, B,* and *C* are not correct because expired medications should be handled according to facility policy; they do not have to be reported to MedWatch.

**35. B:** Choice *B* is the correct choice. U-100 insulin contains one hundred units of insulin per milliliter; therefore, there are ten units of insulin in one tenth of a milliliter of insulin. If a patient is to administer three tenths of a milliliter of U-100 insulin, or 0.3 ml, then the patient will be injecting thirty units of insulin. Choice *A* is the number of units in a 0.3 ml dose of a U-500 insulin. Choice *C* is the number in a 0.3 ml dose of a U-200 insulin. Choice *D* is the number of units in a 0.3 ml dose of a U-300 insulin; therefore, Choices *A, C,* and *D* are incorrect.

**36. C:** Choice *C* is the correct choice. Household wastes are solid wastes per the RCRA definition. Although household waste might contain hazardous materials, it is excluded because handling and disposal under current RCRA guidelines would be impractical, considering the amount that is generated in households across the United States. Choice *A*, F-listed waste, is incorrect because these are hazardous non-source-specific wastes and are therefore regulated under the RCRA guidelines. Choices *B* and *D* are also incorrect because they are both hazardous source-specific wastes that include pharmaceutical wastes and are therefore also regulated under the RCRA guidelines.

**37. C:** Choice *C,* Vigamox, is the correct choice. Levaquin is among a class of antibiotics known as fluoroquinolones, which also includes the ophthalmic medication Vigamox. Cross sensitivity is common among medications in the same class; therefore, someone with an allergy to Levaquin (levofloxacin) is likely to have a reaction to Vigamox (moxifloxacin) since they are both fluroquinolones. Choice *A,* Duricef (cefadroxil) is a cephalosporin. Choice *B,* Cleocin (clindamycin), is a lincosamide. Neither Duricef nor Cleocin are fluoroquinolones; therefore, Choice *A* and Choice *B* are incorrect. Zyvox, Choice *D,* is also incorrect because it is in a class of antibiotics called oxazolidinones.

**38. D:** Choice *D* is the correct choice. Common side effects of the urinary analgesic Pyridium include rash, pruritus, dyspepsia, nausea, anemia, headache, and discoloration of the urine. Choices *A, B,* and *C* are incorrect because rhinorrhea (runny nose), diarrhea, and vomiting are not common side effects of Pyridium.

**39. D:** Choice *D* is the correct choice. When a recall has been issued for a medication, medical device, or dietary supplement, the manufacturer will provide specific information regarding the affected products such as the NDC number, lot number, package size, and expiration date. Choices *A, B,* and *C* are incorrect since the NDC, the expiration date, and the package size, while helpful, do not give the exact batch of product that has been affected by the recall. In addition, if the issue lies with the raw materials, then multiple lots, multiple NDCs, and multiple package sizes might be affected. It is the lot number that provides this information; therefore, Choice *D* is the correct choice.

**40. B:** Choice *B* is correct because the pharmacy technician should inform the pharmacist regarding any warnings and alerts when performing an order entry. The pharmacist has the duty to verify drug interactions and collaborate with the healthcare provider to change the medication if needed. Choice *A* is not correct because revising the patient's profile is not a safe action unless the patient's condition or medication therapy has changed. Choice *C* is not correct because overriding a drug interaction is not within the scope of practice for a pharmacy technician. Choice *D* is not correct because any alerts during order entry should be referred to the pharmacist, who will contact the healthcare provider if needed.

**41. C:** Choice *C* is the correct choice. Anaphylactic reactions are allergic reactions in which the medication elicits a systemic immune system response. Signs of anaphylaxis include skin rash, runny nose, sweating, rapid heart rate, hives, and swelling of the tongue, which can constrict the airway, making it difficult to breathe. Choice *A* is incorrect because, although anaphylaxis has the potential to be fatal, it is most often treatable with a shot of epinephrine. Choice *B* is incorrect because anaphylaxis is a rare allergic reaction. Choice *D* is incorrect because anaphylaxis typically occurs within minutes of administering the medication

**42. D:** Choice *D* is correct because rivaroxaban is an anticoagulant used in the prevention of deep vein thrombosis. Anticoagulants are among the most common medications involved in adverse drug events (ADEs). Choice *A* is not correct because carvedilol is an antihypertensive medication used in the treatment of high blood pressure. Carvedilol is not in the class of medications most commonly associated with ADEs. Choice *B* is not correct because acetaminophen is an analgesic, anti-pyretic medication commonly used to treat mild pain and fever. Acetaminophen is not associated with an increased incidence of ADEs. Choice *C* is not correct because levothyroxine is a synthetic hormone used in the treatment of hypothyroidism. Synthetic hormones are not associated with an increased risk of ADEs.

**43. A:** Choice *A* is the correct choice. Medications that are returned to stock are still dispensable since they were never picked up by the original patients. These medications must be returned to the inventory, any insurance claims reversed, and they must be relabeled with a return-to-stock label so that they can be used for the next patient. Choices *B* and *C* are incorrect because medications that are deemed non-saleable or non-dispensable include medications that have been expired, damaged, or adulterated. Choice *D* is incorrect because medication that has been returned to the pharmacy after being dispensed is deemed non-dispensable. Regardless of the reason it was returned, the law does not permit medications that have left the pharmacy to be dispensed to another patient, as the handling and storage conditions after leaving the pharmacy are unknown.

**44. B:** Choice *B*, MedWatch, is the correct choice. MedWatch is the reporting system that allows the reporting of adverse reactions to medications. Choice *A* is incorrect because the CDER, or Center for Drug Evaluation and Research, performs clinical reviews of the reported events. Choice *C* is incorrect because MedWatch collects the reports, but the collected information is compiled in the FDA's Adverse Event Reporting Systems database (FAERS). FAERS does not collect the initial reports. Choice *D* is incorrect because, although both MedWatch and FAERS operate under the FDA, the FDA does not collect the initial reports.

**45. D:** Choice *D*, olmesartan, is the generic equivalent to Benicar and is indicated in the treatment of hypertension; therefore, Choice *D* is the correct choice. Choice *A* is incorrect because rosuvastatin, or Crestor, is a cardiovascular agent indicated in the treatment of hyperlipidemia. Choice *B*, glyburide (Diabeta), and Choice *C*, pioglitazone (Actos), are both indicated for the treatment of type II diabetes. Choices *B* and *C* are therefore incorrect.

**46. B:** Choice *B* is the correct choice. Any entity that collects controlled substances for disposal must be registered with the DEA. Choice *A* is incorrect because medication receptacles and kiosks must be in a secured location; this is usually inside a DEA-registered waste collector facility such as a hospital, law enforcement agency, or pharmacy. Choices *C* and *D* are also incorrect because controlled substances should be collected and returned in discreet liners or envelopes to prevent diversion of the medications.

**47. A:** Choice *A* is the correct choice. Insulin is often dosed in units, but physicians may still write the dose in milliliters. Thus, insulin syringes often have both units and milliliters printed on the barrel to avoid confusion. U-100 insulin refers to the units of insulin per one milliliter of solution. One milliliter of U-100 insulin therefore contains 100 units of insulin. If one milliliter of insulin solution contains 100 units of insulin, then 0.6 milliliters of insulin solution would contain 60 units of insulin. Choices *B, C,* and *D* are incorrect since Choice *B,* 0.4 milliliter, contains 40 units of insulin; Choice *C,* 0.3 milliliters, contains 30 units of insulin; and Choice *D,* 0.2 milliliters, contains 20 units of insulin.

**48. B:** Choice *B* is correct because 100 mcg (micrograms) are equal to 0.1 mg (milligrams). To avoid medication errors, dosages with decimal points should include a leading zero. Choice *A* is not correct because 1 mg is equal to 1,000 mcg, 10 times the intended dose. Choice *C* is not correct because dosages with decimal points should be written with a leading zero. A prescription of .1 mg can be easily confused with 1 mg. Choice *D* is not correct because 1.0 mg is an incorrect conversion for the intended dose, as shown above. Additionally, the use of a trailing zero can lead to a medication error.

**49. B:** Choice *B* is the correct choice because off-label use of medications is a common practice in pharmacy. Choice *A* is incorrect because these types of indications are not FDA-approved. Choice *C* is incorrect because drug manufacturers are only allowed to market a medication for FDA-approved indications. Choice *D* is incorrect because drug label cannot promote any indication that has not been approved by the FDA.

**50. D:** Choice *D* is the correct choice. The NDC code is made up of three segments: the labeler code, the drug code, and the package code. The first segment is referred to as the labeler code; it is specific to the manufacturer and is assigned by the FDA. The second segment refers to the specific drug, while the third segment refers to the package size. Choice *A* is incorrect because the NDC code is made up of three segments rather than two. Choices *B* and *C* are incorrect choices because the FDA requires all unfinished and finished drug products be assigned an NDC code including bulk powders, drug components, and APIs, but these products do not necessarily have to be approved for use by the FDA.

**51. C:** Choice *C* is correct because 1.0 mg is written with a trailing zero, a prescription practice that can lead to dosage errors. Trailing zeros should be avoided because a dosage like 1.0 mg can be easily mistaken for 10 mg. The prescription should be clarified to ensure the dose is meant to be 1 mg. Choice *A* is not correct because "take 1 tablet" is written appropriately. Numerical values are acceptable. Choice *B* is not correct because PO is an acceptable abbreviation; PO refers to "by mouth." Choice *D* is not correct because #30 refers to the quantity of tablets to be dispensed. This is written correctly.

**52. B:** Choice *B,* vitamin D, is the correct choice. Vitamin D works with calcium to prevent bone loss and improve overall bone health. Choice *A,* fish oil, is a source of omega-3 fatty acids which, in conjunction with a healthy diet and exercise, can help reduce triglycerides. It does not help maintain bone health. Choice *C,* iron, is incorrect because it is a dietary supplement indicated in the treatment of anemia caused by iron deficiency. Echinacea, Choice *D,* is incorrect because it is an herbal dietary supplement recommended to boost immune system health.

**53. A:** Choice *A,* Lyrica, is the correct choice. Lyrica is a Schedule V controlled medication that is indicated for the treatment of fibromyalgia. Choice *B* is incorrect because Horizant is an extended-release formulation of gabapentin indicated for the treatment of post-herpetic neuralgia and restless leg syndrome. Choice *C,* Amrix, is incorrect because it is an extended-release formulation of the muscle relaxer known by its generic name cyclobenzaprine; however, it is used to treat muscle spasms and not fibromyalgia. Choice *D*, Relafen, also known by the generic name nabumetone, is also incorrect because it is an NSAID indicated in the treatment of arthritis.

**54. D:** Choice *D* is the correct choice. Roman numerals are often used in pharmacy to indicate the quantity being prescribed. For this prescription order the prescribed quantity, XVI, is 16 tablets. The Roman numeral X stands for 10, the Roman numeral V stands for 5, and the Roman numeral I stands for 1. The placement of the I to the right of V indicates addition; therefore, X (10) + VI (5 + 1) = 16. Hence, Choice *D* is the correct choice. Choice *A*, 13 tablets, would be written XIII. Choice *B*, 14 tablets, would be written XIV. Choice *C*, 26 tablets, would be written XXVI.

**55. C**: Lantus, Choice *C*, is the correct choice since it is the only medication listed here that can remain stable refrigerated or at room temperature for up to twenty-eight days. Choice *A*, Tresiba FlexTouch, is an insulin pen that can remain stable refrigerated or at room temperature for up to fifty-six days after opening. Levemir vials, Choice *B*, are stable up to forty-two days under the same conditions. Choices *A* and *B* are therefore incorrect since they are stable for greater than twenty-eight days. Toujeo, Choice *D*, should not be refrigerated after opening, but it is stable for up to forty-two days at room temperature. Therefore, Choice *D* is also incorrect.

**56. D:** Choice *D* is the correct choice. Reconstitutable drugs are generally more stable in their dry powder form. Reconstitution of a medication increases the potential for microbial growth and decreases the stability of the medication. Choice *A* is incorrect because, while some reconstituted medications such as antibiotics and injectables require refrigeration to maintain stability after being reconstituted, not all reconstituted medications require refrigeration. Choice *B* is incorrect because diluents that are used to reconstitute medications can decrease the medication's stability, which may vary depending on the diluent used. Choice *C* is incorrect because single dose vials (SDVs) of medications are intended for only one dose to be drawn after reconstitution even if the entire volume is not being administered. SDVs do not always contain preservatives; therefore, multiple draws can introduce bacteria and affect the stability of the medication.

**57. C:** Choice *C* is correct because compounding sterile products that will be administered to several patients or be used by the same patient multiple times is categorized as a medium-level risk. Choice *A* is not correct because low-level risks include manual mixing of up to three manufactured products to create one sterile product. Choice *B* is not correct because a high risk level is assigned to the process of making a sterile solution from non-sterile bulk powders or mixing sterile ingredients in a device that is non-sterile prior to producing a final sterile product. Choice *D* is not correct because "severe" is not a recognized risk level.

**58. C:** Choice *C* is the correct choice. Per the Title 21 Code of Federal Regulations, the DEA schedule of a medication is required to be on the stock bottle but not on the medication container that is dispensed to the patient. Choices *A*, *B*, and *D* are incorrect because the medication container that is given to the patient has federal labeling requirements that include the prescription number, the patient's name, the prescriber's name, the date the medication was filled, the directions for use, and any auxiliary labeling explaining cautionary information.

**59. C:** Choice *C* is correct because the pharmacist should be informed of prescription duplications for controlled substances. Tylenol #3 is a Schedule III controlled substance that is strictly regulated to avoid misuse. Choice *A* is not correct because refusing to fill a patient's medication is not within the pharmacy technician's scope of practice. There may be special circumstances surrounding the new prescription that a pharmacist needs to verify. Choice *B* is not correct because dispensing controlled substances should be carefully monitored and regulated to avoid misuse. Choice *D* is not correct because calling the healthcare provider to clarify the new prescription is not the role of the pharmacy technician. The pharmacy technician should inform the pharmacist of the concern.

**60. A:** Choice *A* is the correct choice. The amount of progesterone powder can be calculated by multiplying the strength needed per suppository by the number of suppositories needed. Calculate as follows:

$$100 \text{ mg per suppository} \times 35 \text{ suppositories} = 3{,}500 \text{ mg}$$

Because the question asks for the answer in grams, covert 3,500 milligrams to grams. Since we know 1 gram is equivalent to 1,000 milligrams, set up the equation and solve for *x*.

$$3{,}500 \text{ mg} \times \left(\frac{1 \text{ g}}{1{,}000 \text{ mg}}\right) = \frac{3{,}500 \text{ g}}{1{,}000} = 3.5 \text{ grams}$$

Therefore, 3.5 grams of progesterone powder will be needed to prepare thirty-five 100 mg vaginal suppositories. Choices *B*, *C*, and *D* are incorrect amounts of progesterone powder.

**61. B:** Choice *B* is the correct choice. The first step in the wet method is to make the mucilage by triturating 2 parts water and 1 part gum. Choice *A* is incorrect because non-sterile emulsion preparations are composed of ingredients that are immiscible, such as oil in water or water in oil. This type of mixture is therefore thermodynamically unstable and usually requires an emulsifying agent for stabilization. Choice *C* is incorrect because both the wet and dry methods of emulsion preparation use a ratio of 4:2:1; however, it is 4 parts oil, 2 parts water, and 1 part gum. Choice *D* is incorrect because neither the dry nor the wet method requires the addition of heat. The beaker method requires the oil-soluble and water-soluble components to be mixed separately, then heated to approximately 70°C (158°F), and then mixed.

**62. C:** Choice *C* is correct. Cold chain systems are protocols established to ensure that the proper storage and temperature requirements of vaccines are maintained throughout the shelf life of the vaccine. Choice *C* is the correct choice because patients are simply vaccine recipients and are therefore not involved in the cold chain. Choice *A*, vaccine administrators including physicians, clinics, and pharmacies, is incorrect because administrators are the last responsible party in ensuring the cold chain is maintained. Choice *B* is incorrect because the cold chain system begins with the vaccine manufacturer. The vaccine manufacturers are responsible for ensuring the storage and temperature regulation of finished vaccine products as well as raw materials during the entire manufacturing process. Choice *D* is incorrect because vaccine distributors are the second step in the cold chain system and are responsible for ensuring that temperature requirements are maintained during storage and transport of the vaccines once received from the manufacturer.

**63. A:** Choice *A* is correct because personal protective equipment (PPE) should be applied from the most contaminated to the least contaminated areas. The bouffant cap should be donned after the shoe covers. Choices *B* and *C* are not correct because the gown and mask should be donned after hand hygiene is performed. Choice *D* is not correct because sterile gloves are donned after entering the clean room.

**64. A:** Choice *A* is the correct choice because under no circumstances can Schedule II prescriptions be transferred. Choice *A* is the one incorrect statement. Choices *B*, *C*, and *D* are incorrect choices because they are true – Schedule III-V controlled prescriptions can be transferred one time between individual DEA-registered pharmacies that do not share the same patient database (or multiple times if the pharmacies do share the same real-time database) and the verbal transfer must be communicated between two licensed pharmacists.

**65. C:** Choice *C* is correct because all errors, including near misses, should be documented using an incident report. Tracking errors helps to identify systemic problems. Choice *A* is not correct because informing another pharmacy technician is not indicated. The pharmacy technician should report the near miss to their supervisor. Choice *B* is not correct because near misses should be documented to analyze and improve systemic processes. Choice *D* is not correct because a healthcare provider does not need to be informed of a near miss during the dispensing process.

**66. C:** Choice *C* is the correct choice. The gauge or lumen size of a needle refers to the diameter of the needle. The smaller the diameter, the larger the gauge; therefore, the needle with the smallest lumen is Choice *C*, the 30 G needle. Choices, *A*, *B*, and *D* are therefore incorrect.

**67. A:** Choice *A* is correct. Visual indicators that an oral suspension has lost stability include precipitate formation, caking, and color changes. Choices *B* and *C* are incorrect because loss of stability caused by chemical changes can affect the overall therapeutic potency of the oral suspension and result in pH changes; however, these effects are not visually apparent. An analysis of the compounded preparation would be needed to determine if the preparation has retained its potency and to verify changes in pH. Choice *D* is incorrect because an oral suspension that has lost stability due to a chemical change may show visual signs of toxic byproducts caused by the degradation of the active pharmaceutical ingredient and excipients; however, there may be some byproducts that are not observable as well.

**68. C:** Choice *C* is the correct choice. Coumadin (warfarin) is available in nine different strengths, which can enable multiple dosing variations. The available doses of Coumadin include 1 mg, 2 mg, 2.5 mg, 3 mg, 4 mg, 5 mg, 6 mg, 7.5 mg, and 10 mg. However, there is not a 4.5 mg tablet. Since 1 mg, 7.5 mg, and 5 mg tablets are the available strengths of Coumadin, Choices *A*, *B*, and *D* are incorrect.

**69. B:** Choice *B* is the correct choice. Most oral syringes are marked every tenth of a milliliter, which enables precise dosing, while dosing cups, dosing spoons, and medicine droppers are marked in ¼ or even ½ milliliter increments. Choice *A*, dosing cup, Choice *C*, medicine dropper, and Choice *D*, dosing spoon, are incorrect since these devices are not labeled as accurately as oral syringes.

**70. D:** Choice *D* is the correct choice. A drug that is missing its lot number would be considered a mislabeled drug and would therefore prompt a Class III drug recall. The missing information is a violation of FDA regulations; however, it is not likely to cause significant harm to the patient. Choices *A* and *C* are incorrect because both are examples of Class II drug recalls. Choice *A* is incorrect because, while the bottle contains the correct medication, it contains two different strengths of the medication. This error might lead to the patient receiving the incorrect amount of their cholesterol medication.

Cholesterol medication, while important, is not a lifesaving medication, and therefore this error is not likely to have a significant adverse effect on the patient's health. Choice *C* is also incorrect because a medication not meeting quality assurance specifications such as weight is not considered a significant enough risk to the patient to warrant a Class I recall, but it is more significant than a Class III recall. Gabapentin is not considered a lifesaving medication; therefore, not meeting the weight specification is not likely to cause significant harm to the patient. Choice *B* is incorrect because the presence of particulates in an injectable medication would be considered a Class I recall since it has the potential to cause a life-threatening embolism.

**71. A:** Choice *A* is correct because a near-miss event is an error that is caught before it can cause harm to the patient. The purpose of a pharmacist verification is to ensure that the prescription label matches the hard copy prescription and to ensure that the correct medication will be dispensed to the patient. Choice *B* is incorrect because an adverse effect is defined as an unwanted or dangerous reaction *after* using a product or medication, but the medication in the scenario has not yet been given to a patient. Choice *C* is incorrect because a sentinel event happens after a patient has taken the medication. A sentinel event results in loss of a limb, disability, or death. Choice *D* is incorrect because a side effect is an undesirable effect that happens after the patient uses a medication.

**72. B:** Choice *B* is correct since Synthroid is a narrow therapeutic index medication and is indicated for the treatment of hypothyroidism. Choices *A* and *C*, carbamazepine and phenobarbital, are both narrow therapeutic index medications; however, they are anticonvulsants indicated for the treatment of seizure disorders. Therefore, Choices *A* and *C* are incorrect. Vancomycin, Choice *D*, is a narrow therapeutic index medication as well; however, it is used to treat bacterial infections such as methicillin-resistant staphylococcus aureus (MRSA). Thus, Choice *D* is also incorrect.

**73. D:** Choice *D* is correct. The international normalized ratio (INR) values can range from zero to five with an optimal value between two and three. An INR value above three can lead to excessive bleeding; therefore, hemorrhaging is the result of a warfarin dose that is too high. DVT, stroke, and pulmonary embolism are all serious conditions in which the blood is clotting too much. These conditions are likely to occur in a warfarin patient whose INR value is less than two; therefore, Choices *A*, *B*, and *C* are incorrect.

**74. D:** Choice *D* is the correct choice. Flocculating agents are electrolyte-based additives that neutralize suspended particles, creating a uniform suspension that helps to slow down the rate at which the particles settle. Choices *A* and *C*, levigating and wetting agents, are incorrect because they are additives used to decrease surface tension in suspensions, enabling better dispersion of the active ingredient. Choice *B*, viscosity enhancers, slow sedimentation by thickening the suspension, making it less fluid. Therefore, Choice *B* is also incorrect.

**75. C:** Choice *C* is the correct choice. The given NDC code is in the standard 5-3-2 FDA format. To convert the NDC to one that can be processed by an insurance agency, the 5-4-2 format, a leading zero must be added to the second segment. Therefore, Choice *C*, 54321-0987-60, is the correct choice. Choice *A* meets the 5-4-2 format requirement, but the zero added to second segment of the NDC was placed at the end instead of in the beginning. Choice *B*, 054321-987-60, and Choice *D*, 54321-987-060, are incorrect because they don't have the 5-4-2 format.

**76. B:** Choice *B* is correct because the United States Pharmacopeial Convention (USP) is the organization responsible for developing Chapter <797>, a regulation that monitors facilities that prepare, store, and dispense compound sterile preparations. Choice *A* is not correct because the FDA (in addition to state boards of pharmacy) is responsible for enforcing compliance with USP <797>. Choice *C* is not correct because the Environmental Protection Agency (EPA) is an organization responsible for protecting human health and the environment. Supplies used for cleaning pharmacy equipment and surfaces must meet EPA standards. Choice *D* is not correct because the Occupational Safety and Health Administration (OSHA) is responsible for monitoring the implementation of mandatory infection control guidelines.

**77. D:** Choice *D* is the correct answer because DEA regulations prohibit refilling a Schedule II controlled substance. Choice *A* is incorrect because federal regulations permit Schedule V controlled substances to be refilled for up to one year from the date written. Choices *B* and *C* are also incorrect because Schedule III and IV controlled substances may be refilled five times or for up to six months from the date written, whichever comes first.

**78. A:** Choice *A* is the correct choice. Coalescence is a breakdown of an emulsion in which the interfacial tension between equally distributed droplets is disrupted, resulting in fusion of smaller droplets into larger ones. Choices *B* and *D* are incorrect because this breakdown results in a preparation that is therapeutically ineffective, and it is irreversible. Choice *C* is incorrect because the internal and external phases do not completely separate.

**79. C:** Choice *C* is the correct choice. For a capsule to be acceptable, its weight variance must be ±5% of the average capsule weight, which was determined to be 0.287g. Multiplying the average weight, 0.287g, by 95% (or -5%) will yield the minimum acceptable weight for the capsule. Multiplying the average weight, 0.287g, by 105% (or +5%) will yield the maximum acceptable weight for the capsule. Therefore, the acceptable weight range is 0.273 g to 0.301g:

$$0.287g\,(95\%) = 0.273g$$

and

$$0.287g\,(105\%) = 0.301g$$

Choices *A*, *B*, and *D* are therefore incorrect, as they fall outside the 5% margin of error.

**80. B:** Choice *B* is the correct choice because the amount of the active ingredient does not change with precipitate formation; this is the only option that is NOT a potentially fatal consequence of precipitate formation. Precipitates can form in intravenous solutions that have been improperly reconstituted with chemically incompatible diluents or inadvertently mixed with incompatible medications during intravenous delivery of the drug. Choice *A* is incorrect because the chemical interaction that occurs can result in the delivery of a medication that has been inactivated, leading to therapeutic failure that can be harmful if the condition being treated is a serious one. Choice *C* is incorrect because this type of chemical incompatibility can also result in the administration of potentially life-threatening toxic compounds that may have formed in the solution. Choice *D* is incorrect because precipitation particulates can enter the bloodstream, causing fatal embolisms.

**81. A:** Choice *A* is the correct choice since DEA Schedule I controlled substances include medications that have a significant abuse potential and no legitimate medical purpose. DEA Schedule I controlled substances, including heroin and LSD, are illegal; therefore, they cannot be prescribed. Choices *B*, *C*, and *D* are incorrect choices since the substances controlled under Schedules II, III, and IV all have legitimate medical purposes.

**82. A:** Choice *A* is correct because the dispensing process is a check in the overall medication dispensing process that involves verifying the prescription label against the original prescription. The pharmacy technician must ensure that all components match before dispensing the medication. Choice *B* is not correct because the verification process is performed by the pharmacist. During this step, the pharmacist compares the NDC number against the stock bottle, ensures the drug being dispensed matches the illustration image, checks the prescription label against the hard copy of the prescription for accuracy, and ensures all other checks have been accurately completed. Choice *C* is not correct because the point-of-sale check is the step where an additional patient identifier is requested before handing the medication to the patient. Choice *D* is not correct because prescription drop-off is the first step in the multiple check system. During this step, the pharmacy technician ensures the components on the prescription are accurate and the patient is correctly identified and matched to the information on the prescription.

**83. C:** Choice *C* is the correct choice since amber vials or dark-colored stock bottles are the best way to prevent photodegradation of light-sensitive medications. Choices *A* and *B* are incorrect because photodegradation can occur in light-sensitive medications within minutes of exposure to artificial or natural lighting. Choice *D* is also incorrect because exposure to light can break down both the active ingredient and any excipients or fillers.

**84. B:** Choice *B* is correct because independent double-checks, cautionary labeling, and computerized alerts are all safeguard strategies for handling high-alert medications. Independent double checks ensure that high-alert medications are checked with another pharmaceutical staff member before dispensing. Cautionary labeling ensures that high-alert medications are tagged with high alert labels, indicating that further checks are required. Computerized alerts caution the pharmacy technician to double check the prescription information before dispensing the medication. Choices *A, C,* and *D* are not correct because pharmacies should stock high-alert medications in smaller units, volume, or quantities.

**85. D:** Choice *D* is the correct choice. The CMEA was enacted to curb the abuse of the decongestant pseudoephedrine (Sudafed), which is used to make the street medication methamphetamine or meth. The CMEA covers OTC medications that include pseudoephedrine, phenylpropanolamine, and ephedrine. Choice *A* is incorrect because phenylephrine or Sudafed PE is an OTC decongestant like pseudoephedrine; however, it is not a precursor ingredient to methamphetamine and is not restricted by the CMEA. Choices *B* and *C* are both incorrect because cold medications that contain the ingredients dextromethorphan and guaifenesin may have purchase age restrictions depending on the specific state; however, they are not restricted by the CMEA.

**86. D**: Choice *D* is correct because the first step in performing hand hygiene with soap and water is to wet the hands thoroughly. This helps create lather when the soap is applied. Choice *A* is not correct because hand hygiene, whether it is with an alcohol rub or soap and water, should be performed every time medications are prepared. Choice *B* is not correct because alcohol-based rubs do not remove bacterial spores. Choice *C* is not correct because hands should be washed with soap and water for at least 20 seconds.

**87. A:** Choice *A* is the correct choice. Storage information, including proper temperature and any excursions permitted, is printed on the manufacturer's drug label. Choice *B* is incorrect because controlled room temperature is defined by USP as a temperature range between 68°F and 77°F (20°C to 25°C). Choice *C* is incorrect because temperature excursions for room temperature medications are five degrees Celsius or nine degrees Fahrenheit above and below the controlled room temperature range (15°C to 30°C or 59°F to 86°F). Choice *D* is incorrect because 20°C to 25°C is equivalent to a controlled storage temperature between 68°F and 77°F, which is the normal room temperature range. The proper storage temperature of refrigerated medications is between 2°C and 8°C (36°F and 46°F).

**88. B:** Choice *B* is the correct choice since a patient should only receive enough medication to get them to the next ANC draw. A patient receiving ANC labs every two weeks should therefore be dispensed no more than a two-week (14-day) supply. Choice *A* is incorrect because a 7-day supply would not get the patient to the next ANC draw. Choices *C* and *D* are incorrect because 30-day and 90-day supplies far exceed the amount needed to get the patient to the next ANC draw.

**89. C:** Choice *C* is correct because bupropion, an antidepressant, is commonly confused with buspirone, an anti-anxiety medication. The recommended tall man lettering for bupropion is buPROPion. Choices *A, B,* and *D* are not medications that are commonly confused with others and are not part of the recommended list for tall man lettering.

**90. D:** Choice *D* is the correct choice. Choice *D,* SL, means to place under the tongue or sublingual. Choice *A* is also an oral route of administration; however, PO means by mouth and does not indicate that the medication should be placed under the tongue. Choice *B*, OS, is incorrect since it is the sig code used for an ophthalmic route of administration, specifically, to the left eye. Choice *C*, AU, is incorrect because AU is the sig code used for otic routes of administration, meaning both ears.

Greetings!

First, we would like to give a huge "thank you" for choosing us and this study guide for your PTCE. We hope that it will lead you to success on this exam and for your years to come.

Our team has tried to make your preparations as thorough as possible by covering all of the topics you should be expected to know. In addition, our writers attempted to create practice questions identical to what you will see on the day of your actual test. We have also included many test-taking strategies to help you learn the material, maintain the knowledge, and take the test with confidence.

We strive for excellence in our products, and if you have any comments or concerns over the quality of something in this study guide, please send us an email so that we may improve.

As you continue forward in life, we would like to remain alongside you with other books and study guides in our library. We are continually producing and updating study guides in several different subjects. If you are looking for something in particular, all of our products are available on Amazon. You may also send us an email!

Sincerely,
APEX Test Prep
info@apexprep.com

# FREE

## Free Study Tips Videos/DVD

In addition to this guide, we have created a FREE set of videos with helpful study tips. **These FREE videos provide you with top-notch tips to conquer your exam and reach your goals.**

Our simple request is that you give us feedback about the book in exchange for these strategy-packed videos. We would love to hear what you thought about the book, whether positive, negative, or neutral. It is our #1 goal to provide you with quality products and customer service.

To receive your **FREE Study Tips Videos**, scan the QR code or email freevideos@apexprep.com. Please put "FREE Videos" in the subject line and include the following in the email:

   a. The title of the book

   b. Your rating of the book on a scale of 1-5, with 5 being the highest score

   c. Any thoughts or feedback about the book

Thank you!

Made in the USA
Middletown, DE
18 February 2023

25166700R00084